Row to Alaska

By Wind & Oar

A retired couple's adventurous row up the Inside Passage

By Pete & Nancy Ashenfelter

Dedication

To Sam and Sarah McMillan of New Aiyansh, British Columbia, who saved our lives with total disregard of potential damage to their boat or injury to their bodies. We are forever in your debt.

First Edition. Anderson Publishing Inc. Printed in U.S.A. ISBN 0-945989-22-9

Acknowledgments

A warm thank you to:
Mary and Steve Gropp, who inspired us to undertake this adventure.

Geremy Snapp, who designed and constructed Surfbird, and who encouraged us to follow our dreams.

Jo Bailey-Cummings, whose enthusiastic interest gave impetus to our journey.

Tom Kincaid, who first published our articles on boating, and later featured a series on this rowing trip.

Kate Parish, who painstakingly helped edit our scratchings.

Dave Parish, Geremy Snapp, Allen Cooper, Gwen Cole, and Tami of Big Bay Marina, who shared their pictures.

And to everyone along the "Inside Passage" who extended hospitality and encouragement.

TABLE OF CONTENTS

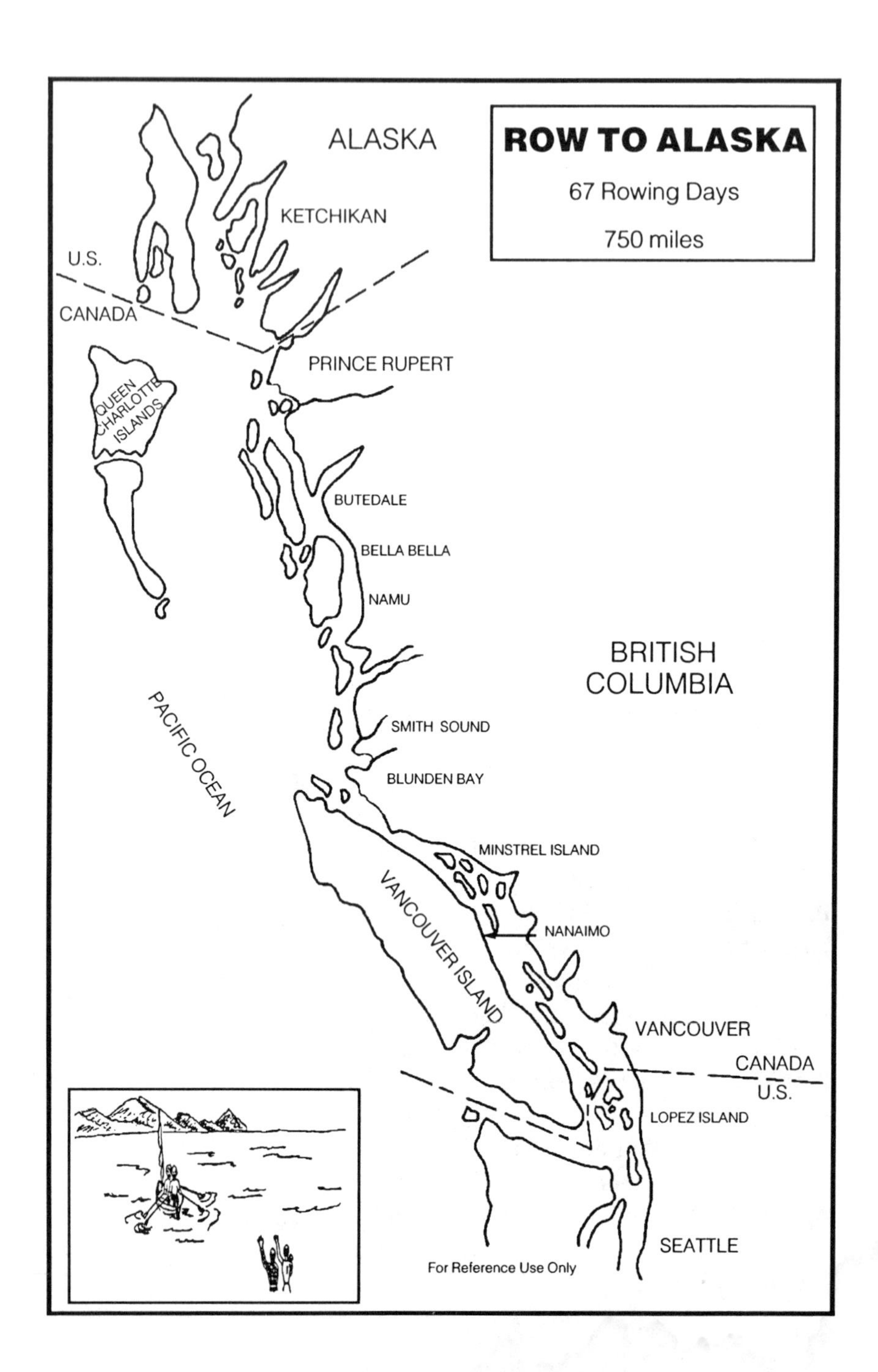
ROW TO ALASKA
67 Rowing Days
750 miles
ALASKA
KETCHIKAN
U.S.
CANADA
PRINCE RUPERT
QUEEN CHARLOTTE ISLANDS
BUTEDALE
BELLA BELLA
NAMU
BRITISH COLUMBIA
PACIFIC OCEAN
SMITH SOUND
BLUNDEN BAY
MINSTREL ISLAND
VANCOUVER ISLAND
NANAIMO
VANCOUVER
CANADA
U.S.
LOPEZ ISLAND
SEATTLE
For Reference Use Only

PROLOGUE: (Pete) "THAT SOUNDS LIKE SOMETHING WE'D LIKE TO DO."

"It's getting to be too much," I shouted, as our seventeen-foot open dory bucked back from each oncoming wave. "Let's head back to that rock and get behind it." We rowed directly into the threatening wind. It had picked up in less than fifteen minutes from a light following breeze to gusts over twenty knots head-on. Salt spray mixed with the pelting rain. Although we strained hard and fast on our two sets of oars, we saw by the shore that we were getting nowhere. I had turned away from the wind to make myself heard, bobbing my head toward a small island behind us, just offshore. Nancy nodded ready agreement. We both immediately pulled hard on our windward oars to turn through the three-foot, rain-filled troughs so we could run with the wind to shelter.

After about fifteen minutes, pushed by the wind and rain, we made the lee of the rock. It was about fifty feet in diameter, fifteen to twenty feet high, ringed by a lower base of foam-covered, jagged, rocky outcroppings and topped by a cluster of dwarfed, wind-bent spruce and cedars. The wind whipped around both ends of the rock, but left untouched a small space directly downwind, just large enough to give us relief. In the ebbing tide, the rock lay offshore about fifty feet. In two hours we would be aground if we remained there. We sat in the rain, washing gently against the rocks from the actions of the wind and waves. We watched the beach bottom come slowly closer to ours and waited for the wind to slacken. From up on the rock on the windward side, through the rain, I made out some of the buildings of Ketchikan, Alaska, our destination. The distance was about three miles — about seven hundred and fifty miles from our starting point near Seattle, Washington.

Less than two hundred feet away were two shorefront homes. Around us, the low-scudding clouds darkened the early afternoon. Inside the houses, soft lamp light let us see people going about their daily activities. Wood smoke whipped from the chimneys. The occupants showed no curiosity about the hunched-over, yellow-hooded, wet rowers sitting in a small open boat just offshore in the lee of their island. Nor were we the least bit concerned about their problems.

Since our capsizing three weeks earlier in a quick, ferocious storm just south of Prince Rupert, both Nancy and I were more chary about being out in stiff weather. Only yesterday, we were blown off the water by a drenching, thirty-knot storm that took all night to blow itself by. The capsizing took away a lot of our starch. Here, in these last miles, despite the nearness of our destination, we quickly turned for the nearest shelter to wait.

Our trip had taken two-and-a-half months. Most of the days were spent rowing, eight to sixteen hours a day, depending on circumstances. We'd come through fog, fast currents and tidal rapids, around ocean headlands, among hundreds of islands, through several violent squalls and one full-fledged vicious storm. Rain found us on more than fifty of our days underway. Each night we had to make a camp where we could also find a suitable anchorage for our boat. We became expert at wet camping and soon found we were too tired at the end of each day to lose sleep over the constant threat of a hungry bear.

We saw mile on mile of beautiful coastline and hundreds of wilderness islands, most uninhabited. We met many kind and interesting people and shared scores of wildlife experiences. More than anything else, we shared an adventure that would remain a high point in our lives.

What happened to bring us to the lee of this small island in an open sea-dory? What happened that would move two retired senior citizens to undertake what proved to be an extremely difficult, frequently risky, often uncomfortable, always interesting extended adventure?

By the summer of 1981 all of our eight children had reached adulthood and moved out of our home. Both Nancy and I were thinking of winding down our current professions to do some things different and interesting. We were apparently "ready" to receive some casual comments made that summer by two of our friends that their son was rowing to Alaska. They shared part of a letter they had received from him. Since we had sailed in some of that area, we mentioned that we would like to talk with him when he returned. That was about the extent of our interest at that time.

That fall we were invited to our friends' home to meet their son, Steve Gropp, and see the slides of his trip. He talked and shared his passage. The scenes of the islands and headlands, coves and camps, sunsets and surfs comprised a mosaic of rugged, remote beauty seldom seen closely by humans, for these are lands and islands largely unconnected by roads and rarely touched by passing boats. Many of the coves and bays were accessible only by a row boat or kayak.

In the warmth of our friends' living room both Nancy and I were interested, maybe even intrigued. Driving home, Nancy said, "That sounds like the sort of thing we'd like to do." I was thinking the same thing.

"I wonder if we could do it?" I replied. After a few more comments, we dropped the subject to talk about something else.

As the winter wore on, we talked more of making such a trip. We started serious research concerning such things as the route, likely weather and places where we could re-supply. The more we looked into it, the more we realized that this wasn't to be just an extended outing. It shaped up more as an expedition.

The boat route from Seattle to Alaska is seldom without weather problems for even the largest of ships. The term "Inside Passage" is misleading, for while it is in fact inside for much of the way, the protection that seems logical from the Gulf of Alaska weather is more often non-existent. Rather, the narrow channels of the passage act as funnels for the winds to concentrate and blow through, frequently at accelerated velocities. Too, the route transits some of the toughest water passages in the world-Johnstone and Queen Charlotte Straits, Queen Charlotte Sound, the Pacific Ocean around Cape Caution and Ivory Island and the notorious Dixon Entrance. These facts were easily set aside as we fantasized our outing in the early stages of our thinking.

We knew we had to cover about 750 miles on these "inside" waters and open ocean. We hoped we could sail part of the way, for cruise-sailing had been one of our pastimes for the past ten years. We learned that the route to Alaska via the Inside Passage winds through some of the Northwest's most beautiful scenery. The idea of making camp every night, we thought, would be no different from the many we have made and liked while backpacking in the mountains. All along in our eleven years of marriage, Nancy and I have enjoyed physical activities that have involved our "doing." We have sailed a lot among the islands of Washington State and British Columbia, Canada, including a tempestuous circumnavigation of Vancouver Island. We have hiked hundreds of miles in the Cascade and Olympic Mountains. We both work out regularly to stay in good physical condition. By nature neither of us courts danger simply for the thrill, but we like the satisfaction of completing something difficult, especially when it involves experiencing the out-of-doors.

As we moved along in our research we shifted our thinking from "if" to "when." The summer of 1983 worked out well for us: A good time to change our professions. Nancy was a junior-high school teacher/counselor, I retired from careers in both the Navy and business.

It became clear that success in our undertaking would hinge more on preparation and determination than on strength. Neither of us had ever rowed anything larger than a dinghy. We didn't even prepare for that, figuring that conditioning would come from application.

We knew the distance we wanted to travel — about 750 miles. We estimated about two-and-a-half months would be needed. We wanted to be off the water before September, the traditional start of the northern storm season. June 9th was chosen as our starting date. The pace of preparation quickened as our countdown narrowed. We were more than committed. By June 9th we were as ready as we felt we could be, probably a little scared, but positively excited. We had little idea of all we would discover and experience. We did have a lot of reason to believe we were in for an unusual and memorable experience. We were not disappointed.

PART I: (Nancy) "WE'VE TALKED ENOUGH. TIME TO PUT WORDS INTO ACTION."

I don't know when we made the final decision to row to Alaska, or if we even did. We sort of drifted into it. Viewing Steve's slides definitely whetted our appetites. For a year the subject kept entering and exiting our conversations. Eventually, we talked about actually doing it. We fixed on the summer of 1983 as the time. But first we had to acquire a boat.

Pete had researched the project thoroughly, and concluded that a seventeen to eighteen foot dory would be best for such an undertaking. Having built only one boat in his life, a twelve-foot, flat-bottom skiff, he did not feel competent to build an ocean-going dory. We looked for a skilled craftsman who might be interested in our project and commissioned Geremy Snapp, owner of the Upright Boat Works on Lopez Island. We made a commitment to something — a tangible — a wooden boat designed for the express purpose of taking us to Alaska. We had talked enough. We put our words into action. Once started, there was nothing to do but keep going.

Geremy fit the boat into his schedule for completion by mid-May. We planned to leave in early June, as we wanted to be off the water in Alaska before the weather turned winterish around the first of September. We had a lot to do to get ready. We were going to row to Alaska!

Friends who knew of our upcoming adventure wanted to know how we were preparing for the physical and emotional stresses of such a trip. Were we rowing every day? Were we lifting weights? Perhaps we should be seeing a psychiatrist. Most of our older friends were convinced we had gone bonkers. One of my friends, a woman about five years my senior, could not imagine anyone undertaking such insanity. She said, "All I want in life is my own bed and my grandchildren." Her words hit me with volcanic impact. Now I knew why I was taking this risk. Although many of my peers shared her goals, I figured when it gets down to the safety of bed and grandchildren, you can haul me away by the feet.

Retirement loomed around the corner and both of us wanted to partake in a physically demanding adventure before settling into a new routine. Pete had worked for over forty years, and I a total of twenty, in and among raising children. We were ready for a change. This trip seemed a good transition into a different life-style.

Preparing for the expected physical strains had really been a lifelong process. Pete had been running for over eighteen years and he swam three-fourths of a mile three times a week. My past experience as a physical education teacher and my lifetime involvement in sports helped me stay reasonably firm, although avoiding weight gain was, and is, a continuous struggle. My conditioning during the past three years had been in the form of regular workouts and light weight lifting at a local fitness salon.

Both watch our caloric intake (between intervals of chocolate binging) and we are physically active with hiking, swimming, walking and calisthenics. Both are of small stature. Muscles do not ripple sensuously on our aging frames. We allowed that we would receive ample warm-up and conditioning for the sustained pull to Alaska during the first few weeks of the actual trip. "We'll start out slowly and pick up speed as we build strength," Pete concluded, as we were laying out our course one day in preparation for buying our charts.

Early on, we purchased wrist braces for Pete, who suffers from mild arthritis. We reasoned that he could then immobilize his joints if the stress of rowing proved to be too great. For the same reason, we asked Geremy to design narrow-bladed oars to eliminate the feathering action and reduce the amount of wrist rotation.

Being compulsive list-makers, we quickly developed seven categories for necessary supplies and equipment: camping and fishing gear, clothing, emergency and navigational aids, First Aid supplies, food, ground tackle (anchoring gear) and personal supplies. As we began to build our lists of items under each heading, it became obvious that a lot more research and planning would be essential.

So like pilgrims to Delphi, we spent an afternoon with Steve and Mary Gropp at their island home in the San Juans. We interviewed, questioned and took notes. As we shared a pot of tea, they recalled some of their experiences and problems and gave us practical hints and suggestions along with a detailed sketch of how they anchored their boat out from shore each night. In her willingness to share, Mary reached into their closet and dragged out their beat-up Goodrich Xtra-Tough boots, which she claimed were indispensable items on their voyages. They recommended a cast iron fry pay (indestructible), a bailer (indispensable) and adequate rain gear — the commercial fisherman kind, not the lightweight sailing type. They stressed the need for plastic, plastic and more plastic to bag, double-bag and then bag again. "Nothing can be kept completely waterproof — you'll see."

With our lists and sketches in hand, coupled with their warm encouragement, we left to catch the ferry home.

The trip was now beginning to materialize into reality for me. I began to grasp the concept, for maybe the first time, that we were really going and what it might be like. Our friends warned us of all possible pitfalls: grizzlies, terrifying rip-tides, whirlpools, storms, wolves. What am I doing? I thought.

Here I am, a mother of eight, an ex-teacher and counselor of junior high school kids; a woman in her midway years. What am I doing taking a risk like this? In a way, my questions both queried and rejoined. Our children were all adults now. My teaching years were behind me. Only menopause loomed ahead, and I couldn't see that as something to anticipate eagerly. It was my turn for adventure, even if it involved some danger. With those thoughts surfaced, it was time to stockpile provisions.

The first category, Camping Gear, did not involve too many new purchases as we had backpacked in the Washington wilderness areas for many years and owned most of the equipment vital to survival. We did add two rain tarps, one to cover our two-person tent for protection against heavy rainfall and one to create a "cooking tent" away from our campsite to discourage bears or rodents from coming too near our sleeping area. We spent hours on the latter, stitching seams to form pockets in which to insert rigid poles and nylon line so we could erect it quickly and efficiently. (It lay in the boat during the entire trip – never used.) We had trial tarp raisings on the back lawn. We hammered stakes and pulled lines taut to create rainproof shelters while the May sun shone warmly on our backs.

To complete our camping category, we threw in two 2-1/2 gallon plastic water containers so we could always carry a three-day water supply aboard, a black plastic shower bag in which water could be sun-warmed (ha!) to provide hot baths ashore and 2,000 waterproofed matches, which I had laboriously dipped in paraffin one by one.

Canadian fishing laws require that all non-commercial fishing lines be attached to a pole or winch, not to the boat, so we purchased a thick salmon pole and reduced it to a stub. We fastened an old reel to this and carried the stub along with a small hand net and many lures, worms, jigs and sinkers. This was to be our dinner meal ticket for most of our trip.

Space was a major factor in our decisions to add or eliminate items. When it came to clothing, we knew we would live in jeans topped by layers of T-shirts, sweat shirts, wool sweaters and rain gear. We both shuffled through our closets and dressers to drag out the oldest, most worn and generally bedraggled clothing we owned. We didn't kid ourselves about the conditions we would face. We expected to be dirty and damp most of the way up the British Columbia coastline. We optimistically added shorts and swimsuits and pessimistically threw in long underwear, woolen hats, gloves, wool pants and wool jackets.

Our family insisted we throw in survival suits, those bright red-orange, bulky "spacemen" overgarments used by commercial fishermen. They also urged us to carry a VHF radio for emergency calls to the Coast Guard. We resisted both because of space limitations, impracticality and/or high cost. Geremy offered to lend us his survival suits and our family would not allow us to refuse. At Pete's retirement celebration, he was given a parting gift of a hand-held VHF radio by his concerned fellow employees. So we added those items to our pile of flares, life jackets, whistles, tide and current books, charts and compass. It never occurred to us to throw in a B.C. ferry schedule or shipping schedules, but it might have warded off potential disaster.

First aid supplies were easy to compile, but when it came to dental emergencies, Pete suggested I contact my dentist of the past thirty years. During a tooth-cleaning session, he urged me to get a prescription for a wide-spectrum antibiotic along with some oil of cloves, cotton and toothwax to combat any toothache or broken tooth. It was my fervent hope that none of these goods would be employed, as I doubted our tooth repairing skills, especially in a rocking boat or on a rain-soaked island. "Open wide now. This may hurt a little."

My next stop was at the office of our family physician, whose casual approach to practicing medicine has always appealed to us. We've liked his philosophy that the body is a miraculous self-healer, so why interfere? Being an ardent back country enthusiast, he prescribed the suggested antibiotic along with some medication to alleviate the pain of muscle strain or injury. He longed to go with us and looked like a disappointed boy denied his outing as I left his office.

That evening, discussing our plans with a friend, our judgement was sincerely questioned. "I sure hope you know what you're doing," he said. As I nodded assurance, I heard my inner voice respond without conviction, "So do I."

While poring over our charts, it appeared that we could be out of touch with civilization for as long as forty days. We didn't know whether there were any services between Bella Bella and Prince Rupert, a long stretch of watery wilderness. Because of this our food had to be carefully planned. Our space limitations did not allow for much variety, so our menus would have a sameness about them, altered only by the variety of seafood we hoped to hook or scrounge from the water and beaches. We planned breakfast around orange Tang, oatmeal with dried milk and brown sugar, pre-mixed pancakes with butter and syrup and coffee. Lunch would be rye crackers (purchased in foot-wide wheels), peanut butter, cheese (when available), lemonade, fruit, chocolate bars and dried fruit and nuts. My eldest daughter, Jami, had shipped us a carton of delectable dried figs, apricots, coconut, macadamia nuts and carob-coated nuts and raisins from Hawaii. We hoped dinners would be our "catch-of-the-day" along with beef bouillon, rice or potatoes, carrots or other veggies we could purchase along the way. Bisquick pan-bread with butter and honey and hot chocolate were to be dessert. I looked forward to this feast, as calorie counting had been a daily routine for at least ten years. Our daughters thought this was a helluva way to lose weight, but I eagerly anticipated the pleasure of eating as much as I wanted, including daily chocolate bar snacks, while losing weight!

There were no problems involved with assembling the equipment for ground tackle, which is a boating euphemism for anchoring gear. If you have ever boated, you will recognize the aptness of the word tackle.

Anchoring or weighing anchor frequently involves a hassle with stubborn or twisted line and incredibly heavy and resistant pieces of chain, attached always to an awkward unstable anchor.

The final category, Personal, contained some items which fell under the heading of idealism: sketch pads, cards, cribbage board, stationary. These were all tossed in with the hope that we would find some lounging time on soft, warm sandy beaches where we would pen long letters home, casually sketch the wildlife or idly play cribbage to pass the empty hours. As it turned out, our most restful times awake were while we were rowing in no-wind conditions — a treat not often experienced. We carefully selected twelve books which neither had read, so we could switch and always have fresh material.

Pete decided to abandon his lifelong cleanshaven look to avoid the painful scraping of cold salt water shaves, so our toiletry needs boiled down to toothbrushes, toothpaste and combs — although some would debate Pete's need for a comb.

Having assembled all of the above plus camera, zoom lens, film, batteries and binoculars, we faced the task of waterproofing. Taking Steve and Mary's advice we stuffed everything in garbage or zip-top bags, then double-bagged for stowage in large "waterproof" sacks constructed for white-water rafters. We had a sack for each category, plus individual bags for our sleeping bags, tent stakes, shovel and axe. Food was broken into a bag for each meal. The binoculars and camera had their own inflatable sports sacks, which theoretically would float if necessary. One did; one didn't.

The enormous pile we had created filled the floor space in our small family room. "We better haul it all into the living room where we can lay it out like the shape of a boat," said Pete. "I'll measure off seventeen feet and you stack the gear in the imaginary bow, stern and under the seats." I felt a bit as I had as a child, when my sisters and I would while away full days being Buck Rogers in our make-believe space ships, but I stuffed it all in the vague shape of a dory, then stepped back to survey my work.

"It all fits, but where do I sit?" I wailed.

Envisioning a boat settling in to its gunwales, we decided to eliminate some items which had been included as backup supplies. We also broke down the food bags and mailed a large box of supplies to ourselves at Bella Bella, near the halfway mark of our journey.

We looked at each other over the mound of provisions. Everything had been tested except the rowers. Departure was imminent. Eight months of detailed planning and preparation lay on our living room floor ready to be moved to our boat. In three days our home would be occupied by our summer renters. We were more than committed. The clock was now running. The promise was for far more than we ever expected.

PART II: (Nancy) LOPEZ TO NANAIMO: "THIS DOESN'T SEEM TOO TOUGH."

June eighth dawned as a clear, potentially lovely day. Looking out our second-story bedroom window, I recorded the sweep of Lake Sammamish's north end a mile below our home. The waters were quiet and still below their morning blanket of soft white mist. I absorbed the beauty of our tiny garden: the delicate mauve of the clematis vine snaking its way up the fence; the flashing red of the salvia, the pert yellow marigolds, blue petunias and flowing white allysum. I tucked this scene into the recesses of my mind to pull out later when I needed a reminder of serenity and stability.

....

On the leeward deck of the ferry taking us to Lopez, accompanied by three of our adult children: Bobbi, Jay and Martha, the late afternoon sun blessed us with its warmth. We would not be able to say that very often during the ensuing two and a half months. We were each involved in private thoughts. Is this the last time I'll see these three precious people, I mused. The ferry pushed through sparkling blue waters, seagulls wheeled overhead and sailboats skimmed silently alongside. We'll be an intimate part of this beauty soon – what could be more rewarding, I thought.

Once off the ferry, we drove the short distance to the county park, our departure point. There, we secured a campsite for the night then tramped a mile through the woods to Geremy Snapp's home and boatyard to launch the boat for its upcoming journey.

"It's so small," said Bobbi as she peered into the gleaming white hull.

"What beautiful lines she has." Jay admired Surfbird through his architecturally trained eyes, understanding the lovely flow and sweep of her design.

"Are you really going to row to Alaska in that?" Martha shook her head in awe as the reality of our undertaking sank home for perhaps the first time.

It did look small and vulnerable, but what the hell – no risk, no

PART II - LOPEZ TO NANAIMO

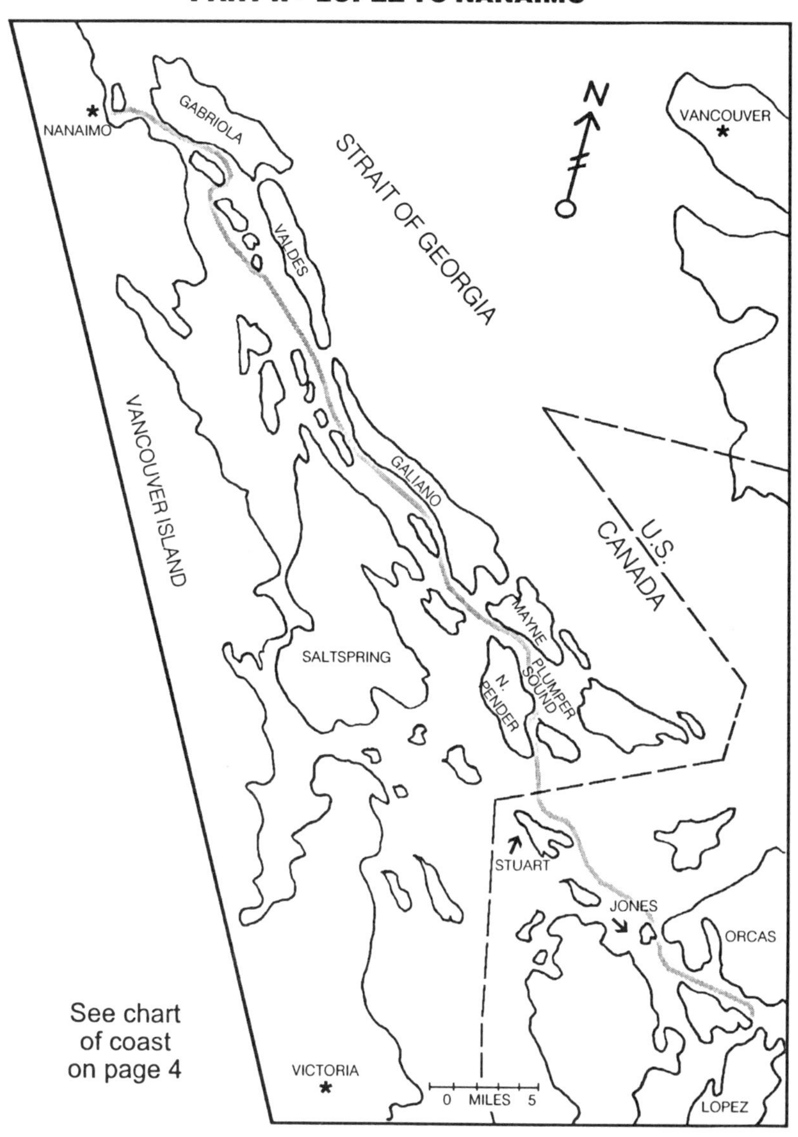

See chart of coast on page 4

personal growth or pleasure. Right? Right!

Geremy was proud of his creation. He ran his hands down her curved planks with obvious affection. She was a beautiful boat. I remember thinking: We have to trust one another, lovely lady. I hope we're both up to that faith.

She did look frail sitting in the grass next to the boatyard shed. She was somewhat squat, clean white outside, oiled natural wood inside and close to the ground. The mast was stepped, the sail rattled and flapped in the soft June breeze. I don't know what we expected, but she most certainly didn't look like she was going anywhere.

The time had come to stop talking and get under way. True, this wasn't her initial launching. A week earlier, we had slid her into the water in front of Geremy's home. No champagne, no band, no bunting. Pete and I had climbed aboard, fixed our oars and started to row — the first time ever together. Surfbird had flown through the water. Though light for her size, she weighed close to two hundred pounds. We were amazed at how easily she had rowed and how readily she had responded. We had been thrilled with her performance. Somehow, though, the same thrilling feeling didn't emerge as we now saw her sprawled in the grass. Maybe it was because the "moment of truth" was here. Fish or cut bait. Call it off now or take the next step.

"Nancy, can you help me stow the sail and mast in their case?" Pete was lifting the mast out of the boat. With the help of all hands, we wrestled the boat down to the waterfront, over the bank and into the water. The transformation was immediate. Like a swan waddling into the water or a seal hunkering on shore, Surfbird was out of place on dry land. Once in the water, she became a thing of beauty, truly in her liquid element. Her gentle sweeping lines, from her proud thrusting stem, through her stable midships to her graceful raked stern were lovely to behold. She was ready and so, suddenly, were we. "Let's row up to our campsite." Pete coiled the bow line and nodded for us all to climb in.

Jay and Martha commandeered the oars. Pete and I shared the forward seat and Bobbi perched on the stern seat and directed traffic with orders of, "Pull on the left oars — now on the right!" Port and starboard were not in her vocabulary.

Back at the park, a half hour later, we secured the boat, unloaded the car and hurried back to the ferry landing where we ordered our "last supper" at the tiny hamburger stand.

In but a few minutes the ferry Kaleetan swept swiftly in from behind Upright Head and nuzzled into her Lopez slip. We all exchanged hugs, kisses and "I love yous." Martha slipped a small bag of chocolates into my hand and the three of them dashed for the car. As Jay pulled the car slowly forward in the ferry line, every window erupted with confetti, poppers and streamers. The quiet Lopezians must have felt invaded. It was quite a send-off. We waved good-bye until the small figures on the upper deck faded from view. My eyes were blurred with tears. A lump settled near the bottom of my throat and sent warning signals to my brain: I wonder if I'll ever see them or their siblings again. Maybe I truly have lost my sanity.

We turned and walked back up the hill to the park, saying little, absorbed in our own thoughts, hand in hand for support.

By 9:00 P.M. the population of the campground settled in for the night. That is everyone but us. We lay in our bags alert to the soft slapping of gentle waves against the piles of driftwood randomly stacked on the shoreline a few feet away. Each was only partially aware of the prodigious undertaking ahead, but we suspected it might change our lives. That thought kept us awake, mostly in our private worlds.

Sometime around 2:30 A.M., the soft sounds of the surf altered to the slap, crunch, slap, crunch of wood hitting wood. We each awakened at the same time to the change. We sat upright and quickly examined the new noise, then pulled on our jeans and boots and scrambled out of the tent to find Surfbird grinding into the logs with each swell of the incoming high tide. Pete secured two stern lines and pulled them in opposite directions to fend her off from possible damage. He also tied off the threatening log. With the boat out of danger, we climbed back into our bags and dropped off into sleep until early morning. Midnight checking of the boat and her moorings were to become routine drills as we worked our way north. The situation frequently called for action from one or both of us.

Dawn urged us out of the tent into a gray overcast day and also into our first lesson on how not to store food. (The second lesson was to occur the following night.) The plastic canister packed full of gooey peanut butter had somehow become disconnected from its lid. Our favorite sandwich spread had oozed onto every plastic bag and jar in the breakfast sack. Every container had to be taken from the waterproof sack and scraped to remove the sticky brown residue. The sack itself had to be turned inside out and cleaned — not an easy task without hot running water.

After breakfast, we trial-loaded the boat for the first time. To our amazement everything fit. Our concerns had been for naught. Then, we unloaded her to be able to walk her out to the low-tide line. We were anxious to get underway, but needed Geremy's strong arms to help lift her into the water.

We heard the Snapps approaching even before they hove into view around the point. The outboard on their small skiff heralded their approach, and in minutes we were helping them off-load our sail-wrapped mast and Geremy's two survival suits. With the help of two boys visiting the park, six of us carried Surfbird about a hundred and fifty yards across the tidal muck to float her for the start of our passage to Alaska.

Geremy and Pete made repeated trips to the beach to bring down our gear while I started stowing. This became one of my daily chores. We quickly filled in the space under the bow cover with the tent, tarps, sleeping bags, axe, charts, tarp poles, personal gear, First Aid bag and books. Next to my forward seat was the camping gear, dinner bag, clothing, foul-weather gear, fishing supplies, one plastic water container and our life jackets. The breakfast bag nestled under my seat. Next to each of us was lashed our individual orange survival suit on one side and floatable packs containing our camera, lenses, film, batteries, binoculars and small VHF radio on the other. Pete had the lunch bag and second water container under his seat and on the stern seat were secured the sailing rudder, two anchors, a float for the pulley system and four hundred feet of coiled yellow polypropylene line for anchoring. Beside each of us on top of the seats lay the sail-wrapped mast in its canvas cover on one side and two extra oars on the other. Later, when we had stepped the mast, we gained some shifting-about room on our seats. But now there was scant room for the two rowers and their four eight-foot oars.

As we climbed in to cast off, Geremy pulled out his many-bladed Swiss Army Knife to make a last minute touchup to the boat. "Do you have one of these aboard, Pete?" He asked.

"No, not one that fancy. Just my ordinary pocket knife."

"Here, take this," said Geremy, quickly unstrapping his and handing it to Pete. "You'll find a hundred uses for it." And, he was right.

At last there was nothing to do but start rowing. We backstroked out, turned the boat about, waved good-bye to picture-snapping Geremy and his wife, Celia, and started out on our great adventure. It was eleven-thirty, but neither of us was hungry. After three years of talking and eight months of detailed planning, we were finally moving north.

A light wind and flooding tide were with us and the oars handled easily. It felt good. I'm sure we both wore small smiles as we pulled away. Lopez Island faded slowly into the background. A seal popped up its head to look at us. We considered it a good omen. "This doesn't seem too tough," I noted.

"Nope — it's all pretty smooth so far." From our trial row a week earlier Pete's right rear cheek was near blistered. Now he had it tape-covered and sat on a polyurethane pad, infinitely more comfortable. It was to be three weeks of hard rowing before his tenderness gave way to occupational toughness.

By the end of the first day, we developed our rowing system. From our positions (amid-ship and stern thwarts, for the purist) we each rowed our own set of oars. Pete sat on the stern thwart and set the pace and controlled our direction. From my position amid-ship, I matched his pace. The big problem with rowing is that you can't see where you're going. My job was to turn my head to see where we were headed and pilot us around and through obstacles. "Pull harder on your port oar," I would shout. "Heavy on your starboard!" In particularly close situations, especially to avoid shallow rocks, I stopped rowing altogether to assist with detailed piloting. I would turn to kneel on my seat and yell out commands over my shoulder. "Hard on your port. Now straight ahead. Slightly to your starboard. Back down!"

The oars took on separate identities. They became "his and hers."

After a few weeks our hands could discern if we had mixed our oars, port from starboard or Pete's with mine. In such cases, things weren't right until we switched the incorrect oar into its "home" hand.

Eagles and seals became our constant companions. They accompanied us every day. The magnificent birds wheeled in giant circles overhead and the inquisitive pup-like mammals emerged from the depths to peer at us with their insatiable curiosity. They helped us feel less alone.

I felt ripples of excitement somewhere in the vicinity of my stomach as we pulled into Harney Channel between Shaw and Orcas Islands. We're really going to do it, I thought. It was an exhilarating moment.

Our destination for the day was Jones Island, a state marine park. It peeked out from behind Orcas Island in mid-afternoon as we cleared Pole Pass, cruised past Deer Harbor and turned Steep Point. There was enough space on the dock for our little boat, so we secured mooring lines and started to pull heavy camping gear and food bags up to a campsite on the hill above the dock. This process was to be reversed each morning and repeated over seventy times in the days ahead. People on the dock remarked on the precision and unison of our rowing — "Right professional." Neither of us had the energy to say this was our first day of rowing anything all day — much less together. We had only rowed four hours, but we had covered seven and a half miles. Not bad for a start.

Bed looked wonderful. We fell in, proud and weary. Our day's end thoughts were: This is going to be fun.

Snarls of fierce intensity shattered our sleep. "What was that?"

"I don't know," Pete mumbled. "There aren't any bears on this island — probably a dog." I drifted back into a half world of semi-consciousness where dories bobbed on choppy bays and gulls circled overhead on arched elastic wings.

Again the vicious growling and snapping aroused me from sleep. The sounds were near — too near — and I envisioned fanged wolverines slashing through our skimpy netting to attack our bodies imprisoned in sleeping bags. "Pete! Pete!" I hissed. "Whatever it is, it's near!" He jerked reflexively to one elbow and flashed a light toward the offensive sounds. The creatures scuttled away into the woods. We slept until morning.

The evidence of our night visitors was sprinkled on and around our picnic tables where we had carelessly left our heavy waterproof sack of breakfast food. Thinking there were only deer on the island and small rodents, we had assumed neither could nor would work through the fortified double-thick bag. We had overlooked raccoons. Thus our second breakfast was a fascinating blend of orange Tang, oatmeal, hot chocolate mix, coffee and pancake powder, lightly coated with peanut butter residue from yesterday's experience. The bag was punctured by several holes just large enough to admit a tiny leathery hand. It took over an hour to sort and rebag everything, toss the unusable, patch the outer bag with aluminum ducting tape, wash and dry the bag and repack. A lesson well learned. From then on everything resembling food was placed in the boat and anchored off-shore for the night.

We shoved off on the early morning tide accompanied by the good wishes of the boaters who had also spent the night at Jones. The calm waters enclosed our oars with little resistance as we pulled further from the shoreline and out into San Juan Channel. Our goal for the day was Bedwell Harbour, home of Canadian Customs, across three-mile-wide, often turbulent Haro Strait. It was not to be attained this day. Instead, we received another lesson learned over and over again: Take each day as it comes. Face changing conditions and deal with that change now! Forget goals. Handle each minute's situation as well as you can. Survival became the name of the game.

The wind picked up in the long sweep of the channel. We soon found ourselves battling white-capped waves blown by twenty-knot gusts against the incoming tidal current, which resulted in three-foot high tidal rips. Since we hadn't tested either our capabilities or the boat's, we decided to pull for a small islet and wait for calmer waters. The strong push of the current denied us that option as well. We were swept back down Speiden Channel, the boat bucking and bobbing on the roiled waters. "Pull hard!" Pete yelled over his shoulder. "We've gotta get ashore!"

"I'm pulling! I'm pulling!" My God, I thought, are we really crazy to undertake this voyage? Here we are on our second day out and we're in trouble. What will it be like in Georgia Strait or on the two stretches of open ocean?

The islet became unattainable as we were pushed out into the now pulsating current. Fear was set aside by the sheer physical effort of gaining ground. "We're not getting anywhere!" I screamed.

"Nope – can't make it – better cut back to Cactus Island."

Water sloshed over the gunwale and into my right shoe. "Pete," I screeched, "we're taking on water. We've gotta get to shore – anywhere – fast!" Sweat rolled down our sides as we pulled with all the strength we could muster. How I wished I'd lifted heavier weights last year. But now, all we could do was pull with what muscles we had.

It took us two hours of gut-wrenching work to gain ground against the wind and current and pull into the lee of Cactus Island. We secured to a private dock, seemingly deserted by its owners, and crawled onto the sun-warmed wood to collapse spread-eagled until our bodies recovered. We devoured our lunch ravenously and watched the current build to six or seven knots. It had been a hard pull. For the moment, we were both drained of energy. "My God, if we have many days like this, we'll each weigh about eighty-five pounds," I quipped. Pete weakly nodded his agreement.

In tidal streams such as the one we had just passed, the required effort became easily quadrupled over a "normal" rowing stroke. We often had to stroke twice as fast and pull twice as hard to get through the situation. On one occasion, we couldn't let up that pace for a little over two hours – a fair physical exam, among other things.

As the day wore on, we made some sorties away from the dock to test the waters rushing between our little islet refuge and John Island. Twice, we were over-anxious to be under way, and twice the current whipped us down channel. "Third time's a charm," said Pete. "Let's row the back eddies close to shore and see if we can work up the side of the island." It worked for about ten minutes. A large rock forced us to turn out and — whoop-the current grabbed us and gleefully spun us back down and past our refuge. It took double-time rowing to break out of its clutches and reattain the safety of our dock.

It wasn't until late afternoon that the current subsided enough to let us pull across the channel and row through John's Pass into Haro Strait. This body of water, often formidable in our sailing days, was now flat calm and benign. We pulled swiftly up the coast of Stuart Island and slid into the still waters of Prevost Harbour.

The sun was low on the horizon by the time we set up camp and ate dinner. We had only enough energy to clean the dishes before falling into our bags for the night. Again, only seven-and-a-half miles, but twice as hard as the day before. At this rate we would get into top condition fast. At an equally fast rate we were learning about currents and winds experienced at water level in a small wooden boat.

The night was quiet. No snarls nor scampering feet interrupted our sleep. We awoke refreshed and ready to tackle the strait that delineated the border between the United States and Canada. The actual boundary was about midway between the land masses of Stuart and South Pender Islands in the middle of a big ship channel — the main channel between Vancouver, B.C. and the Pacific Ocean. We expected to lunch in a foreign country.

As we loaded for departure, a friendly retired couple offered us three abalones they had wrested from the rocks the previous day. If you have ever captured these elusive delicacies of the sea, you know they do not relinquish their rockbound positions without putting up a good battle. The gift and good wishes which accompanied it warmed us.

During the time we remained or touched into inhabited sections of the islands and British Columbia coastline, we were to be showered with tokens of encouragement, positive thoughts and warm hospitality by the people we encountered. The rugged independent settlers of this wildly beautiful coastline understand and appreciate fellow adventurers. This was to be demonstrated to us time and time again.

We crossed Haro Strait uneventfully. No ships threatened us. The waters were calm and the wind nonexistent. Even the ever-present line of rips near the Canadian side was less roiled than usual. We passed through the mildly churning waters with ease.

Rip tides, caused by shifting and conflicting tidal currents, aggravated by the wind and sometimes bottom configurations, are present throughout the waterways of the Pacific Northwest. Most are charted, and therefore somewhat predictable, but they are nevertheless frequently startling in their intensity and apparent life of their own. They often run as rampaging rivers; frequently as noisy, sometimes roaring, as they build and subside and move into and out of channel areas and around islands and headlands. The waves of their chop sometimes build to over three feet, completely devoid of the customary rhythm of traditional waves. We encountered tide-rip areas daily all the way to Alaska.

We passed into the protected waters of Bedwell Harbour just before noon and checked through Canadian customs before heading to the laundromat, showers and delectable cheeseburgers.

The pleasure boaters whose vessels lined the multi-fingered slips at Bedwell Harbour wandered past our little dory, clucking in amazement at our undertaking. People wanted to be a part of our journey. The captain of the 78-foot sailboat, Harambe, out of Seattle, pressed us to take an old piece of cargo netting to cover the gear stashed forward of my rowing station. He thought it would help hold it in if we capsized. (Heaven forbid!) He also gave us grease for our squeaking oarlocks. A warm-faced man in a small cruiser gave us an enormous apple he had developed in his orchard in eastern Washington. It was a new strain of the Washington Delicious and the most succulent apple we had ever enjoyed.

By late afternoon the harbor current was running northward, so we slipped away and swept through the narrow pass separating North and South Pender Islands and entered Plumper Sound. Its name always reminds me of the strong ties between Canada and England. What could sound more English than Plumper? Most of the tidelands and shorelines here are considered Crown Lands, though private homes and docks dot the coastline.

We felt intrusive as we tied up to a small private floating dock off Mayne Island on Navy Channel. It was near 7:00 P.M. and we were out of strength and a helpful current. A rapid scanning had indicated no public campgrounds available in these more populated Gulf Islands. We could see no public beaches. We decided to ask permission to use the dock. No one answered my knock on the door of the cabin on the hill above the dock, but on my way back I encountered a gentleman who gave us permission to spend the night. We pounded our abalones into tenderness before frying them quickly over our backpacking stove and sat back to enjoy their succulence while the dock gently bobbed beneath us.

As dusk descended, a smiling gent paddled up in his canoe. He stopped to say hello and ask us about our boat. He was to be the first of many Canadians we met who had left former professions or occupations to settle into a new and simpler life-style. He had designed and built his home on Mayne Island and loved his new life of gardening and fishing. We heard his cheerful whistling as he paddled out to drop a line. "There goes a happy man," said Pete.

The first ferry passed by around 9:00 P.M., a half-mile away and completely unexpected. Our floating bed rocked violently from the wake. We shot upright instantly as though we had been in an earthquake. My hand shot out of the plastic cocoon we had created from our tarp, clutched one of the dock edges and held on until the water calmed. How jolting – out of our first deep sleep! Another ferry passed by at 10:00; another at 11:00 and the last churned by at midnight – each time after we had fallen back into slumber.

We arose at 4:00 A.M. to catch the last three hours of flood tide. Feeling unrested, we piled our gear into the boat and headed toward Montague Harbour, a provincial park about eight miles away on Galiano Island, where we hoped to have breakfast. In the starless pre-dawn darkness, the water was calm and black, the nearby land mass formless and blacker. We rowed quietly and easily, guiding on some distant blinking channel markers. The air was heavy and unmoving. With the aid of the slight current, we moved past Mayne and out into Trincomali Channel, neither of us saying much. Our reveries were suddenly shattered by the blast of an out-of-sight ship's horn in Active Pass, about a mile to the east of us. By now it was light, and clear to us that we were in the middle of the channel used by ferries and some deep-draft ships headed for the open sea via the Strait of Juan de Fuca.

Instantly, and as one, we started pulling hard to get out of the channel. At the same time a menacing gray-green ship carrying export logs rounded out of the pass churning directly toward us, her deck cranes angled as the arms of some gigantic monster, her engine pounding and a big bone in her teeth. If at first our motivation was concern, now it was fear. We were such a small target, so difficult to see, especially on this calm early Sunday morning when an alert watch was unlikely in the wheelhouse. We strained harder and harder, unable to judge his course accurately. By now we could easily make out the name above the frothing white bow wave, Southern Express. Express was apt. She appeared to be aimed right for us. Now we were panic rowing, unable to budge from a point dead ahead of her bow. She was coming fast, slicing clearly for our midships. I was unaware of any physical feeling and pulled frantically at my oars. By mere inches we seemed to move across her bow. While we felt close to standing still, frozen on her bow, she charged toward us. Slowly now, her starboard bow came more clearly into view, then abruptly, her beam.

As quickly as she came, she passed by about a hundred yards away, a Nanco freighter out of Moravia, unaware, I'm sure, of the two sweating, sprint-spent rowers left bobbing violently in her wake. We both slumped over our oars, winded and suddenly let down. Pete's head glistened wet with running sweat. My whole body felt damp. This entire episode had lasted maybe twenty minutes, more like one of those quick, vivid, frustrating dreams experienced in that half-sleep just before we awaken – at first we're not sure whether it happened or not. So we bobbed in silent relief. "Whew," I breathed softly. "Do you suppose there is any way we could have known that was coming?"

"I don't think so," answered Pete. 'I probably should've brought along a Canadian ferry schedule, but I don't know how you can tell when freighters are going to pass by."

"Well, that one was a little too close."

"I'm hungry," said Pete. "Let's get into Montague."

"I'm with you. I could down a whale." And I think I could have, blubber and all.

The deserted crescent beach created from crushed clam shells shone glaringly white in the early morning sun and crunched with every step. As the water receded with the ebbing tide, clams were revealed everywhere. They squirted water vertically, sometimes over twelve inches high. We couldn't harvest them, however, because of PSP warnings. Almost all the beaches in the inland waterways where there was heavy boat traffic were closed to bivalve harvesting either because of Paralytic Shellfish Poisoning (PSP) caused by an organism carried in "Red Tides," or because of bacteria from human contamination.

Because we had pulled onto a very shallow shelf beach, Pete decided to anchor out to avoid going aground. So after a filling and satisfying breakfast, he headed out to face his first experience with Surfbird's ground tackle. We had purchased almost 400 feet of light yellow polypropylene line because it was strong and floated. It was also lighter to carry than nylon line. No one mentioned that it snagged. It snagged on rocks, driftwood, shells, portions of the boat, us and mostly on itself. It developed knots and tangles with no assistance from human hands. Sometimes it even seemed to come alive, writhing and contorting all on its own.

Pete is a patient man (How else could he have survived years of marriage to me?) For two hours he sat offshore calmly pulling all 400 feet of line through loops and knots over and over again. I heard an occasional, "God Almighty," but not much else. I sat on the beach writing in my journal, reading, enjoying the warm sun, secretly glad that I was not the one wrestling with the stubborn line.

"From now on we'll prepare our anchoring lines on the beach," Pete pledged when he finally finished his chore. "But this system is going to work OK."

By 1:00 P.M. the tide had slackened and began to flood again. We pulled north toward Wallace Island, that wonderful spot where the book, Once Upon An Island was created. It had a magical place in my imagination, as the author's homesteading experiences had been imprinted so vividly. The wind was blowing gently from directly behind us, so we pulled into a tiny cove of that island to rig Surfbird for sailing. This was the first time. She took to the breeze nicely and moved at about three knots. It felt good to both of us to drift north in a gentle, sun-warmed breeze.

In less time than it would have taken rowing, we reached Hall Island where we docked at another private float and asked the owners for their permission to camp ashore. Permission granted, we set up camp on a dry grass knoll overlooking their dock and Saltspring Island beyond. The couple owned this fifty acre island. I wondered what it would be like to live on your very own island dependent only upon yourself and your spouse. No ferry served their island. Everything had to be brought over from Ganges, county seat and the biggest shopping center on Saltspring.

Today, with the aid of our sail, we had covered seventeen miles — a record so far — and gratifying to us since we had spent about three mid-morning hours back on the beach at Montague Harbour. By now we found we could row steadily at a rate of two knots in little or no current or wind. Our hands were callused and our shoulders, legs and backs strengthened. We could, when called on, maintain an even stroke for four hours without stopping, but usually tried to break each hour. We programmed energy snacks for mid-morning and mid-afternoon. With a light following wind we often set sail and rowed simultaneously at three to three-and-a-half knots. An estimated twelve to fifteen- knot tail wind could move us at about four knots, but any wind much over eighteen knots was uncomfortable and dangerous.

We estimated wind speed by the appearance of the water's surface. The Beaufort Scale (see Appendix B) spelled out the conditions fairly accurately.

Bed time arrived early for us, as we were always exhausted from the combination of early rising, fresh air, lots of food and hours of rowing. Neither of us read very long after writing in his or her journal. Our eyes kept dropping shut, even before the sun had set. Tonight was no exception. Dinner consisted of crackers and peanut butter. We were tired — too tired to cook.

An otter slithered in and out of the water as we quietly slipped our lines at 5:00 the next morning. The lovely creature appeared to take great joy in this playful interlude. We were excited to be so close to his watery playground.

We rowed and sailed past Reid Island and the Rose Islets, marveling at the orange-splashed sunrise peeking through Porlier Pass from the Strait of Georgia. We fairly glided past the Pylades and Ruxton Islands before pulling into the protected bay of the provincial park called Pirates' Cove on DeCourcy Island. Here we prepared a late breakfast and waited for slack current before heading around the back side of Mudge Island rather than attempting the dangerous passage through Dodd Narrows. Waters rip through this narrow pass at nine knots during maximum current — too fast to handle comfortably in our little vessel. Even slack current does not produce quiet waters for long in this constricted passageway.

Before we entered the shallow waters of False Pass, we passed a herd of seals resting on some offshore rocks. We counted at least thirty-five gray and a few speckled animals. As we stroked by, they all slipped into the water to accompany us. Shiny black and mottled gray heads appeared to be swimming Labrador Retrievers as they popped up just off our stern to stare at us with unquestionable curiosity. Six seals separated from the main herd and surfaced repeatedly nearer and nearer to our boat as we moved down channel. They stared and stared, pushing their shoulders high up out of the water cocking their heads to achieve a better view of our passing. Occasionally one would surface so close that it would frighten itself and flip back under in a rush of froth. They followed us for about an hour, giving us much pleasure in their companionship.

Boats drawing more than three feet could not move through False Pass until full flood tide, so we wended our way alone through the kelp, past two sailboats at anchor outside, awaiting their turn. We could move, for at most we drew five inches of water, fully-loaded. Exiting into a broader waterway, a stiff breeze from the stern filled our sail and moved us smartly past a smoke-belching lumber mill and into Nanaimo Harbour.

Newcastle Island Passage

PART III: (Pete) NANAIMO TO LASQUETI ISLAND: "FIRST WE HAVE TO CROSS THE STRAIT OF GEORGIA."

Nanaimo is a bustling port town nestled on the eastern shore of Vancouver Island. It lies due west of Vancouver, B.C., across the Strait of Georgia. In years past, because of its natural harbor behind Newcastle Island, Nanaimo became an Indian settlement. There they could easily snare the salmon that abounded around the smaller tide-swept outer islands. Later came the loggers to harvest the islands' abundant evergreen forests, followed by miners who drilled the coal deposits that lay under the town and harbor. In the days of steamships and steam engines, Nanaimo was one of Western Canada's main coaling stations, serving the coastal steamers that trafficked to Vancouver and Victoria, as well as the logging trains that worked the many timber camps. As one of England's dominion frontiers, it is not surprising that Nanaimo's coal mine and the island under which it extends were both named Newcastle.

Today, the mining and logging are gone, replaced by two large active mills, sport fishing and a ferry terminal that links this portion of Vancouver Island directly with the city of Vancouver on the mainland. Newcastle Island is now a Provincial Marine Park available only by boat. Its seven hundred-plus acres are dominated by a dense virgin evergreen forest, crossed occasionally and ringed by soft forest trails that access the many rocky outcroppings that surround the island. Each of these outcroppings harbor tide pools and pocket-beaches piled with driftwood and broken shells.

Newcastle Park was a logical place for us to lay off our oars for a day. We were five days out from our start on Lopez Island, having covered the seventy miles without much wear and tear on our bodies. Already we were stronger and leaner and more callused – both our hands and our seats.

From my journal: "We both started out wearing gloves but now don't use them. Our back, shoulder and arm muscles no longer ache at the end of a day, but we both note that our wrists and lower arms are still a little sore." I was glad to hear Nancy talk of the same soreness, for it was in the wrists and hands that I expected to aggravate my arthritis. My greatest apprehension about our undertaking was that it would flare to the point of forcing us to give up our goal. At Nanaimo, I could believe my aches and pains were normal and not arthritic. Though by now quite callused, our hands were slightly swollen — a condition that didn't leave us for another couple of weeks. There was no discomfort despite the swelling. By now, after about a week of rowing, we could row a couple of hours straight in moderate conditions without stopping, although we found it best to take a break at least every hour for the pleasure of some chocolate, or to observe better what was going on around us. Our bodies had also become more conditioned to the ground, letting us sleep better. We quickly learned to adjust around rocks and other lumps that invariably surfaced and grew during the night. Our small air mattresses fast qualified as Beautyrest substitutes.

Up to now, it all seemed quite easy. We'd had some intermittent rain and also some sun; not much wind. "This is nice," I commented as we rounded into Nanaimo Harbour. "From what we've seen so far, this should be a pleasant summer." We had sailed the six miles up channel from Dodd Narrows, secured the sail and broken out the oars. Rowing across the front of the town felt good — maybe even kind of special. I remember thinking, "We've come about a tenth of the way with no significant problems. Our boat is plenty seaworthy, good and stable even in twenty knot winds, easy for two to row when not against the wind. Our boat and us — we can do it." I think we both had felt even a touch of pride as we had moved up to the park dock. I had even fantasized as Horatio Hornblower, "Look smartly now lads. We'll not be seen as a Houligan crew." Rowing, we found, gives lots of time for musing.

We laid over a day in the park to take care of a lot of little things. I cut off part of the tiller for easier handling, re-bound the Beckett pulley to make it easier to raise and lower the sail. Nancy re-packed all the watertight bags to accommodate the order and frequency of use — things we used most and first each day on top, and so on.

Both at the park and during a brief grocery stopover at the public dock in town, quite a few people came over to see our boat and talk with us. All reacted with some expression of wonder. Most were encouraging. "That's great!" "More power to you!" "Gotta hand it to ya — y'r doin' somethin' while ya can," and so on.

"People here seem to appreciate challenge," Nancy noted, as one approving fisherman walked back to his boat. We felt encouraged.

While Nancy picked up some groceries, I organized our charts for the next leg. I kept folded and in order of use about five days of charts held in a flat, clear plastic waterproof container that we could use while rowing. The top chart was immediate reference and the bottom chart next. That way, we didn't have to change charts in the wind or rain — we simply had to flip over the container. The remainder of the charts were rolled up and stowed

PART III - NAMAIMO TO LASQUETI

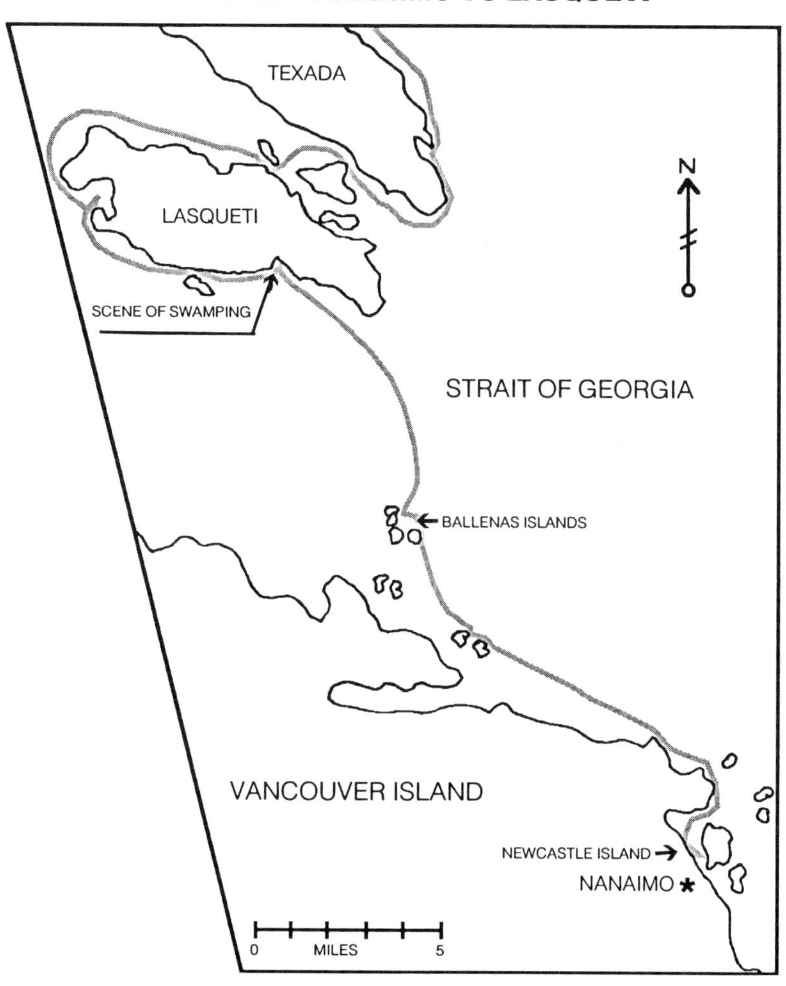

See chart
of coast
on page 4

in two waterproof tubes.

In our planning, we had thought that we could use small scale — larger area-charts, and thereby cut down the number we needed to bring. We had reasoned that we would row only ten to fifteen miles each day, and would therefore be able to see and discover suitable anchorages for our overnight camps. We had failed to consider the full reality of the slowness of rowing. An hour of steady rowing could easily be used to explore a small cove for a site that would be above the high tide line, flat enough for our mountain tent and secure enough to provide a protected anchorage for the boat. More detailed charts, we found, saved us a lot of rowing time — especially at the end of the day when we were tired and hungry and still had two hours of chores ahead to make camp, fix dinner and set up the anchoring system.

Years ago, on a sailing stopover in Nanaimo, we had found a very knowledgeable chart dealer operating out of a small magazine and book store on a crooked side street. He interested us because of his detailed familiarity with Canadian Pacific waters and the fact that he had never traveled to any of the places he knew so intimately. From our earlier experiences we had found his counsel to be accurate. "Let's find our chartman and fill in some details of our larger area charts. I'll find room for them someplace." Probably because she rowed mid-ship, and therefore farthest forward, Nancy fell into the role of cargo master-stower and unstower — and chart handler while underway. She was also more flexible physically for the contortions demanded of stuffing into and pulling out of the bow.

I agreed, "This may be the last place we'll find enough selection for what we need." An hour after we entered his store, we walked out with about 35 more charts and a lot better feeling about our trip. From those earlier sailing days, we were fairly familiar with the waters for the next hundred miles, but after that, everything would be new. Though we now had about seventy charts, we would later wish we had even more of larger scale.

The chartman had been enthusiastic about our trip. "I sure would like to see where you're going — beautiful country I hear. Some trip! I wish you well." As he rolled up the charts, back to us, he mumbled, "Maybe someday I'll go up there."

"Interesting man," Nancy commented as we walked up the street. "Sad that he travels mostly in his mind." I agreed somewhat absently, for now my mind was on the next leg, the Strait of Georgia.

That next section weighed heavily on both of us. For northwest boaters, this body of water is the most notorious. Separating Vancouver Island from the Canadian mainland, the strait runs just that way — straight — for about one hundred and fifty miles. It is a slot between two parallel mountain ranges fifteen to thirty miles across. What makes this slot so precarious is its direction — northwest to southeast, the directions of our most violent winds. Worse, these winds can come up with little warning and last for several days. There is ample distance to permit buildups to gale force and winds of that velocity occur frequently. Add heavy tidal current, chop and frequent rain and you have quickly worked into a setting for a memorable experience. Anyone who has crossed the strait more than twice in a small craft has a horror story to tell. All we asked for was a period of four or five calm hours.

On our day off at Newcastle, the strait was calm and the sun intermittently warm through some broken clouds. We hiked the five miles around the island, breathing deeply the moistness of the needled forest floor. In the quiet of ancient firs and cedars, slanting sun shafts highlighted the green moss and ferns. We interrupted several deer, a pair of flickers and a bright, red-topped pileated woodpecker intent on working his snag. Wrens and chickadees gleaned the tree branches and cones as though they were passing down a buffet table. After sitting for five days in our rowing positions, it felt good to stretch our legs. Though we were getting plenty of exercise, I missed my running routine.

As we came to pocket-beaches we looked in the tidal pools for orange and purple starfish and the other small world creatures that come to life in between tides. At one such east-facing beach, Nancy looked across at the flat calm strait. "This would have been an ideal day to cross. I hope this weather holds for two more days."

"Yeah, that would at least see us across the worst part," I replied.

The next morning was overcast, with a light southeast wind. We wanted to leave at slack low tide – around nine o'clock so we broke camp and started loading around eight. Each of us made several lugging trips over the quarter mile between our camp and the dock. On one such trip, as I returned up the gangway ahead of Nancy, I heard some commotion down on the dock near her. She had dropped her load and now ran toward the end of the dock. "Stop that!" She shouted. "Get out of here! Shoo!" I turned, just in time to see a crow in flight, making fighter-type attacking runs on an obviously wounded white dove. The frightened dove was finally forced into the water, where it somehow managed to flop its way under the overhanging end of the float. The crow, working off the end of the dock, was joined by a screeching seagull. In loud confusion, they made short, airborne thrusts under the dock, clearly in for a kill. They both jumped to nearby pilings as Nancy charged down on them, and they told her off in no uncertain terms. Next thing I saw, Nancy had reached in under the dock and pulled out the wide-eyed, cowering dove. She walked up the dock with it cradled in the front of her sweatshirt. "Those damn heartless birds!" She threw to no one in particular. She carried the dove up to a thicket of bushes and gently placed it under some thick cover. "Maybe it will be able to fly after its wings dry. Poor thing."

We left Newcastle on the flooding tide so we could work our way west about fifteen miles to an island jumping-off place. At that point, we could narrow our crossing to about seven miles to Lasqueti Island, and then cross the remaining six on another leg. That was a lot better than a fifteen mile crossing, for at our speed that could mean up to ten hours of rowing. A lot could happen in ten hours, especially in the Strait of Georgia.

Once we were outside the harbor and past the low entrance rocks and islands, we found a light southeast wind – enough to help us, but not enough to let us sail with any authority. "Let's row – sail and see if it works," Nancy suggested.

"Worth a try. We might be able to pick up a knot or two." The light wind was steady and enough to fill our sail. We moved up the coast at about three knots – very pleasant. We approached the two Ballenas Islands around six, the wind having steadily picked up throughout the afternoon. Around two we stopped rowing and sailed, running with a building sea within sight of our destination. The wind strengthened, now with gusts to twenty knots.

"We better take down the sail. We're lunging too much," I shouted as I moved to break out my oars. Nancy quickly released the halyards and struggled to lash the sail and boom – half balancing and half clinging to the swaying ten-foot mast.

"Let's get around that point of the island," she said, laying into her oars in rhythm with me. Rowing in a white-foamed sea was a new experience for us. We both glanced regularly over our right shoulders to judge our progress toward the rocky, spray-shrouded island. We seemed to be standing still.

"Pull harder, Nancy," I shouted.

"I'll try," she yelled back. Slowly we inched toward the point.

"Just a little bit more," I kept repeating, mostly to myself, straining as hard as I could.

A long half-hour later, wet with sweat, we rounded the point into a sheltered, crescent-shaped sandy beach. Looking around, we saw no signs of life. This was a restricted area belonging to the Canadian Navy. We hoped they wouldn't mind our using a small part of their beach for a night. We needed the advantage of the island off-shore position for our jumpoff the next morning. By now it was seven-thirty and we were tired. While Nancy built a fire and fixed dinner, I set up the tent and anchored the boat. It was ten P.M. when we finally climbed into our bags. Some time during the night I awakened to sheeting rain on our tent and a howling wind. "Damn!"

We were up at five-thirty, but disappointed to see whitecaps out on the strait. We decided to wait until afternoon in hopes that the tide change would bring a change in the wind. "Let's go look for some water," Nancy suggested. We followed a couple of old, disused trails, but found no water and no sign of recent human activity. By now it was raining hard.

"I'm going to walk up to the far end of the beach and see what I can find to eat," said Nancy. "Want to come?" Her voice came to me from within her yellow hood.

"No. I think I'll get some things ready to go." When I reached our tent, the collected rain bulged some low spots in our blue rainfly. How to get that water into our container? I had no funnel. Looking around, I soon found a clam shell, scoop-shaped, about four inches across with a kind of spout. Several hundred dips later, sitting in the pouring rain, I finally filled one of our plastic containers. I was satisfied with the effort.

After a cold lunch under a dripping cedar, we decided to try a crossing. The rain continued heavily, but the wind seemed to have slackened. We rolled up the wet tent and packed and loaded everything into the boat and started out. Our bay was calm, but the minute we broke out from our mask of land, the wind hit us. Eighteen to twenty knots on our starboard beam and two to three foot breaking waves. Almost simultaneously, we responded, "We have to wait til morning." We turned and headed back, saying nothing more. The calm of the bay was welcome, but neither of us was happy with the prospect of setting up our wet camp.

"I don't know what it will taste like, but I found a dinner," yelled Nancy wading up the beach toward me. What she had found was a moonsnail feeding along in about one foot of incoming tide. When feeding, the snail extends out of its shell to form an almost translucent beige muscular ring. It looked much like a submerged vacuum cleaner. It stretched perhaps fourteen inches across, pulsating as it gathered its edibles from the water. When challenged, it withdrew its mass back up into its shell, which is about the size of a Big Ben alarm clock, but much more attractive in its conch design. Being all muscle, it was strong, and even when cooked extremely tough. It was a dinner, but not one of our best.

We were up at four the following morning, feeling that we could go. The rain had stopped and the wind seemed slight. We ate a quick breakfast, broke camp and headed out. "Looks OK," I said, glancing across the strait, though obviously it was going to be a wet gray day. Lasqueti Island, a low, dark, mist-shrouded blur, lay seven miles north. We rowed past the second Ballenas and on out into the strait. "Let's see if we can sail," I suggested, for we had about twelve knots of wind. We moved nicely, though with no keel we set steadily to port — westward. About half way across, instead of slackening as we knew morning winds frequently do, the wind picked up to fifteen knots, then eighteen, then twenty. By now, we moved at about three knots, but lunged off of the parallel wave top as the wind gusted. We began to take spray over the starboard side. "Let's reef," I yelled into Nancy's yellow hood. She struggled to hold onto the mast while she worked the sail. We were about three miles from our target, a small harbor at the south end of Lasqueti. I shouted over the wind to Nancy, both of us facing forward, "The fastest way to get there is to sail, but I don't know how much longer we can do it safely."

"I don't like this at all," She threw back, clutching both sides of the boat to steady herself. After another half hour, it became clear that we were sliding too far north to make the south end of the island. I tapped Nancy on the shoulder, shouting against the wind. "I think we should head up the island and run with the wind until we find some sort of cove out of the storm." She nodded quick agreement, so I turned northeastward, letting the sail out. With the wind now at our backs, Surfbird picked up to four knots, but felt much more stable. Slowly, the island came to us, but only to reveal rocky cliffs and spray-covered, foam-charged rocks and outcroppings. We kept our heading for another half hour but found no place to duck into. Five minutes later, Nancy turned to me.

"There," she was pointing up ahead, "over there — looks like a narrow cove with a beach." I turned over to head where she pointed. As we came closer, a small cove broke away from the rocky cliffs, maybe a hundred yards deep and fifty yards across. I headed into it. Too late did I see the log-strewn pounding surf at its head. No place to turn, and with too much speed, we went on in, happy to rush toward shore.

"Drop the sail!" I shouted over the wind. Nancy responded quickly as I hauled in on the sheet, but it did nothing to slacken our speed. Surged by the surf, we were thrown to a grinding stop on a sandy beach. As quickly as we landed, the force of the wind and water pushed us broadside to the beach. Immediately, a breaker broke over the side, half-filling the boat with water. "Try to push us off," I shouted. "We're gonna swamp! Get the stern out!"' I had thrown my oars into their locks and was trying futilely to back-row off the beach with no effect whatsoever against the breaking, pounding surf and the flooding tide. Nancy jumped out and was quickly thrown down into the surf by a breaker. The same breaker filled the boat to my waist. I jumped out too, only to be thrown down beside Nancy. We both staggered against the waves to push against the boat. Shoulder deep in water, we managed to get the stern out. Too late. A breaker over the stern filled the boat with water. As if giving up, Surfbird settled on the bottom, her stern six inches under water along with all her contents. The mast and bow stem were all that showed, While all this was going on, I worked to hold off a thrashing thirty-foot spruce log that the surf was attempting to throw onto Surfbird. While Nancy somehow held off one end I found a line and tied it around the other end. We both hauled the log, Volga-boatmen-style, up the beach.

"We've got to get our gear out of the boat," I yelled, running drunkenly back down into the surf, half dragging and half leaning on Nancy. We both wobbled back in, oblivious to the coldness of the water or the sting of the rain-filled wind. Sometime in our approach the rain had started again, and it was pouring hard. It didn't make much difference, for by now we were thoroughly soaked.

At the far head of the beach were strewn hundreds of bleached logs, thrown like matchsticks by previous storms, now all above the high tide line. "Let's get our gear up there," Nancy shouted, pointing to some twenty-five yards away. To salvage our gear, we ran transfer relays from boat to logs. Food bags, sleeping bags, tent bag, photography bag, personal bags, oars, tiller, sail — on it went, fifteen, twenty, thirty trips each. We didn't count. We just ran, unloaded and dumped, two blurred figures in hooded foul-weather yellows and water-filled, knee-high, brown rubber boots. On successive trips to the boat we found things washing in: a sun hat (there's a laugh), a glove, a fish-bashing club, a floor board, another glove and so on. We finally cleared the boat of everything: floorboards, loose seats, a tangled mess of anchor line, fishing gear, rudder, clothes, everything – and all of it soaked. And there on the bottom, now under nearly two feet of water, lay Surfbird. With the rain pouring down on us and the wind and surf pouring in on us, we both stood together, facing into the wind, slack – armed staring down at Surfbird, as though we were facing an open casket in a bizarre nautical funeral. "We better call the Coast Guard," Nancy mumbled, mostly to herself. "It's over."

"No, by God! We're going to get out of this somehow," I flung back. But it did look like our trip was ended. We were both too drained to cry. "When we came into the cove, I thought I saw a cabin up on the top of that cliff," I said pointing to the south wall of the cove. "Let's go see if we can find some help, or some kind of shelter."

Off we slogged, not caring that our boots were filled with water, not knowing exactly what we wanted if we did chance to find someone. Just off the beach we found some old car tire marks in the mud, and a trail leading up into the forest in the general direction we wanted. We found signs of activity but nothing recent: a pile of plumbing pipes here, an old rusty stove there, a stack of water-soaked rough lumber off the trail, a plastic-covered stack of something. The trail wound upward around some huge old trees as well as among these piles of oddments, making a natural bed for the now gushing runoff stream. After maybe fifty yards, I stopped and turned, holding my hand out to Nancy, "Listen, do you hear something?'

Throwing back her hood, she cocked her ear up-trail. "I hear music."

"So do I. Where's it coming from?"

"Up that way." She pointed up and out toward the cove. A minute later, we broke out over a ledge to look down on a one-room, weathered, cedar-sided cabin nestled among the rocks. It was sheltered by several large evergreens and overlooked the cove perhaps a hundred feet below. From its outward appearance the cabin might have been empty, for the chimney was lifeless. But music definitely came from within.

I stepped onto the small porch, maneuvering around some empty cartons and a small pile of bark. It was around seven-thirty in the morning. I knocked. No answer. "How strange." I turned to look at Nancy.

"Knock again – harder," she replied, now blue-lipped and shivering. This time I pounded, the third pound producing a crack in the door that revealed a woman, hair uncombed, barely awake, clutching a robe to her throat. In absurd unison, we tried to explain who we were, how we happened to be there and I know I included the ridiculous question, "Do you mind if we use part of your beach for awhile?"

"My God," she said, "come in and get out of those wet things. I'll start a fire and put on some coffee. You look miserable." Had those words ever sounded better?

"We better take our boots off out here," Nancy said, pouring about a quart of water out of her left boot.

In a few minutes, the small barrel-shaped metal stove radiated its warmth. From the far corner, dressing with her back to us, "I'm Diane. My husband, Errol, is away, but he'll be back this afternoon. I work up in False Bay and I've got to run now to work. I overslept." Brushing her hair, she turned, "You make yourselves at home here — you have to find wood outside — there's some piled up the hill. There's some milk in the cooler, still fresh and some bread and eggs and cans of stuff under the counter. Water's out in the rain barrel. I'd love to talk with you but I've gotta run. I won't be back until late tonight."

She struggled into her cardigan and made for the door. "Please stay tonight — we've plenty of room and we can visit in the morning. I'd really love to talk with you." With that she was off, walking or driving to work, we didn't know which.

"If you go down and get our clothing bag, I'll fix us some breakfast," Nancy said, peeling off her wet sweater. We'd been up since 3:30 — four long hours! We were both starved.

Inside, our clothing bags were miraculously dry. Dressed in dry clothes, we nestled up to the stove to eat scrambled eggs, fresh buns and hot coffee. The world was now a far better place.

By noon, after several trips down to the boat, we had dried our food and personal things in the cabin. By one o'clock, the storm had passed, the tide was out and the sun broke through to reveal Surfbird isolated high and dry on the beach, filled with clear quiet water. By two, I had most of the logs in the cove covered with tarps and tent, pots and pans, charts and chain, line and lumps of water-warped bags of staples, all drying, including our soggy sleeping bags. Like a baker of giant pastries, I worked up and down the logs, turning this, spreading out that, to encourage the drying process. In between turns, I bailed out Surfbird. Later Nancy helped after she'd repacked our things in the cabin.

Around mid-afternoon, we were joined by a man and his dog. The man was in his early forties, bearded, his long hair blowing to the wind. He was dressed in near-white jeans, an equally faded flannel shirt. He stood in worn-over clodhoppers that were once brown leather. "Hi. I'm Errol and this's Paka. Diane said I'd find you here. Anything I can do to help?"

"You sure can. We need your strength to move the boat closer to the water." I wanted it out far enough to be afloat at six next morning. Surfbird is heavy and awkward for three men to move, but somehow we three managed to move it out about twenty-five yards. I then set up the anchoring system to hold when the tide came back in.

While we were moving the boat, we were entertained by Paka, a remarkable miniature black poodle type. He loved to chase sticks thrown over the logs. It was the way he chased that was amazing. He didn't run, he bounced — stiff-legged, like a gazelle, but at lightning speed, brushing the top of every log with all four feet. Errol threw and off went Paka — zap! Bounce,

bounce, bounce. Paka didn't tire of it, but Errol soon did. A great show while it lasted. We later heard from Diane that on one occasion, Paka misjudged a leap at great speed and came down jaw first on one of the logs suffering a brief concussion.

By five, everything was dry and the boat reloaded, ready for an early departure next morning. "C'mon up and we'll have a drink and fix some dinner," Errol urged. "Diane won't be back 'til late."

Errol was pretty laid back. He made his living – such as he wanted – doing odd jobs for the scattered permanent residents who lived on the south end of the island. Prior to moving to Lasqueti, he had been a computer programmer and software specialist in Vancouver. He was, we were to find, the first of a number of educated, professional people who had bagged the pressures and fast pace of urban life for a different drum beat in a more remote setting.

While waiting for the dinner that Nancy was preparing, Errol showed us some of Diane's work – poetry and watercolors of local beach and forest scenes. Both Nancy and I were impressed by her talents. Diane has since written us that she has sold some of both. We're sure we will hear more of her.

Errol insisted that we try some locally produced "white lightning" while we joined him in listening to his favorite tape by Pink Floyd. It seemed that we covered a wide range of philosophy as we ate and talked before we surrendered to the warmth, the lightning and the long day. We never did hear Diane come in, though she had to trip around us to climb up to their sleeping loft, and she said she wasn't very late. We had seen the day turn from high expectation to near disaster, and certainly our all time spiritual low. With everything dried and restowed and Surfbird afloat and undamaged we felt renewed. We slept well that night with Paka curled on our feet.

Next morning, Nancy and I were up at five and anxious to go. We planned to fix breakfast after a couple hours of rowing. Diane and Errol came down to the cove to see us off. "What are you going to do today, Errol?" Nancy asked.

"As little as possible," he responded with a grin.

"Nice people," I said, as we pulled around the point outside their cove.

"I'm sure we'll never forget them," Nancy replied. "What a lovely morning. Nice day for a row." And once again we were underway.

We planned to pass around the north ends of Lasqueti and Texada Islands, but by the time we had reached the north end of Lasqueti, the weather had turned again. It socked in and rained hard, accented by loud rolling thunder. "I don't see any relief on the west side of Texada in case the wind comes up," I said, as we lay-to between two small islands, waiting out a squall. "The only harbors appear to be south. I think we should go down around the south end of Texada. We'll lose another day, but it'll be safer. This weather's too unstable."

"OK," Nancy agreed. "Just hope the rain stops. I'd like to get out of my yellows eventually."

As we headed south, the wind picked up – not much, but enough of a headwind to slow us to about one knot. "At this rate, it will take us five hours to reach Tucker Bay. That looks like the first protected place to make camp." The headlands seemed to stand still. It took us over six hours of steady rowing. The rain stopped but we had rowed for eleven hours and were tired. Most of the afternoon was given to our own thoughts. Nancy was beginning to feel sharp pain in her hands and wrists from the constant pull of the oars.

The cove was shallow and rocky, which meant we had to anchor quite a ways out – another long haul to lug all our gear over mossy, basketball-sized rocks. We had just started to eat our rice/carrot/fish/stir-fry, when the sky opened up. Faster than we could tell about it, our fire was squelched and our dinner washed afloat in our plates. We still had our tent to put up and it was now dark.

It rained hard all night. Breakfast was cold and silent. As if we weren't already down enough, some creature during the night made off with our only pot lid.

A detailed search of the area failed to produce it. We broke camp and loaded up, everything sodden. Once more we struggled over the same slimy rocks. Both went about our chores mechanically; neither broke silence. We rowed out and southward, still saying nothing, both discontent, wrapped in our own thoughts. The rain had stopped though and the water was now calm. For easily an hour we rowed on, each of us transfixed by our wake – silent – hearing only the rhythmic dips of the oars. I remember thinking, the strait is calm – it would be easy to head back.

Nancy stirred first from her spell. "D'you hear the loon?" She asked, pointing leftward. "I think she's over in that cove." I didn't hear it, but Nancy hears better than I. As we looked, a seal poked his head up about fifty feet off our stern, and then another. We started to row again and they followed. "They're so darn curious," Nancy commented. "They look like puppies swimming after us." We four stayed in convoy for maybe ten minutes as we worked our way across the channel to the Texada side.

"Look how the sun is hitting that vine maple up on that rock outcropping," I said, pointing off to our right.

"Coming out of that mossy rock, it looks like a postcard," Nancy replied, "absolutely beautiful."

We rowed on for awhile, maybe fifty feet offshore, both just looking at the cliffs and trees just off to our right. The morning sun warmed our backs. "Maybe we've seen the worst of it," I volunteered. "It couldn't be any worse. Let's see if we can make it across Malaspina Strait today."

"We said we were going to make this trip. Let's finish what we started," Nancy answered. We picked up our beat and sat a little straighter.

PART IV: (Pete) LASQUETI TO SONORA: "THERE SEEMS TO BE A PRICE FOR EVERYTHING."

Though only a mile, rowing out across Quarry Bay started our juices running early. The bay is located on the B.C. mainland, about ten miles east of Lasqueti and Texada Islands. The wind was stiff against us; we bucked hard against two-foot white-capped waves. We were somewhat rested, despite having spent the night perched on a barely tent-wide rocky outcropping. Its green mossy topping did provide an element of luxury, and it didn't rain all night. "Maybe this wind will back to the south after we get outside and help move us north," Nancy offered. As we nosed out into Malaspina Strait it became clear that her forecasting skills still needed work. The wind did change, but to veer to the northwest and to pick up some strength – against us.

"Let's turn back and wait it out. Whadda you think?"

"Yeah. This is too hard," Nancy returned. We had pulled for about a half hour and had gained less than a quarter of a mile. With the wind, we returned quickly around the north head of Quarry Bay and found shelter in a niche along a darkly jagged rock cliff. So Nancy could fish to pass the time, I rowed slowly around in our small shelter. After awhile we traded positions. We each caught a nice bottom fish, enough for our supper. In time, filtered sun worked through the patchy morning fog to warm us. In response, we sat back to read for awhile, followed by an early lunch, in hopes we would be able to row all afternoon.

"Let's try it," I said, as I pushed down my last bite of peanut-buttered pilot bread, "I think the wind's slackened." It had, indeed, but not to give us pleasant rowing. It was twelve to fifteen knots, the waves about two feet. Still, we moved up the coast: dip, pull, pause, dip, pull, pause. Two hours later, we were only halfway to Cape Cockburn and displeased with our progress – only one mile for two hours of hard work. "Let's pull into shore and look for a place to rest."

"I'm all for that," Nancy answered. "I need to make a potty stop anyway." We were about a half mile offshore, cutting directly across a bight toward the cape. As we rowed in toward shore, we found a small cove, well sheltered from the wind. The short beach, in between two rock outcroppings, was fine-graveled and clean. At the head or the beach was a soft, natural tent site and an abundance of dry driftwood. For real pleasure, we each found bathtub-size tidal pools on the rock outcroppings, filled with fresh, clean salt water warmed by the early afternoon sun. "Absolutely ideal. Let's stay for the rest of the day. This is a bit of paradise." Nancy was ecstatic with our find and I was equally impressed. We first laid out all of our gear, including about two thousand soaked wooden matches. With the boring job done, we bathed in Roman-like luxury and lounged in the afternoon sun, reading and dozing, all things right with the world. Our two fish, broiled over an open fire, made our dinner and capped the day, a beautiful red-orange sunset providing a perfect backdrop for our glimpse into heaven. This afternoon was the perfect realization of our visualized trip to Alaska: warm, beautiful summer days, friendly waters, magnificent vistas and comfortable camp settings. A brief moment in Camelot.

We awakened to a clear day, breakfasted and sat back to enjoy our coffee in the warm morning sun as we looked out on the now docile Malaspina Strait. There was virtually no wind, but for the next three hours the current would be working against us. We could row against it though, and we would have the current and possibly a southerly breeze with us all afternoon. With twenty-one miles to go to Westview, we had a long day ahead.

Preparing to load our gear, we found the outgoing tide had left Surfbird afloat, but penned inside of four protruding, barnacle-covered rocks, each far too big for us to move. If we couldn't free the boat, we'd have to wait for the rest of the tide to go out and then enough incoming tide to refloat her — a period of about eight hours. We didn't want to lose that time today. Nancy lifted and pushed on the bow and I lifted and pulled the stern, trying to get the keel up onto the lowest rock. "We've got to move fast before the water runs out and leaves us stranded," Nancy urged. The first two attempts produced no results. The boat was just too heavy. On the third try, getting my shoulder deep under the transom, with a great push from Nancy, we edged the corner of the keel up onto the rock — a toehold. About eight more Herculean efforts by both finally worked the keel up onto the rock. Now, all we had to do was slide the length of the keel along and over the rock. The bow at this time was afloat, riding about a foot lower than the rock-held stern. We each took a side at the stern and tried lifting and pulling in unison while balancing our footing between the rocks and the bottom.

"Ugh! Ugh!" Each effort gained about an inch, until the boat, finally balanced in air, perched on top of the rock. After the stern dropped down into the water, the rest came easier. Twenty minutes of extreme effort freed the boat and left us weak, but happy to be once more in charge of ourselves.

"By God! We did it!"

"Seems like we always have to have something bad with the good," Nancy answered. "There seems to be a price for everything."

The sun did stay with us, and a light southerly breeze let us sail much of the afternoon — our record day for the entire journey — twenty-one miles in seven hours.

PART IV - LASQUETI TO SONORA

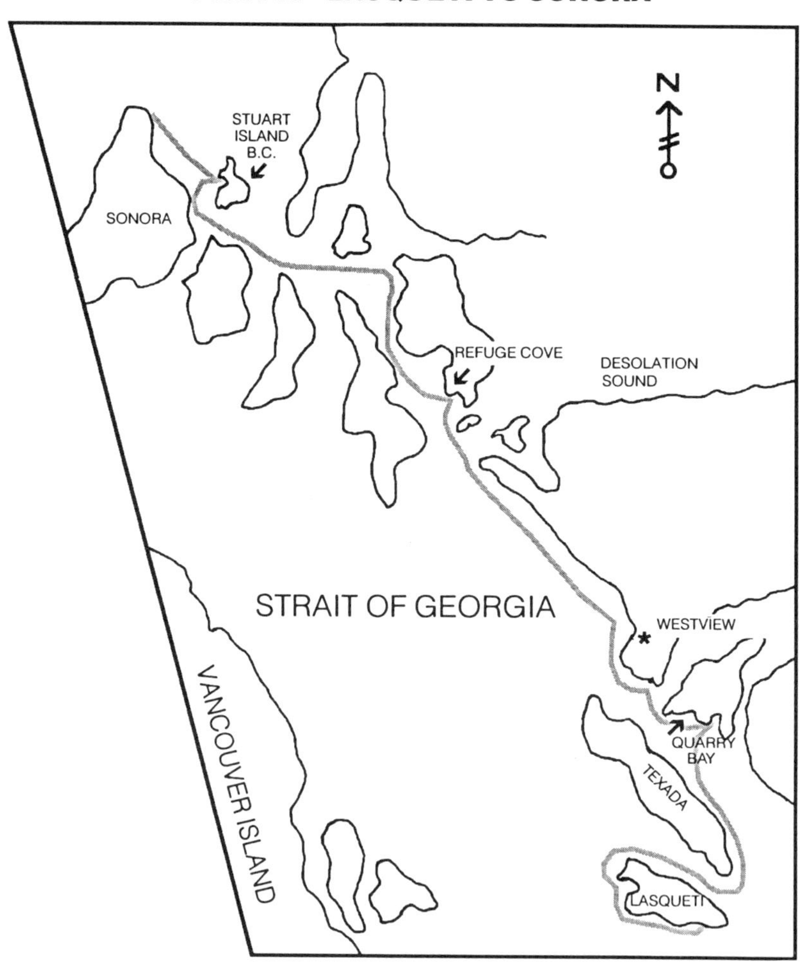

See chart
of coast
on page 4

Rowing up the coast, offshore twenty-five to fifty yards, permits a unique perspective of a coastline. What appears as a fairly straight shoreline on charts, especially larger area charts, turns out to be a series of rocks and coves and projections out into the water. The larger projections become headlands — something to be gone around. Our whole trip to Alaska became an unending series of those headlands. Often we could see as many as eight ahead or astern, the farthest often blending into haze. To see them in number meant that they did not extend out into the water very far. More importantly, these shorter projections would not be characterized by strong currents. Major headlands, often identified on charts as "points," almost always guaranteed strong flood and ebb currents. Playing the currents and back-eddies were an important part of our journey.

In the distance headlands lose clear definition, taking on rounder, smoother lines. The end always disappears into the water. These round smooth curves and lines — take on clear shapes, such as an alligator's head and body, or a grizzly taking a drink, a beaver swimming, human faces and noses and so on. Looked at behind us, a headland appeared quite different from its approaching profile. At far distances, ahead or behind, they often shimmered as mirages, suggesting islands instead of points of land.

Naming the headlands by what we saw was a constant diversion, providing both interest and conversation. Frequently, what we thought and hoped would be our target point ahead proved simply to be another headland, often one of several to go around before finally reaching our goal. When this happened, one of us usually reacted. "Oh my God! We still have another two miles to row."

We were north of Lund, a remote recreation settlement on the B.C. mainland, working toward an area called Desolation Sound. A gusting rain had stayed with us all day. The heavy gray clouds hung darkly just beyond arm's reach. The force of the wind beat the rain against our backs and into the rolling waves. Beyond a hundred yards the water and the rain merged into solid grayness. Whenever we turned to see ahead, rain slopped into our hoods and trickled down. Though often only a hundred feet away, even the black-treed shoreline stayed veiled and rain-streaked.

Our immediate goal was to find a campsite. We'd been looking for the past four miles and had found nothing. We hadn't spoken for over an hour. Unacceptable campsites required no verbal confirmation, especially in the rain. We both knew. We just rowed and looked and rowed some more. "Guess we have to cross the sound." Nancy broke the silence as we neared the end of the strip of shore we'd been hugging. "It's three hours more, but we know there's a cove there."

"I don't like the three hours, but I don't see any choice. Can't get any wetter," I replied. "How do you feel?"

"Tired and hungry," Nancy responded, "but let's go. The sooner we get there the quicker we can eat and curl up in the tent."

We had rowed for eight hours, the last three of which had been hard against a steady northwest wind across Desolation Sound. All around us now, steep rock walls dropped sheer into the gray water. "Let's try the lee side of that island ahead," Nancy offered as we pulled into a large cove, sparsely peopled at one end. This was our last hope for a campsite this day. "Maybe there'll be something there." As we approached, we could see no place to camp near the buildings at the end of the dock. Through the rain we heard the muffled sounds of a generator and a superimposing rock beat coming from a well-chromed cruiser tied up at the small dock.

Probably have their heater going so they'll be warm as they step out of their massage shower, I thought as we pulled away for the rain-shrouded island in the middle of the cove. After studying the situation around the dock, I looked at our chart, all wavy under its clear plastic covering. "It appears there might be a smaller cove out near the tip of that island. Let's go look."

Nancy nodded as she stroked to turn the bow toward the island. "Guess we'd better. There's nothing here." As we edged around the island, maybe half a mile, we came upon a strange sight. In the cove that we had seen on our chart, we saw a grid laid out on the water, about a hundred feet offshore. Four or five lines separated by about thirty feet. Each of these lines was held afloat by a buoy placed approximately every twenty feet along its length. The entire grid formed a rectangle, about three hundred by one hundred-fifty feet. It resembled an odd sized floating football field.

We moved around the grid toward a small frame building onshore that extended out over the water. From inside we could hear a generator operating. A door leading out to a small covered dock was open, so we rowed to it. I climbed out onto the dock and poked my head inside. At the far end I saw a man working, and at the same time he saw me. He stopped doing whatever he was doing and approached, a bearded young man wearing fishermens' bib foul-weather pants over knee boots. I'm sure he wondered who I was, especially as I was approaching from the water side. "Hello," I said. "My wife and I are rowing to Alaska, and we're looking for a place to put up our tent for the night."

"Jesus," he muttered as he poked his head out to see Nancy sitting in the boat. "You're going all the way up in that?" shaking his head, "Jesus! Sure not for me. Jesus! A place to camp?" turning back to me.

"Do you suppose we could spend the night on that side of the island?" I asked, pointing across the small cove.

"I don't own it, but I'm sure it's OK. 'Sides, who's going to say anything in this rain? Help yourselves—Jesus." With that he turned to go back to his work.

We did find a kind of level mossy site just big enough for our tent, having first rigged our big orange tarp over it. Because of an apparent layer of kelp on the bottom of the cove, I couldn't get the anchor to hold in any of about ten tries. When I changed from our Bruce to our pronged Danforth anchor, I found a bite, but I'm sure into the kelp. Fortunately our boat is relatively light and there was no wind. It rode OK all night.

As I was completing the anchoring-out process, still sitting in the boat, the man from the building approached me on a raft powered by an outboard motor and equipped with a boom and hand winch. "What are you doing here?" I asked, sweeping my hand from the building out over the grid.

"This is an oyster farm," he said. "We farm oysters," he added, as though to clarify his first statement. "We grow Pacific Oysters originally imported from Japan many years ago. This is an off-bottom farm. We have trays — four or five hanging down on a line from those long cables you see over there, a suspension down about every ten feet."

"How many are you growing, and how long does it take to grow an oyster?" I asked.

"Thousands. Oysters can live to about twenty years, and I've seen 'em almost a foot long. Mostly, we harvest in two to three years, when they're four to six inches long. Good flavor then, and tender."

"Why here?" I indicated in this cove.

"Shallow bottom and muddy — the trays stay suspended even at low tide, and the tides bring a good food supply for the oysters twice each day. No big waves to really disturb anything. Good place to grow cultured oysters."

"Good market?"

"We seem to be able to sell all we can produce. Main thing is to make sure we can harvest every year. Well, we're both getting wet, and I've got work to do. I've got to take in some oysters off some trays now. Some that are ready for shuckin' and shippin'. I like your boat, but all the way to Alaska? Jesus!" He pulled away and I completed my anchoring.

"Learn something every day," I mused.

We slept in the rain, breakfasted in the rain, packed in the rain and headed out in the rain. Not much different from an oyster's life, I thought as we turned on up the narrow channel.

All day the clouds clung to the water, hiding the heights of the nearby shorelines. In this gray world above and below, the dense evergreens that closed us in on each side of the channel washed black. "It's like rowing in a tunnel," Nancy observed as we worked along.

The wind was behind us, ten to twelve knots. It had shifted from the day before. The waves, though only about a foot high, were choppy against an oncoming current. We had to work to make progress. This was now the third day and second night of uninterrupted rain. Neither had much to say. We were simply pulling for a cove up ahead about ten miles, our day's destination. "Maybe, at least we'll find a decent campsite," Nancy said, as much to herself as to me.

"God, I hope so," I responded mostly to myself. "I could use some sun too — or at least some dry."

We found neither. The only possible site was on a small low island southeast of Sonora Island. It was partially covered with low salt-water grassy plants that grow among the rocks. Very high tides leave little of this island showing.

Anchored nearby was a small fishing boat, a large, black, tarp-covered flat-nosed aluminum skiff. Its single occupant was fixing his supper in the uncovered stern area, smoke rising from a small woodstove. About the time we got our tent and tarp up, he rowed over in his dinghy. He was not alone. Sitting in the bow was a large, black, long-haired dog, about a hundred and fifty years old, obviously having trouble maintaining his balance even in this quiet backwater. "He won't let me leave him – wants to be with me all the time, but mostly, he sleeps, especially in rough water. Been with me more years than I can remember. I come over to pick some glasswort and goose tongue. I cook it up for dinner every night I can find any. You oughtta try it. Here I'll show you." He approached shore and climbed out of his boat, still in the rain.

We tried it and it was OK, a bit salty with a biting tang. It became a familiar addition to our routine dinners and gave us minerals and vitamins missing from our normal fare. He picked some for himself and returned to his boat without saying another word. "Strange man," Nancy observed, "appears lonely and vulnerable yet almost unfriendly – except to tell us about the grass. I hate to think of the day he loses his dog – and that day can't be far away."

Most evenings, after dinner, we crawled into our tent. We were most often on a densely forested shoreline. There was usually no place to walk and we had put in a full physical day. We read every night until we dropped off, always while daylight was still full. This far north, darkness ran from about 10 P.M. until 4 A.M. Regardless of the day's events or circumstances, our natures let us be cheerful and social most of the time and especially during this evening period. We never seemed to run out of things to talk about. But afternoons, while rowing, usually included long periods of quiet time when each of us was content with our own thoughts. Even during these periods, an unusual happening or observation would pull us back from our woolgathering and pick up a conversation.

PART V: (Pete) SONORA TO MINSTREL: "WHIRLPOOL! WHIRLPOOL!"

On this voyage, Sonora Island is a turning point, like: "Go north on Main Street until you come to 85th and then turn left." We had worked our way north inside Vancouver Island, among the hundreds of beautiful islands that lay off the British Columbia mainland. Spectacular scenery surrounded us: islands, inlets and snow-capped mountains plunge deep into sparkling blue waters. Scores of hidey-holes provide protected anchorages for the many pleasure boaters who find their way up into these still rather remote wilderness waters. Shielded from the cold Pacific Ocean by Vancouver Island, waters in these parts, though tidal, hold heat from the sun. As a result, from mid-July through mid-September, both the salt water and lakes are comfortable for swimming – almost tropical. We have sailed many times in these waters, each time seeming to surpass the last in beauty, pleasure and pleasant surprises. Sunny days provide the best memories. For us on this trip the sun had ceased to exist for the past two weeks. Beauty is hard to see through days of constant rain – but we knew it was there.

At Sonora Island the route turns left – west to traverse across Northern Vancouver Island. Actually, we were to head a little north of west for about a hundred miles, until we came to the Pacific Ocean, at which time we would turn north again.

Charts of the area around Sonora Island show rapids. Some have names like Yaculta and Dent and Greene Point and they pass such places as Whirlpool Point and Mermaid Bay. These rapids are narrow passageways through which large volumes of water must pass, four times daily, twice each way. Some of these rapids reach a velocity of twelve knots at maximum flood or ebb. Right outside of Big Bay on Stuart Island is the confluence of waters out of the Dent Rapids from the west and Arran Rapids in the north, converging through the narrow Barber and Gillard Passes to form the Yaculta Rapids running south, like two rivers joining. Where they converge, large fast-moving whirlpools form. Here, we wanted to be especially cautious.

At Big Bay we checked our current tables and found that slack current would be at 4:30 A.M. next morning. It would take us about half an hour to row out into midstream and another half hour to pass through the

PART V - SONORA TO MINSTREL

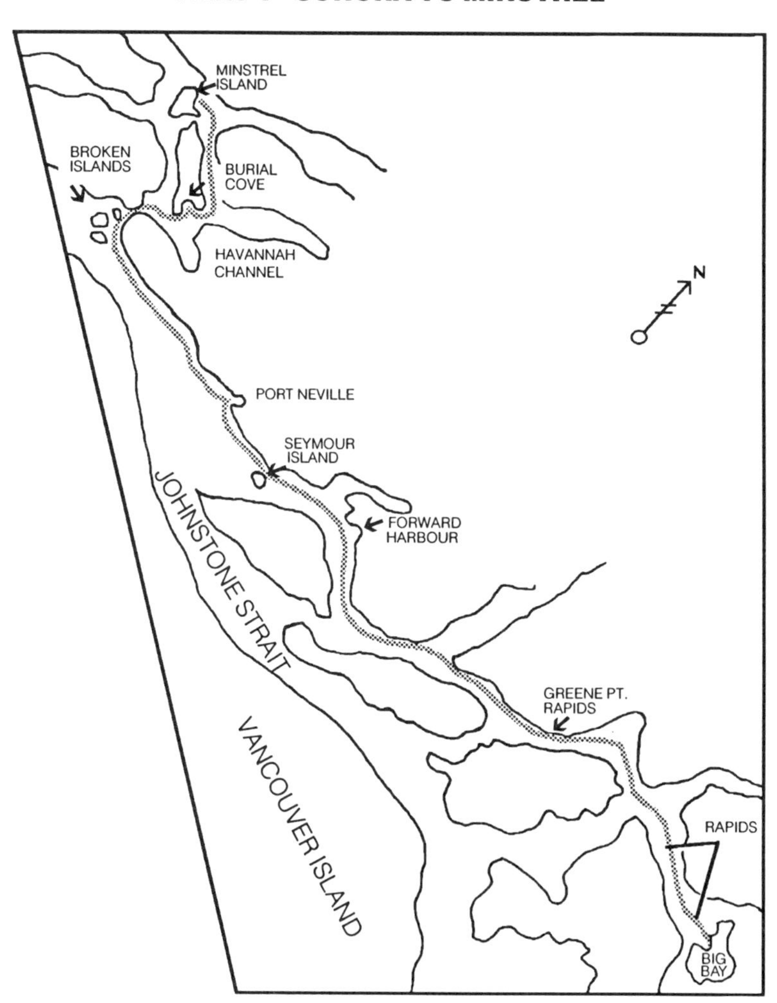

See chart of coast on page 4

first narrows.

Up at 3:00, we breakfasted, loaded and were out by 4:00. It was still dark. The ceiling was completely overcast. As we approached mid-channel, the pull became surprisingly difficult. "What's going on?" Nancy shouted. "The current is supposed to be slack."

"What's that noise?" I shouted back, half turning while still rowing hard. The noise was like a fast-rushing river, only now it became a roar. Faintly, out of the west, we saw what appeared to be a foot-high wall of turbulent white water snaking across the channel toward us. In an instant we were hit by that wall and shoved backward. At the same time, the stern of the boat turned clockwise, at first slowly and then quickly whipped, pushing the starboard rail over.

"Whirlpool! Pull hard on your left oar," I yelled, straining as hard as possible on my own left oar. Shortly, that whirlpool let go, only to be replaced by another. We spun. Then we spun again. Then again. "Harder!" I yelled, "Or we'll be moved miles down stream." After the first turbulence, the waters weren't as riled. The current was strong though, and we had to pull hard to loosen the grip of each whirlpool: hard, fast strokes, easily forty a minute. At times our rears never touched the seat. Our legs and arms became simply part of our oars. After half an hour of this, in first light, we saw that we had made absolutely no progress. "We're standing still!" I shouted. "Row harder! We've got to make that island over there by the flashing light!" By now we were both soaked with sweat. Every muscle ached. Feeling had left our hands and our lungs screamed for air. A stroke a second! "Don't stop! We're gaining on it. Pull!"

"As hard as I can," Nancy managed, following me stroke for stroke. Slowly, the island came to us. Finally, Nancy grabbed onto an overhanging cedar bough. We pulled ourselves into a little niche in the island, secured the bow and stern lines to branches and both folded onto our seats. After a few minutes our normal breathing returned and the pain in our shoulders, wrists and legs subsided. I glanced at my watch. "We were an hour in that cougar." I grabbed deeply for air. I could still manage little more than a whisper. "That was tough."

"More like a whole day," Nancy returned. "I've never worked harder. I don't understand what happened."

"Let me see that current table." Nancy pulled it out of its case and handed it to me. "I see now. How dumb can we be? We forgot to correct for daylight saving time. We hit that current at max flood!"

"Oh damn — no wonder! How stupid! Let's have our morning snack now. I'm starved." It was only 5:30 A.M.

The rushing waters soon subsided and turned in our favor. We pushed out and passed with the current through Dent Rapids, an easy eventless pull. We wanted to get up to Cordero Island, about twelve miles away. Cordero defines the east end of the Greene Point Rapids, a good place to start tomorrow's row.

Shortly after our real mid-morning break, it started to rain and continued through lunch and all afternoon. "Looks like another wet tent night," Nancy muttered as she checked her trolling line. So far, we had dragged a line every day and not caught any salmon. Lots of fresh firm bottom fish had found their way into our frying pan, but we continually hoped for a salmon — a real delicacy for us.

"Hope we catch something soon," Nancy said. "I don't want to hunt for clams or mussels in this rain."

We were just off Channel Island in Cordero Channel, about eight miles west of Stuart. So far we had taken probably ninety percent of our evening meat from the water: Fish, clams, mussels, oysters, often garnished with wild onion, goose tongue and glasswort. Most often we caught bottom fish: Greenling, blue and copper rockfish, tomcod and an occasional small sole. We had no crabs because a crab trap was too bulky to carry. Every day, almost all day, we dragged our line. Rather, Nancy dragged her line, for she is the inveterate fisher. Today was no exception. "Hold it, Pete. I've got something on." Nancy had dropped her oars and picked up her pole. "It's heavy, whatever it is. It's not fighting." She continued to reel and we both stared at the line climbing out of the water. "I can't believe the weight," she added. "Get the net ready in case."

"Look at that," she said, trying to hoist her prize out of the water. "Get the net under it — quick! Oh my God! Have you ever? Can you get it in? Hurry!" What she had was about a twelve-inch greenling on her hook. But at sometime in the process, a thirty-inch lingcod had tried to swallow the greenling. He had half-succeeded and was still holding on. She had both.

"He's too big for the net," I cried. "Pull him a little higher." Each time I came up with the net, he managed to flip out.

"Hurry," Nancy urged. "Don't know how long I can hold him!"

By now I was over the rail so far that my elbows were submerged. I tried to scoop the net deep then up over the lingcod's tail. When I'd get him half in, he'd flip out. This time I went deeper and Nancy horsed as high as she could. The fish slapped violently and the small greenling tore off the hook, neither into our net. "Damn!" Nancy shouted. "Damn! Damn! So close! This just isn't our day."

By 4:00 P.M. we were still skunked. "I don't like the looks of this," Nancy said, as she checked her lure for the umpteenth time.

"What's that ahead, over there on that tree?" I was pointing toward the shore, about fifty feet to our left.

"Looks like a new sign of some sort. Let's go look." As we moved closer, we could see a hand-painted sign, fairly new: RESTAURANT. The arrow pointed directly across the channel. On the other side, less than a mile away and low to the water, we made out a small building, like a houseboat, for it looked to be afloat. "Let's row over and see," Nancy urged. "Maybe that's the floating restaurant we heard about back at Big Bay." As we crossed the channel, through the steady downpour, we approached a fairly new, shingled, un-painted one-story house afloat on logs, fronted by a broad dock. One other boat, a runabout, was secured up the float closer to the shore. As we came alongside, a smiling bearded man approached to take our bow line.

"Hello. I'm Reinhardt Kuppers. Welcome to Camp Cordero. Come in before you get any wetter. You might want some fine German cooking."

Nancy beat him through the front door, squishing in with the speed and agility of a sheepherder headed for town. When I came in, Nancy introduced me to Doris, Reinhardt's wife, a warm, outgoing, obviously hard-working woman in her mid to late thirties.

The Kuppers had emigrated from Germany to Canada, and after a brief stay in Vancouver, decided to try to make a go of it in a more remote setting. Here, on the north bank of Cordero Channel, completely on their own, they built this compact floating lodge. A nice, wood-warm restaurant looked out over the water. Their lodge included three cozy guest rooms, all immaculate. Doris' menu made us think we were in a small Bavarian inn. When they showed us a compact, cedar-paneled room complete with two ship's bunks, Nancy and I chorused without consultation, "Is this room available tonight?"

After a marvelous schnitzel dinner, complete with spatzle, schnapps and a round of "Ein Prosit," we turned in, warm, filled and brimming with good feelings and fellowship. Never had the rain sounded better — outside, heard clearly through the open window for all of a minute before we both dropped into deep sleep. Next morning, we quietly cooked our own breakfast in Doris' galley and slipped away around 5:00 A.M. as we wanted to pass through the rapids at slack current. The rain had stopped, replaced by a heavy gray fog, making it difficult to distinguish any landmarks. Out in midstream we heard the muffled sounds of two trollers' small diesels, pushing north for the fishing season. We couldn't see them and we knew they couldn't see us, even on their radars. "Let's listen, and when we hear no engines, we'll shoot for the other shore and hug it until we reach Wellbore Channel," I whispered. Except for those distant engines, everything was still. I felt we should be, too.

Crossing the channel in the fog was eerie. No sound now, other than the dipping of the oars. No reference points on shore or by the small islands midstream. No current direction. Were we going straight, or in circles? We didn't know.

The shore almost hit us before we saw it. We breathed easier, particularly as we could hear another approaching troller. Many, we knew, used this northern route for their summer passage to Alaska to avoid the treacherous possibilities further south in the Seymour Narrows. "Let's stay in close," Nancy urged. "I don't want to tangle with a fishing boat. One nice thing about fog though: no rain."

"Amen."

"I wonder if there'll be enough boat traffic for Reinhardt and Doris to make it?"

"I sure hope so. If any two people have earned it, they have. Nice people." After about two hours of rowing, the fog began to lift, allowing shafts of sunlight through. The area over the water became a soft golden cloud, wisping above and near us, ahead, behind and on both sides. The green of the cedar and arbutus and the moss on the shore turned bright yellow-green, as though splashed by fairy gold, all touched with droplets of moisture glistening diamond-like in the muted sun. For five minutes, we simply drifted in complete stillness in the wonderland, both letting our oars go, touched as we were by a mystical feeling.

"Where's Snow White's castle?" Nancy whispered. I nodded my head, hardly believing what we were experiencing. Then, as quickly as it came, it went. The fog continued to lift, replaced not by the sun we had hoped for, but by a soft steady rain. "Listen!" Nancy had stopped rowing and was looking over her right shoulder as I turned toward her. "Do you hear talking?"

"I hear something, but I don't know that it's talking. Kind of a babbling. Where?"

"Up ahead on the shore. It must be those crows." Nancy was pointing to a low, small, rocky point just up channel. We stopped rowing to watch, the current idly carrying us toward the gathering.

On the point was a group of about eight crows. They formed a yard-wide circle that enclosed a single crow. They seemed oblivious to us as we drifted toward them. First one crow talked and then the group responded, not loudly, as when "cawing," but more in muted guttural tones. Then another took a short talking lead, to be followed again by the deeper-throated mutterings of the group. By some signal after a particularly active group response, the circle opened up and the group made threatening peckings toward the "defendant." In response, he waddled over toward the shore trees and stopped, about fifteen feet away and sort of hunkered down, stooped-winged, neither standing nor lying, saying nothing. One by one, the rest of the crows flew off, all silent. The lone crow remained until he dropped from our sight as we rowed on. Had he just been drummed out of the corps for some violation of crow code?

In King Solomon's Ring: New Light on Animal Ways, Konrad Lorenz tells about the judicial system he has observed among jackdaws and other corvids. Others, too, who have studied crows, have written of their rather advanced communal systems that have included kangaroo courts for trial and punishment of offenders among their group. "I wonder if we've just seen a crow court?" Nancy asked.

"It sure looks that way to me," I responded. "Whatever he did must have been pretty bad. I wonder if they have punishment to fit the crime? I feel like we've seen an intimate part of birdland – crowland, actually. Do you suppose he gets time off for good behavior? Does he have to leave the group, or just take a lower pecking number?"

It was near noon when we turned north into Wellbore Channel. We searched the shoreline closely looking for bear. Here, a couple of years earlier while sailing, we had seen a black bear feeding on berries on this eastern shore, but that had been in August, and this was the end of June. Where, we wondered, was our summer? By now the rain was steady, falling straight.

"Let's get into Forward Harbour and make a camp. I'm not ready to tackle Johnstone Strait today," Nancy said with a tone of resignation that I didn't care to challenge. For other reasons, though, I quickly agreed. My clothes clung damply and I could feel the chill permeating beneath my multiple layers of clothing.

For foul weather gear we both wore the yellows we had used for years while sailing. Nancy's suit was a heavy, rubberized material of commercial grade, made in Norway. Mine, imported from England, was lighter, more suited to yachting. The jacket worked fine: light, roomy, well-vented and quite up to the demands of this trip. (I still have and use it.) The suspendered pants presented a problem. While rowing, one obviously sits. In our case we sat on fixed seats, not the kind that move forward and backward as in racing shells. Our rowing motion includes a constant twisting on the buttocks. Though slight, this twisting carries with it all the weight of the torso. This constant motion is abrasive on covering garments even though we sat on polyurethane pads. In rather short order on this trip, I had worn through the outer surface and bottom seam of my rain pants. I tried to solve the problem of the leaky seat through the use of silver ducting tape, our universal First Aid for everything. By the time I was through with this antidote, I was sitting on a solid pad of triple layered duct tape, permanently bent to the sitting position. In front, a vertical stripe of tape ran from my crotch to my navel. When I walked, it looked as if I were wearing a lead chastity belt that prevented me from proceeding in anything but a sitting position. Worse, despite all my taping efforts, the seat still leaked. Every time it rained, I would be soaked from waist to knees. Today, I looked forward to drying my pants.

No such luck.

We rowed ashore around the hook of the harbor and pulled the boat up onto the muddy beach so we could go look for a campsite. "You go that way," I said, "and I'll work back toward he hook. With these high tides, we'll have to find something up in back of the treeline." The underbrush along the treeline was dense. After about five minutes, we had each covered about three hundred feet of shoreline. I had found only one possibility. Maybe Nancy was having better luck. "See anything?" I shouted down the beach.

No," she yelled. "Maybe further down."

"Wait a minute. I'll join you." When I caught up with her, she was looking further up the beach.

"I really don't see much of promise in this direction," she said. I wasn't paying attention to her comments as I was looking back at the boat.

"Did you secure the bow line?"

"No. Didn't you?"

"Damn! She's afloat and drifting out!" By then, I was running toward the boat. It was about a hundred yards away. It hadn't drifted far out in the water: about thirty feet. It was moving slowly out, though, nudged by a light breeze. I waded out, fast as I could. In about five steps I was over my boots. Flashing through my mind was the cold thought, Am I going to have to swim? At waist-deep? On tiptoes, (why on tiptoes, I don't know — because the water was cold, I guess,) I grabbed hold of the bowline and moved back into shore.

"This spot down here will have to do, Nancy. It's the only one we've found. The boat would have drifted all the way to the end of the harbor — easily two miles. What a mess that would be."

Working in the rain, soaked inside from the chest down, I managed to get the tarp up over a small, tree-covered, tent-size clearing, just above the tide line. While Nancy unloaded our "waterproof" bags, I erected the tent. On one of the circlings — to drive in pegs, I tripped and fell against a back corner of the tent, bending elbow-like, the two-piece aluminum pole that slanted from the ridge to the base. "DAMNIT!" I fell down between a boulder and a moss-covered deadfall, a sharp pain in my left ankle. "DAMN!" Twisting, I felt no sharpness in the ankle — more a sprain. The pole though, was seriously weakened in the middle, where the two pieces joined. It could no longer hold the tent rigid. My jury-rig was to force the now crimped ends back into tubular form and carve a round wood stiffener that could extend up into each tube. This I did. Twenty minutes later, the pole was repaired to wobbly rigidity and the tent was up, slack-cornered on my side. Nancy had the stove going to boil some water. There was no chance that I could dry out anything for at least another day. I squished over to Nancy to kiss her on the cheek. "Isn't this fun?"

"Well, you did look artful curled around that rock, but don't try to enter any age-group gymnastics. You'll never qualify. Here, drink this." She handed me a steaming cup of bouillon. We stood under our tarp, looking at our well-anchored boat, arms around each other, letting the hot liquid warm us. "Tomorrow will be better."

On such a trip as this, night does not simply pass into morning. One doesn't just go to sleep to awaken refreshed at the start of a new day. Because dinner, in addition to our "daily catch" of solids, usually included two cups of bouillon and two cups of cocoa — a quart of liquid, I had to get up sometime during the night. In a low, two-person tent, that meant:

1. Unzip sleeping bag without awakening mate — usually done slowly.
2. Slide into wet pants while lying on back. (The pants minimize mosquito attacks.)
3. Unzip front — opening mosquito net so as not to awaken mate or rupture bladder.
4. Find, by groping outside tent entrance, and pull on boots. Turn over onto hands and knees and back out of tent. Try not to awaken mate by backing into forward — stay holding the tent up.
5. Grope through the dark around rocks, stumps, roots, branches, holes, until

you've gone a prudent distance. Keep silent at all times. Minimize use of flashlight.

6. Try not to awaken mate by splattering on rock.
7. As long as you're up, go down to the beach and check on the boat.
8. Reverse the process, zipping slowly.

"Is the boat OK?" Muffled, from her sleeping bag burrow.

"Yes. How come you're awake?"

"Don't ask."

Next morning brought us an easy ebbing current down Sunderland Channel. High broken clouds gave us periods of warm morning sun. Our spirits were high. Last night's sleep finally let us gain back our strength from the ordeal two days ago in the Dent Rapids. That took more out of us than we'd thought.

A light easterly breeze let us sail for a couple of hours. We stopped on Seymour Island for relief and a mid-morning break.

Seymour is characteristic of the hundreds of small, uninhabited islands that dot the coast all the way up into Alaska. Usually, they are rock outcroppings thrust up out of the water, covered by dense undergrowth of evergreen salal, wild huckleberry and evergreen seedlings, all towered over by old arbutus, firs, spruce and cedars. Ever present are bleached cedar snags, spiked dead trunks that long ago lost all their green and most of their branches. Now they simply stand tall, providing an unending series of throne-like perches for the magnificent bald eagles we encountered every day.

From Seymour Island we had about five miles to go before we'd enter Johnstone Strait. Sitting on the little island was pleasant. "I wonder what the strait'll be like," Nancy asked. We were both apprehensive about what we'd find. Johnstone Strait had always brought us surprises: rips and strong unpredictable winds. We approached it with a great deal of respect. Today was no exception. Shortly after leaving Sunderland Channel, the current picked up to three-to-four knots moving with us westward. The wind though, had shifted to be out of the west. We had to stop sailing and row against a tough two-foot chop that hit the boat like staccato hammering. We moved in the middle of turbulent chop, the sound more threatening than the resistance. We were relieved to pull into Port Neville, an hour and a half later.

Our chart showed a government dock and store at Port Neville. We looked forward to that, envisioning the purchase of a new supply of candy bars. The dock was there with one outboard runabout tied along the back side. The store, just ashore at the head of the piling dock, was an old, chink-logged building with a porch and covered veranda that faced the water. The building obviously had been built many years ago — sixty? Eighty? Who knows? A faded, handwritten note on the door informed us that the store and gas facilities were no longer in operation, but the Post Office was, from four to five in the afternoon, Monday through Friday. The note was dated 1981. This was 1983. Next door was a house and small farm occupied by Ole Hansen and his family, long-time residents of this spot. Ole was clearly the patriarch of this area.

With their permission, we pitched our tent in a nearby field. Sometime during the night the rain started again, but we didn't stir much. The boat, we knew, would have to be bailed in the morning, but it was safely tied to the float. The rain on our tarp sounded nice.

While eating breakfast, both Nancy and I kept brushing our faces, as though removing cobwebs. We were sitting on a plank we had placed under the overhang of our tarp, just outside our tent entrance. "I feel like something is crawling on me, but I can't see anything," Nancy said, swiping her forehead with the top of her forearm.

"Same here," I answered as I rubbed the back of my neck and my face. "Like something is there, moving, only it isn't." After about forty minutes of this itching and scratching and as the early morning darkness turned into light, I glanced up at the top of our tarp. "Nancy, look." There, clustered so we could see them, were hundreds of small, darting, flying insects. "No-see-ums," I said. "No wonder we've been so bothered."

"They're so tiny. Now I feel like they're all over me. Yukkk! Let's get outta here." Instinctively Nancy reached for the repellent and covered her face, hands and neck. I did likewise before starting a fast disassembly of our camp. It was about seven o'clock. "Let's load the boat and then go thank the Hansens."

The rain continued and the wind was up as we walked to the Hansen's back porch. When Mrs. Hansen opened the door, we were brushed by the warmth of the kitchen stove and the smell of pancake cooking. "Come in and have some breakfast. I'm Lilly."

"We're all wet, and besides, we've..." "Leave your rain clothes outside and come sit. You must be starved. Coffee, pancakes, bacon and some cereal if you want." How quickly we forgot our oatmeal and panbread of an hour ago. Seated at the kitchen table with Ole was their daughter, Lorna, and her fiance, Daniel. The conversation was as warm as the kitchen, it felt good to us. While Ole went to get a weather report on his radio, Daniel asked of our direction.

"We'll turn up Havannah Channel, maybe spend the night in Burial Cove and then on in to Minstrel Island tomorrow."

"Great!" he smiled. "I've got a cabin on the west side of Burial Cove. Not much. No beds and the stove's rusted out. There are probably a few leaks in the roof, but — mostly, it's dry. The door's unlocked and you're free to use it."

In the next room we could hear the crackling and static of Ole's radio, but the words were muffled. Shortly, he returned. "Wind shouldn't be more than twelve-to-fifteen knots, easterly. Intermittent rain. Blustery. Shouldn't get any chop.

"Well, Nancy, let's go give it a try," I said, rising. "I could get used to this kind of fare." We said our goodbyes to this hospitable family, re-donned our wet yellows and headed for the dock.

After an hour of rowing in twelve-to- fifteen knots of tail wind, the wind slackened to about eight knots. "Shall we try to sail?" Nancy asked.

"I'm for it. We've got about seven miles to go. The way the wind funnels down this strait, I'd like to be off the water as soon as possible — no hideyholes either between here and the Broken Islands."

Almost as soon as we had the sail up and I had reached over the transom to lock in the rudder, the wind freshened again, directly astern. We scooted. We covered six miles in an hour and a half. Four knots speed — the fastest our boat had ever moved. It was exhilarating to feel and hear the water rushing by with such speed. Gradually our thrill turned to concern. "The chop's building, Nancy. What do you say we take down the sail. I'm afraid of lunging and taking on water."

"Yeah, let's. It's getting scarey." Nancy quickly furled the sail, while I took in the rudder. We both started rowing.

The last mile down Johnstone Strait was in heavier weather than we liked. The wind built from astern and we rowed into an opposing chop, in the rain, under a low ceiling of gray-black scudding clouds.

With a feeling of relief, we made it around the corner into the Broken Islands, but were immediately stopped cold. The ebbing current out of Havannah Channel was too strong for us. We couldn't make it around Domville Point. We bobbed under an overhanging rock in a bed of kelp, half out of the wind and rain. We hunkered down and ate our lunch and waited for the current to change.

It was about four miles to Burial Cove — two more hours of rowing. At slack current we started out, but right into that same wind that was with us when we came down the strait. By hugging the shoreline and pulling hard, we made progress, but it was slow going — two hours to make two miles. When we turned out to cross the channel, the wind and waves hit us broadside. In this condition, the boat constantly rocked as it moved from the crest to the trough of each wave. We each sometimes grabbed air rather than water on the backstroke, losing our balance as well as our composure.

"This is a long two miles," Nancy muttered. "Wish we had a better chart." She kept glancing over her shoulder looking for the entrance to the cove.

"Wouldn't bring it any closer," I answered. "Think of this as your daily aerobic. Think how sylphlike you'll be. Cabin tonight too. Pulling into a motel. DAMN! It's hard to get a steady bite in this water!"

Four hours after lunch, we pulled into Burial Cove. We sat in the rain and took our bearings. "That must be Daniel's cabin over there." Nancy was pointing to a bleached, two-room cedar cabin nestled among the dark evergreens on the west shore.

"There's smoke coming out of that cabin on the east shore," I said. "Let's go over there and tell 'em what we're doing with their neighbor's place. They might think we're intruders."

"Good idea," Nancy said, as we both pulled on our right oars lo turn toward the smoke. As we drew near, a man approached the shore. "Hello," we hailed. "May we come ashore?"

"Won't you come in for tea? I'm Bob Wood, and that's my wife, Eileen, up there on the bluff. Come in, come in. Let's get out of this rain." Bob was in his boots, so he took our bow line and helped pull the boat up onto the beach. "Ole Hansen radioed to expect you. Said maybe around two, but I knew you couldn't do much against that wind. My goodness! Rowing to Alaska! That's something. Watch your step there, the bank's a little slick in this rain."

Their cabin consisted of two rooms, a bedroom and an all-purpose room. The latter served as kitchen, dining, living and projects room. It was lined with shelves in the kitchen and two walls of books in the living/dining area. The wood range in the kitchen warmed the room wonderfully. We shucked our boots and yellows by the front door and took chairs around their table. Having seen us when we entered the cove, Eileen had put the water on for tea and broken out some cookies. We liked them both immediately.

"What are you doing here in Burial Cove?" I asked. "How did you happen to locate here?"

Eileen picked up the question. "Bob is a Scotsman who found his way to Canada. For the past several years he has been an instrumentation and computer specialist for a Canadian engineering firm that designs and installs pulp mills all over the world. Our last assignment was in Czechoslovakia. Before that we were in Africa. That was an experience. We were most pleased to get out of Czechoslovakia, though. It's not great living in a communist country."

Bob broke in with his rich Scottish burr, "We got tired of living out of a suitcase and the hassle of living in cities. We wanted something more remote. Guess you couldn't find anything more remote than this, eh?"

"But why Burial Cove?" I asked.

"Well," Bob answered, "from living in Vancouver, we got to know about the British Columbia coast and liked it. We wanted to 'homestead,' so to speak, but we also wanted waterfront, so we could keep our boat, fish, crab and that sort of thing you know. We wanted to be rather self-sufficient, and we didn't have much money. Anything we could afford had to be unattractive to most folks – pretty far removed, so to speak."

Refilling our cups with fresh tea, Eileen continued on. "We heard from a real estate agent about an abandoned farm with an orchard and low-bank waterfront – about the size we had in mind. Boy, did he make it sound good. We got in the boat to come see, but first we had to get a chart to even find it. No roads. We're on an island, you know – East Cracroft."

"Boy, what a bloody mess we found," Bob enjoined, his eyes sparkling. "This house, just a shack, was in bad shape – no windows, leaky roof, no water, door half off. The place had been abandoned for years. The orchard – I found some cherry trees a hundred bloody feet high, fighting for light. The farm – all overgrown – the woods taking it back. Oh, my, what a mess, a bloody mess." He stared into his cup while he stirred. He shook his head.

"We were like two kids though," Eileen smiled, "like newlyweds, rather than an old, middle-aged couple. We saw only what it could be — not what it was. And if we offered low, it could be in our price range. Lots of problems and lots of work — we knew before we started, but we made an offer. It was accepted, and here we are."

"We've been here a little over a year now. I don't even want to talk about what this first winter has been like." Shaking his head, Bob continued, "Getting windows in and the door to work were giant steps. I shot a bloody bear right from the door there. My, yes. Eileen's particularly happy today. I finally finished piping water from back up the stream into the kitchen sink — just this morning. No more carrying water. Had to build a woodshed to get dry wood. Last winter we had mostly wet wood and it was terrible, I'll tell you. Now, we've even got an outhouse — it's a beauty — sits up there on the knoll and overlooks everything — even has a fancy oak toilet seat. First class! We're getting there."

"Our kids think we're crazy," Eileen added, "but so far, we're not sorry for our move. We hope to start our house this fall — up there on that bluff overlooking the cove, to the left as we walked up from the beach."

And so we talked, for a couple of hours, the four of us like old, old friends. We were pleased when Eileen invited us to come over for breakfast next morning. With that, we shoved off to cross the quarter mile to Daniel's cabin and a dry night except for a few minor leaks in the roof.

It was mid-morning before we broke away from breakfast. Bacon, eggs, individual small round loaves of home-baked bread and home-canned blackberry jam all combined to put us in a breakfast seventh heaven. "Eileen," I worked out in between bites, "I've baked bread for the past thirty years — all the bread our family has eaten. This is the best loaf I've ever eaten. What's the secret to your chewy texture?"

"Malt vinegar," she said, "two tablespoons, and I use vegetable oil instead of margarine or butter."

Finally, we could delay no longer. Not having many visitors, Bob and Eileen were as pleased to see us as we were to be immersed in their genuinely warm hospitality. During our conversation, Eileen had told us of the unique hunting habits of their cat. "She brings us live hummingbirds, unharmed."

Sure enough, as we walked down to the beach, their cat came up to Eileen with a hummer in her mouth. Eileen accepted it gently and raised it slowly in her out stretched hand, palm up. When her arm was about straight out, the bird flew off, its speed indicating no physical harm suffered. Having observed many hummers at close range we concluded that we had just met a most extraordinary cat.

As we rowed out of Burial Cove, Bob and Eileen stood together, waving us on. "Such a neat couple," Nancy said. "I miss them already. One positive thing about this trip — we're sure getting to meet a lot of wonderful people."

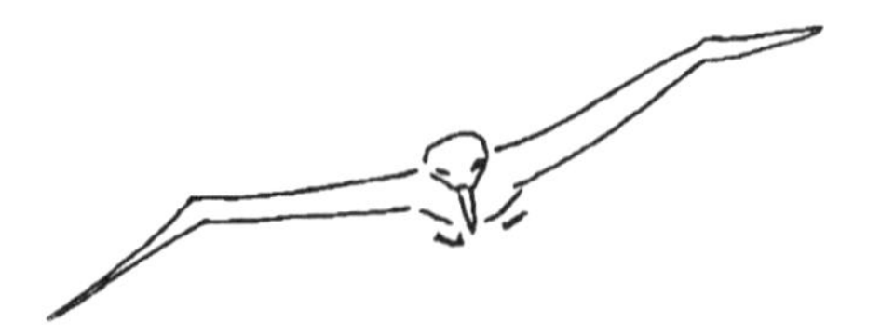

PART VI: (Nancy) MINSTREL ISLAND TO BLUNDEN BAY: "NOW WE'RE REALLY LEAVING CIVILIZATION BEHIND."

"It's risky, but I think I'll light a match."

"Be careful," Pete said. "If you drop it, this place'll go up in a flash." The ancient walls and ceilings in the old Minstrel Island Hotel sagged inward, giving the impression of inexorable movement toward collapse. One could envision past charm, even modest elegance, but no more.

I cautiously lighted our little camp stove and mixed up the usual gruel-like oatmeal. It always improved with a sprinkling of brown sugar and our bodies welcomed its warmth.

We hauled our dirty clothes to the small marina market and while they whirred through the washer in the back room, we shopped for some needed stores.

It was a laid-back Sunday morning. Gulls circled slowly overhead. The smell of freshly brewed coffee wafted out of hatchways and portholes from the boats lining the docks. Lifejacketed kids stood patiently holding drop-lines over the edge of the dock after baiting them with pile worms. It was a good time to reorganize our equipment while awaiting the tide change around noon. We hauled everything out of the boat onto the dock and rearranged the load, stuffing in clean clothes and newly purchased food items. It felt good to establish an order from the chaos. Somehow it gave me the pseudo-confidence of control over my destiny.

We pulled away with the ebb tide amid waves and shouts of encouragement from the boaters still tied to the dock and turned toward Midsummer Island, a fairly large bundle of land, sitting at the bottom of Queen Charlotte Strait. "It feels like we're really leaving civilization behind," I murmured, as the current pushed us rapidly up the channel. "Yeah," said Pete, "I don't imagine we'll see many people from here on until we hit Prince Rupert."

Most recreational boaters don't travel much farther north than Minstrel Island. The strait is known as a fearsome and dangerous place. Winds sweep in directly from the Pacific. There were no boats in sight when a strong wind came out of Knight Inlet to give impetus to our flight. With that realization came the understanding of how totally interdependent we had become. No one could help us if we capsized. No one could pick us out of the water or give us shelter. We were really alone for the first time since

PART VI - MINSTREL ISLAND TO BLUNDEN BAY

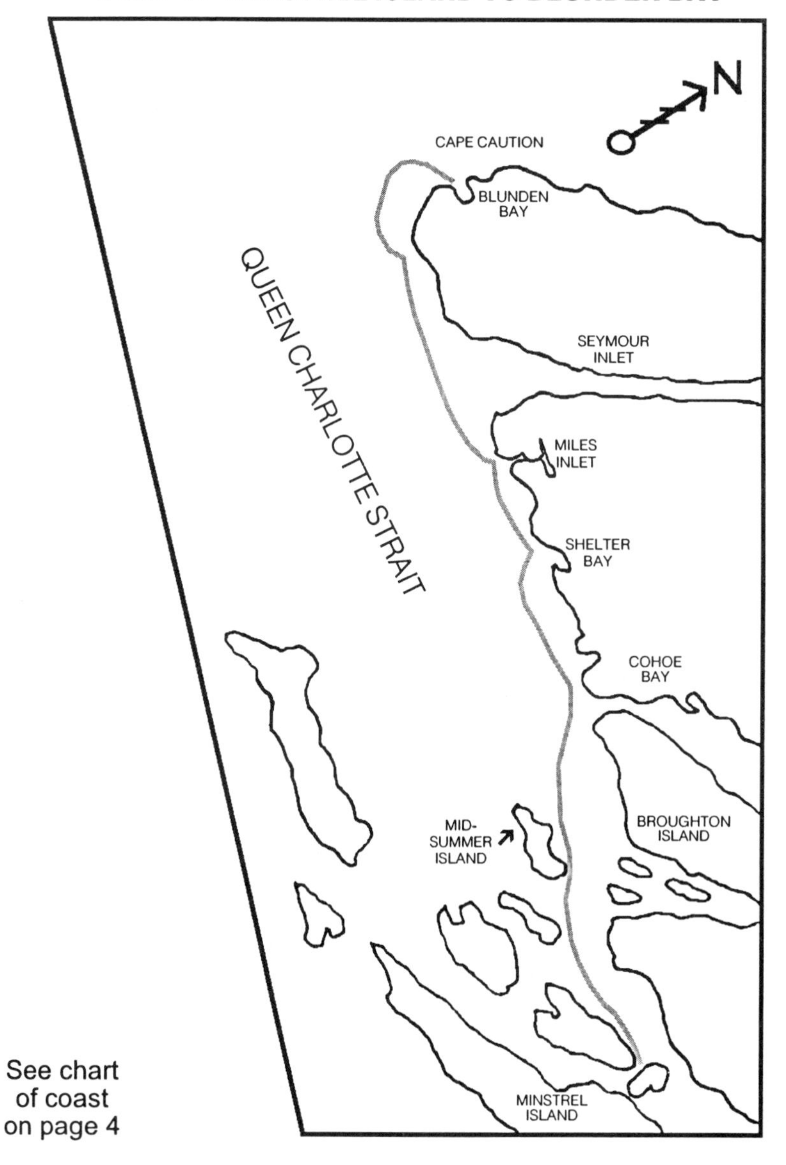

See chart of coast on page 4

leaving Lopez Island and the commercial traffic lanes. We planned to pick our way through the uninhabited islands rimming the strait, and turn the "overhang" of Cape Caution in seven to ten days. We called it the overhang, because on the charts it looked like El Capitan in Yosemite Valley. It appeared to jut way out in the Pacific and then slide back into the Inside Passage and imagined safety. Cornering Cape Caution became a major goal of the trip — a major peak to conquer.

Midsummer Island — images danced in my head — white sandy beaches, light breezes whispering through willow branches, Puck prancing on the beach, grinning mischievously; his famous quote appropriate for our arrival, "What fools these mortals be!"

The image and the reality were not related. Driftwood and tumbled rocks blocked our passage as we struggled to unload and set up camp. Above the rubble was a fairly level campsite complete with cooking rocks — a natural platform on which to set either fire or camp stove. Some minor renovation was needed, so Pete scraped and leveled our tent site while I cleaned two tomcods caught at the Minstrel Island dock. We retired early to a night of wind howling through the trees promising rain and heavy weather in the morning.

In retrospect, after experiencing the delights of the unusually warm summers of 1984 and 1985, we wondered why we didn't just bag it and head for home midway through. But we both have a quality of stubbornness that goes beyond normalcy. Pete calls it determination, but we're both actually damned muleheaded. We like to finish that which we start. If our values had been radically different from one another, we would have had great conflict along the way, but there were surprisingly few crises or disagreements about handling rough situations.

Our hand-held VHF chanted weather information twenty-four hours a day from Vancouver. Sometimes we could hear it, sometimes not. The calm steady voice promised winds dropping by 10:00 A.M. and no winds in the afternoon, so we sat back to savor one more cup of coffee while waiting for those morning winds to slacken. We had concluded early on that we could not wait for good weather, or we would never get anywhere. We just tried to avoid major wind storms and gales. "Wouldn't you know it? It's starting to rain again," Pete groaned.

"We better put on our stinking yellows." By now they were literally stinking and clammy inside, but they would become a lot worse before Ketchikan hove into view.

Hundreds of tiny islets dot the rim of the Queen Charlotte Strait. We had been subjected to multiple horror stories about the dangers of these waters. Fishermen, pleasure boaters and mariners had all warned us of the severe storms in this area. Today the water was benign and bathtub calm. The sun emerged from behind a wispy cloud and warmed our hands as we pulled slowly through the crystalline sea. Two sea otters cavorted on a nearby shore, slithering in and out of the water with sinuous grace. Reflections of twisted spruce, moss-covered rocks and pockets of wildflowers sent shimmering images of green, yellow, lavender and rust into the surrounding glassy waters. Cedar, alder, hemlock, spruce and salal crowded together on each islet to form a dense barrier of underbrush. Heather and kinnikinnick added splashes of color. The rocks plunging into the water were reminiscent of primitive painting. Grey, mauve, orange, black and rust formed into images of wolves, bear, trees and man. "It's calendar art," said Pete. "One of those incredible spots photographers look for to illustrate spring. Let's stop over there on that little islet and eat our cinnamon buns."

One of the enormous pleasures of this trip for me was being able to eat candy bars, granola laced with M & Ms, peanut butter by the tub, mugs of hot chocolate and still lose weight. I have had a lifetime struggle to maintain a trim figure — a struggle I have often lost — so this was Utopia for me. Pete began to look like a survivor of an enforced march, but I loved the feeling of loose jeans and baggy shirts. I didn't even mind my declining bra size.

We climbed onto the rocky surface of an outcropping and munched away on our last-touch-of-civilization — buns. Wonderful! Magnifique! The boat bobbed contentedly at the end of her bow line and we revelled in the beauty of our surroundings.

A distant humming gradually built to a determined drone. Approaching just below the scattered clouds was a World War II PBY. Pete stared in obvious rapture and nostalgia. "Look at that, Nancy; an old P-Boat. Isn't that the most beautiful thing you've ever seen? Nice sound. Pratt and Whitney 1250s with Hamilton standard props. Rattled a lot, but indestructible. Pretty."

"Even prettier than Beavers?" Pete had sucked in his breath with pleasure every time a DeHavilland Beaver, that workhorse of the B.C. and Alaska wilderness, had passed overhead. But today he winged back forty years to his days in the U.S. Navy when he had piloted P-Boats in the Atlantic and Caribbean on anti-submarine duty. It had been an exciting and stimulating time for a young man from Hoquiam, Washington.

"I wonder where it's going? Can't be too many of those still flying. Do you think they could use a mature and experienced pilot?"

"You better apply fast. August is the big 6-0 birthday."

....

Winding through the remaining islets was pleasurable indeed. We were accompanied by seals and myriad water birds. "Looks like rain ahead."

"Here we go again." Into the clammy yellows. The skies opened and it poured. It rained so hard that drops sprang upward from the ocean's surface. We pulled into a protected baylet to escape the full force of the onslaught and dug clams for dinner. Two more otters slithered into the water as we drew near their rocks. Somehow it seemed less onerous to be on land than on water during a downpour. Faulty logic perhaps. Pete's ducting-taped rain pants were not doing their job. Regardless of his preventative taping, they still leaked. On days like this he sat immersed in water, within and without. He too, felt better walking around than just sitting in his private pool. "I wonder if you will be able to rewrite medical history?" I asked. "The only human being to develop a moldy posterior."

"Not funny," muttered Pete, damply.

We approached a lovely sandy beach midday and stopped to get water from a bubbling stream. Most of the water we found now was brown from cedar bark, but here were no problems with consuming it. We had been warned about Giardia, but were lucky to avoid streams infested with that parasite. "Let's stop here and make camp, Pete."

"Oh, I'd like to make it to Aimee Bay tonight."

"This has a lovely beach and a nice flat camping area."

"Let's push on."

I acquiesced, but felt annoyed as the day wore on and we pushed until after six to find a suitable campsite. We always had to estimate the high tide line, find a flat place to set up our tent and a protected spot for cooking, so sometimes the search took hours. Being destination oriented and always feeling that urgency to be off the water before September storms swept in from the Dixon Entrance, we sometimes pushed ourselves harder than necessary.

We were both getting tired — too tired to enjoy our evening stay. By the time we had washed the dishes in salt water and turned into our bags, we were almost too exhausted to sleep. I began to awaken several times during the night with pain coursing up my arms from my two middle fingers. The only way to relieve it was to sit up and let my hands dangle or knead my elbows to relieve the pressure on the ulnar nerve. After five or ten minutes I could ease back down and drop to sleep before the pain won. It also helped to be near collapse.

With Namu about ten days ahead, the days began to blend one into the other, broken only by the variety of camping areas or occasional visits from seals and eagles, our daily companions.

We were out of butter. At home we were constantly aware of nutrition, cholesterol and all those ugly things that animal fats did for the "bod." We used margarine on the table and binged on butter only during the winter holidays. But out here our bodies cried for fats and sweets. The one pound chunks of Canadian butter somehow tasted much better than those pathetic little squares out of the supermarkets at home. We would have swapped my gold chain necklace for a pound or two. Our other provisions were also diminishing, but butter seemed to be our main focus. Huge hunks slathered on syrup-smothered pancakes in the morning and on huckleberry pan-bread in the evening were nonpareil.

Our cut-down salmon pole was rigged with a line which trailed behind us constantly, serving as our principle dinner-catcher. It snagged yellow rockfish, red snapper, tomcod, greenling and flounder but so far, nary a salmon had fallen prey to the lures. It also snagged huge snakes of kelp, They devoured my lures by the dozen.

Pete and I now arose between 4:00-5:00 A.M. to catch the early morning tide. Rowing against the current usually netted us only one knot. With the current we averaged two or two-and-a-half. Our best times were four knots when we had a following wind and strong current – rare, but exciting.

On these early morning tide calls, we rowed for two or three hours then headed ashore and breakfasted, wolfing our food down ravenously. Often the mornings dawned bell clear or with gentle wisps of mist clinging to the treetops. It was often mid-morning before the rain clouds settled down to serious drizzle.

It was just such a morning when we pulled away from Broughton Island back into Queen Charlotte Strait. Wind-twisted trees clung to their rocky islets defying gravity. Pockets of wildflowers: Lupine, Indian paint-brush, golden mules' ears and cow parsnip added slashes of brilliant color. Always the forest merged with the sky in a fringed black-green backdrop.

Some days were all gray: Gray water, gray skies and gray mist clung to the trees and seeped into our tent and clothing. But today was golden. A shaft of sunlight hit the tops of our heads, worked slowly down to our numbed hands and finally flooded the boat. We rowed on until a white sandy beach protected by rocky shelves came into view. We were now on the mainland of British Columbia, near Boyles Point. We could see fishing boats far out in the strait heading north, but none traveled near us. People were not to be a part of our lives for awhile.

Quickly beaching the boat, we ate our breakfast in the morning sun and luxuriated in its rays. "Where do you want to go?" I asked. "I'm going to find a potty room up by that pile of driftwood."

"OK," Pete replied. "I'll head down to the left."

Hanging on to a shred of Victorian modesty, I insisted on privacy for my morning elimination. It became a game to create the nicest environment possible for this daily necessity. Sometimes wet slippery rocks didn't contribute joy to the occasion, but on this morning we each had warm logs on which to sit' and soft clean sand beneath us. Small pleasures became magnified as we were more isolated. In essence, life was stripped down to survival essentials: Food, shelter and dryness were paramount considerations. Friends later asked, "Why on earth would you subject yourself to that kind of discomfort?" Or, "How did you bathe and go to the bathroom?"

We didn't bathe often. There were a few memorable baths, such as the one Pete described earlier when we were near Quarry Bay, but most were hurried dashes into the brine with salt -water soap clutched in hand. If the sun had shone at all that day, we rinsed off with our portable black-plastic bag-shower. If not, we just crusted over with salt. We didn't subject ourselves to this torture too often and really needed a sunny day to wash dirty clothes and dry them on driftwood. With only six or seven days of full sun on the entire trip, opportunities were scant. The tent took on a rancid atmosphere fairly early on – a discouragement to wildlife marauders.

Returning from our morning ritual, we hauled the survival suits out of the boat and spread them on the warm logs to dry. Constant drenchings with salt water hadn't contributed to easy zipper movement. In fact they wouldn't budge. "My God, I hope we never need these things," I wailed. "We'd never be able to get them on. They'd fill up and sink!"

Pete, who is infinitely more patient than I, quietly struggled with pliers, oil and zippers until they pulled up and down once again. A flash of neon red zapped one of the suits and soared off to a nearby branch. Rufous hummingbirds, attracted by the red-orange material, hovered around for the entire drying period, darting in for a close-up view then helicoptering off in a blur of color. The B.C. coastline was heavily populated by these exquisite birds and we were to experience many more close-up observations of their habits.

Later that day we pushed on into Cohoe Cove after 6:00 P.M. We had not learned our lesson about stopping early. The afternoon current change had slowed our forward progress to only a half mile every hour and a half and our projected stopping-over place seemed to be always around one more headland or point of jutting rock. Each evening we perused our charts and tried to pick out a few spots appropriate for camping. Sometimes they were too rocky, murky or steep. It was impossible to tell by the chart. Even when a sandy beach was indicated, it often turned out to be soggy grassland rife with mosquitoes and "no-see-ums." Today our hopes of finding an ideal site were dashed as we rowed into a giant marshland. Acres of shallow waters housed reed-like grass, small aquatic creatures and bugs – acres of bugs – all buzzing and flapping around our heads. A half-buried abandoned barge stuck out of the muck. A sign on its railing read: SPEED LIMIT, 15 MILES PER HOUR. "Don't I wish," I muttered to myself.

To anchor the boat in enough water for it to be afloat by early morning, we needed at least eight to ten feet of water. If not, Surfbird would stand on dry land sometimes for over six hours as we waited for the tide shift. This happened occasionally, as it became unavoidable, but we didn't like our food to be accessible to bear or raccoons during the night. We preferred that they work a little for their food – at least have a brisk swim.

By 8:30 P.M. we still had not found a usable location. The land was either chunks of rock or coursed with rivulets. The mosquitoes and other biting critters were getting to me. I am convinced that some evil person could drive me mad inside of a half hour by enclosing me with a swarm of hungry mosquitoes. Are they ever not hungry? My neck was a solid welt from their bites. Each bit of mounded flesh had merged with another to create one angry, itching mass. Pete didn't seem to mind them as much as I, but I could feel my energy and patience draining fast. "What the hell – let's stop here. The boat will just have to go dry."

"There's no place to set up a tent, Nancy." Pete's voice began to hint annoyance.

"I'm tired and I'm hungry. These damn bugs are driving me nuts!"

"Let's just pull around that corner by the entrance to the bay. Maybe we'll find a better place."

I decided that my pulling one way and Pete another would get us nowhere fast, so I gathered my dwindling resources and pulled sulkily for the corner. As we rounded the rock-strewn barricade, the entrance to a pocket cove opened. Two magnificent bald eagles perched on snags protruding from the clean, white sand beach guarded the entrance. A gravel shelf, just tent-sized, nestled behind some huge protective logs of driftwood and the waters dropped off into ideal anchoring ground. "There is some force that knows when we're reaching our breaking point and provides for our needs," Pete said.

"It sure looks that way," I agreed. I have always believed in the power of one's determination, not an outside or mystical force. I believe that almost anything can be accomplished by doing, and very little by wishing, hoping or endless analysis. But there is always room for the unknown. This little bay coming at such a critical time and several similar incidents later, including one life-threatening situation, opened the door to the possibility of a life force protector greater than we.

We were beginning to feel the first ocean swells. There was a change in the rhythm of the water. Having become used to fighting choppy waves and submitting to the eerie pull of tide rips, this pleasant ride up to the top of a mound of water, then down into the trough, had an easing, almost lulling effect. We were acutely aware, however, that the open ocean was a treacherous place for small open boats. We felt a great sense of urgency to make it safely around Cape Caution. It's very name had hinted disaster. The lighthouse at the cape marks the most westerly site on the British Columbia mainland. Last spring, going over our charts, Pete had set this point as a critical turning point for our journey. "Once we get around Cape Caution," he had said, "we'll have it made. Look how far it protrudes into the ocean. We'll probably have to row about twenty miles that day to make it around."

"Don't tell me about it," I had said. "I may change my mind about the whole damn idea." Ignoring me, Pete had gone on, "Once around though, we can duck into the Inside Passage and be safe from the ocean winds." We had both envisioned a serene protected waterway running from the top of the cape to Ketchikan. Happily, reality sets in small stages of acute, sometimes terrifying, awareness.

The morning row had been easy until a northwest headwind came up and slowed down our progress. We pulled around a hook of land and went ashore to eat lunch, relieve ourselves and refill our water jugs with more tea-colored water. We had sighted a few boats churning up the strait, but none indicated seeing us. I cupped my hands around my mouth and yelled, "GOT ANY BUTTER?" But none had been close enough to hear and answer my plea. Namu would be our next refueling stop.

I began to fantasize about big chunks of solid butter, always sitting atop fresh bread, croissants or cinnamon buns.

The afternoon rain fell softly as we left our luncheon cove and pulled northward alongside the string of Jeannette Islets. The wind had dropped though, so we considered it a fair trade. Our destination was Shelter Bay, a deep slash in the side of the B.C. coast. It was the only protection along this rugged shore until Miles Inlet, our destination for the following day and the last stop before attempting the hard row around the cape.

Shelter Bay had several potential campsites on its southern shores, but with the winds tending to come from the northwest, we decided to pull across to the northeastern corner and peek into what were indicated as lagoons on the chart. Lagoons often were murky and insect-ridden, so it was with some reticence that we made the long haul across the bay. We turned into a well-protected inlet and saw what appeared to be a mirage. "What is that down at the end of the bay?"

"Looks like an incredible strip of pure white sand."

"Can't be. How would it get here? There's no wave action, no white rocks. Besides, we haven't seen sand like that this side of Waikiki." We pulled closer and our mystical beach seemed to shimmer and float above the water.

"It's a mirage."

"I bet it's a layer of scum or plant life on the water."

"Whatever it is – it is beautiful." Our hidden cove revealed itself in all its loveliness: A 300 foot long, pure white sandy beach, set artistically into a background of black-green conifers with giant rocks placed artfully about by a master landscaper. They reflected their lush moss coating into the quiet pools of water surrounding them. A freshwater stream bubbled out of the forest offering clean flat rocks for washing our dishes and clothing. A flock of sharp-tailed sandpipers moved along the tide line, their legs appearing more like wheels than separate appendages. Their tiny chirping voices sounded like chicks in a brooder, amplified when in their incredible fast-action, formation flight.

They allowed me to stalk within a few feet to capture them on film. We had noticed in these remote settings that the birds and animals were much less frightened of our presence than they had been in the more heavily populated areas of British Columbia and northwestern Washington State.

A harbor seal whiffed out his breath as he surfaced within five feet. He pushed his body up shoulder high to peer at us with his inquisitive stare. Two Steller's jays, their vertical slash eyebrows giving them an angry, saucy appearance, scolded us as we set up camp on the soft sand. Throughout our trip these feisty blue flashes would hop just out of reach on overhanging branches and give us hell for invading their territory. They were not above gulping down our handouts of leftover rice or huckleberries, however. They just wanted us to know it was their space, not ours.

A pair of pintails flew overhead, their soft wack-wack-wacks fading into the distance as they passed by. Our days did not seem complete without their passage. We had grown accustomed to their flyovers, at dawn and dusk — always a single pair, never a group.

"Damn!"

"What's the matter?" I queried.

"The tide book says it's a fifteen footer tonight. We'll have to move the tent and all our gear up into the forest. The beach is too shallow for our camp. I should have checked earlier."

"Oh, well, we've made worse mistakes." I looked forlornly at the lovely soft stretch of sand cradling our tent and tarp — all set up and ready for the night. "Let's get it over with," I said with a sigh.

We settled into our spongy, moss-covered forest location that night with the gentle lapping of the tide beyond lulling us to sleep.

The feeling of being in Eden persisted into the morning. We awoke to quiet reflections and the gurgling waters of the stream working down to disappear in the sand. We stretched our stiff bodies and walked out onto the sand.

"It doesn't look as if the tide made it up to our original tent site," I noted.

"Sure doesn't." Pete grabbed the tide book. "Here it is, though — Thursday, July seventh, high tide fifteen feet."

"I hate to tell you, but today's Thursday. You were off a day."

We shrugged off the lost time and started preparations for breakfast with our usual gluttonous anticipation.

Today would bring us within striking distance of Cape Caution. Pete was anxious and a bit edgy about the challenge ahead. We completed loading the boat with muscle power and assorted grunts, groans, "damns" and "get in there, you bastards." Surfbird's stern was barely afloat as we completed the task. She had been high and dry for the latter half of the night in the shallow waters of the lagoon, but nothing had disturbed her contents.

Moving past the Southgate Group of islets and up Schooner Channel was quiet, easy and enjoyable. The PBY passed over us on schedule and Pete gave his expected comment, "Isn't she beautiful?" The morning haze surrendered to the rays of the sun and the western sky was blue. We stayed in the boat and lunched off McEwan Point, moving gently up and down in the ocean swells. We were out in the Pacific itself and we felt the power, now held in check. Rather than attempt the long pull across Seymore Inlet and around the lighthouse today, we decided to turn into Miles Inlet, an intricate channel of rock-lined waterways forming a T on the chart. The inlet was composed of many small pockets, coves and passageways — some so narrow we could just squeeze through without touching the rocky shelves on either side. We explored every pocket, every cove and every passage, finding no flat surfaces for a tent above the projected high tide line. Today we knew it was Thursday and fifteen feet of water would pour into these channels.

In desperation, we selected a last resort at the end of a narrow slot in the steep walls. It boasted a wet grassy knoll with a slanted bed of rotted pine needles and rocks. Our rough estimate of the high tide level put us out of danger we thought – but just barely. We anchored off the rocks in only six feet of water and made the decision to pull out by 4:00 A.M. to avoid going aground. This means we had to be up by 3:00 and load the boat by flashlight, or moonlight, if we were lucky.

Having not caught my usual bottom fish for dinner, I scrounged among the rocks and picked limpets. The little creatures living under their tiny conical hats were tough, but nutritious. With vigorous chewing they were edible, but not our favorite meal. The woods above our nesting spot contained several huckleberry bushes from which I gathered cupfuls of blue and red berries while Pete built a crackling fire against the protective side of a rock slab. I sat in the fading afternoon sun and patched the knees on his jeans. The fire sounded and felt good to us both, as we had been thwarted by rain so many evening before. We sat downing mugs of hot chocolate and hunks of huckleberry pan bread. We felt snug and secure in our hidden inlet.

Although our tent slanted downward, we managed to drop off to sleep. I clung to the uphill slope and Pete rolled against the downhill side of the small blue tent.

"What the —— !" hissed Pete. "Nancy! I have a waterbed on this side. The tide's coming into our tent! My sweat shirt's all wet. So's my mattress. Goddamn!"

There has always been a rather nasty part of me which finds these kinds of situations funny. "What time is it?" I snickered, a short giggling snort following my words.

"I don't see anything terribly funny – it's 11:50."

"Well, roll over to my side and go to sleep. The tide's going to turn in fifteen minutes."

We both awoke at 3:30 A.M. realizing we had slept past our departure time. Pete climbed out of the soggy tent and flashed the light over the steep edge of our rocky base. "My God, the water's almost gone! Hurry and get dressed – then you get in the boat and I'll throw everything down to you!" I scrambled into my jeans and sweatshirt, crammed my feet into damp sox and clammy boots and half-crawled, half-slid down the slick rocks into the boat.

"Hurry Pete! The water's draining outta here fast. Someone's pulled the plug!" Pete stood at the top of the rock and threw. Tent, rainfly, sleeping bags, air mattresses and assorted pieces of clothing rained down on my head as I struggled to stuff them under the canvas cuddy.

"I think that's all of it. Hold the boat in close so I can get in." He slid down the slippery rocks but dropped the flashlight en route. We both watched the light sink quickly to settle benignly on the bottom, lighting the way for any homeward- bound fish or crab.

As the tidal waters deserted the cove, two freshwater streams poured their waters into the emptying basin. The predawn darkness was filled with the sound of the rushing water. We grasped our oars and pulled hard, threading our way back through the maze of waterways and into the ocean's gentle swells. We had escaped entrapment, but just barely. The setting moon and brilliant stars lighted our path across the quiet waters as we pointed in the direction of Seymour Inlet.

This vast body of water empties into the Pacific from deep into the interior of British Columbia. As the waters surge out, they hit the waves of the ocean and create a tremendous roiling effect on the water.

It took us more than an hour to struggle across the churning surface. The experience was somewhat as I had imagined a ride on a bucking bronco — first up and down, then sideways — but always with the underlying swells.

We were both tired after the interrupted sleep, early departure and tough crossing, so we drifted awhile and nibbled on rye crackers and peanut butter. There was no practical place to go ashore to cook breakfast and we wanted to make the turn around the cape before the weather deteriorated.

Huge heads of giant kelp surrounded our bobbing boat. These were by far the most gargantuan species we had ever seen. Their snake-like bodies reached down to the ocean floor where they anchored themselves to twist and sway with the winds and current. Their heads were as large as the seals and sea lions that fed among them. We could imagine ourselves surrounded by the furry beasts instead of the silent plant life.

By noon we began the hard pull to round the corner. The lighthouse loomed very near, but always elusive. The wind began to pick up against us and the waters reacted accordingly. The surf pounded fiercely on the rocks of the cape giving us grim notice of our fate if we veered too close. The mighty sound reinforced our awareness of the awesome power of the Pacific. At least it wasn't raining. "Let's get around this bugger," said Pete, hauling vigorously on his oars.

"I'm pulling. I'm pulling," I responded between gasps for air. We seemed to stand still, bobbing endlessly directly in front of the unmanned lighthouse, but gradually we edged closer and closer to the entrance of Blunden Bay, a protected anchorage directly northeast of the lighthouse.

A great whoosh startled us as we approached the bay — then another volcanic exhalation — and another. "Wow!" I screamed. "Whales! Look at 'em off the port stern!" A pod of leviathans sounded, gusting great geysers of whale breath skyward. Their mammoth flukes slapped the surface with explosions of spray and sound. The Humpbacks were within a half mile of our frail craft and it occurred to us to get off the water — fast! We pulled into the quiet waters of the bay and watched the spectacular display as they cavorted in their liquid playground.

A lovely, clean sandy beach greeted us, complete with warm piles of driftwood on which to dry clothing and gear, rocks filled with plump mussels and freshwater streams emptying into the brine. "Now we have it made," said Pete smugly. "Not quite halfway, but from here on it should be downhill. The worst is behind us now."

PART VII: (Pete) BLUNDEN BAY TO SMITH SOUND: "A QUARTER OF A MILE TO GO. CAN YOU HANG IN THERE?"

Blunden Bay lies about a mile north of Cape Caution; its entrance faces due west into the Pacific. The chart shows this to be either the top of Queen Charlotte Strait or the bottom Queen Charlotte Sound, but the water is the North Pacific. Its weather, waves and currents charge virtually unobstructed across thousands of sea miles from the Asian land mass.

The bay itself is roughly circular, about a mile in diameter. The beach for the most part is sandy, stopped by a dense screen of three-foot-high sand grass that is backed tightly by ancient spruce and cedars, all bent eastward in submission to the persistent westerlies. From a distance, the trees are all black-green, rising from the weathered driftwood logs that line the upper beach from one end to the other. Because of its wide opening, the sea rolled uninhibited into the bay, causing a breaking surf on most of the beach. This was something we had to avoid. Beaching in much surf would swamp the boat and anchoring out would be near impossible.

We found a no-surf area just inside the north point of the bay mouth. That part of the bay rolled onto a shallow shelf, so we had to take care not to be stranded at the time we hoped to depart. The narrow strip of land between us and the ocean rose sharply, first rocks rising out of the swirling water, then higher rocky cliffs, topped by dense, old evergreen trees. Our shelter from the wind was complete and the sandy beach above the tideline about perfect for our campsite.

By the time we completed our arrival chores, it was three o'clock in the afternoon. The high scattered clouds gave us about seventy-five percent sun.

"First thing I want to do is bathe," Nancy announced. "I'm right rancid."

"I'll second that," I answered. We undressed and headed for the surf. It was cold to touch, colder to walk in and near icy to sit in and splash. Our thirty-second bath seemed longer. We did move fast.

Earlier, on a tree near our camp, Nancy had hung a small plastic shower bag in the sun. We had carried it full of water and exposed to the weather every day for the past two weeks. This was the first day with enough sun to warm the water. From our quick bath we ran up the beach to where it hung and let it drain over us. It was warm enough to feel luxurious. It felt marvelous. We followed that with a change into clean, dry clothes. The combination provided a great boost for our spirits. "Let's walk down the beach," Nancy urged.

The beach, all the way around, stretched almost two miles. We two and scores of gulls were its only visible inhabitants. As we walked along, we were in high spirits. We felt strong from our daily regimen and greatly refreshed from our bath and shower. I looked over my shoulder to the ocean, "Look, the whales are still playing out there." Outside, perhaps a half mile offshore, we could see their giant flukes curl into the air and slap onto the water, the distance causing the sound to arrive two to three seconds after the splash rose into the air. Now and then we could hear them blow with long loud sighs. They probably were feeding on small bait fish or plankton, but from our distance, play could not be ruled out. They continued their activity through the rest of the afternoon, never moving from that general area, maybe seven or eight in the pod.

About a mile down the beach we came upon a rock outcropping, twenty feet high and perhaps fifty feet around. A small freshwater stream, more a rivulet, tumbled along and over the top of the rock, working its way down the crevices of the broken surface to the sandy beach. "Look at these," Nancy said. She had walked over to a clump of mussels growing on the side of the rock, just where the fresh water ran onto the beach at low water and into the sea when the tide was high. "Have you ever seen such big ones?"

"They are whoppers." And they were, three to four inches long, an inch and a half across and at least an inch thick. "They apparently like this fresh water diet."

"I'm going to pick some for dinner, " Nancy said. "It won't take many. Let's go back and get a bucket and our water jugs, too. We're getting low." We walked back to camp, picked up our containers and returned. After days of sitting, the leg exercise felt good, made especially exhilarating on this beautiful beach that we had all to ourselves.

While I started the slow run of water into one of our two water jugs, Nancy picked mussels. It didn't take her long to gather enough. "I'll go back and start dinner – OK?"

"Yeah – this is pretty slow – not much of a stream. I'll be at least fifteen minutes." It took more than half an hour. The water was clear and tasted fresh. Now filled, the two seventeen-pound plastic jugs weighed heavily on the walk back to camp. By the time I arrived, the backs of my hands dragged ape-like in the sand. Another shower wouldn't have hurt, either. I was quite ready for dinner. "It's all for you, Nancy-Lou. A glass of wine sure would go well."

"Sorry. We're fresh out. How about a cup of hot bouillon instead?"

"Second best, but I accept."

PART VII - BLUNDEN BAY TO SMITH SOUND

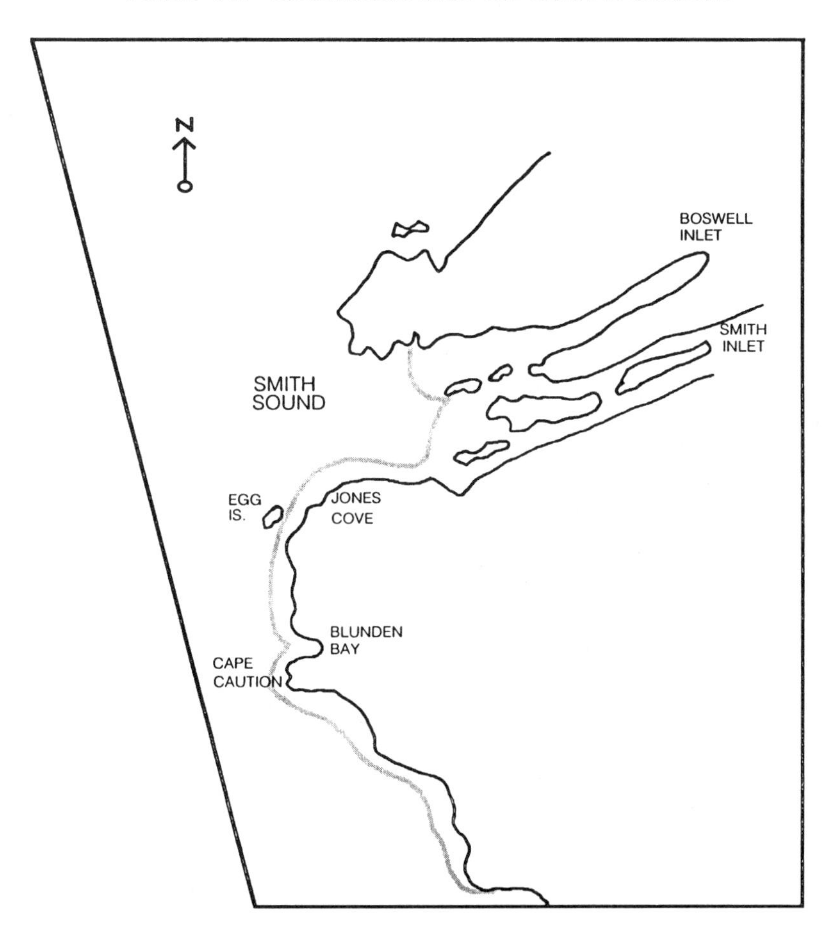

See chart of coast on page 4

The sunset, I'm sure, was beautiful. Neither, though, felt like waiting up for it. We were both tired, but pleasantly so. We felt good about everything in our immediate world. We also were thinking about the minus tide early next morning. We had to get an extra-early start if we didn't want the boat to be trapped on the beach shelf.

I had set my mental alarm for 0330 the next morning, but missed it by twenty minutes. I quickly dressed and ran down to the boat to check out the situation. It was dark outside, but Surfbird's white hull was quite distinct. A quick glance told me we had about twenty minutes more before the ebbing tide would leave the boat stranded. I ran back toward our tent. "Nancy," I shouted, "we've got to move fast if we're going to make this tide. We've got about fifteen minutes."

Nancy had already taken down the tent and was stowing gear. "Let's try," she said and we both turned to, moving quickly and silently, running when steps were needed, jamming instead of packing. Tarp, tent, sleeping bags and clothes. Fortunately, we had stowed our cooking gear the night before. Three trips each. We ran back and forth to the boat, throwing our waterproof bags into the bow helter-skelter.

"Let's go. You take that side and we'll slide her out. She's resting on the bottom." We stood ankle-deep in the water, which was visibly draining fast off the shallow shelf. Small eddies formed around our ankles. When I heaved on my side nothing gave. "May be too late. Try again," I urged. We both lifted and pulled at the same time. After several attempts, Nancy looked over at me.

"It won't budge. Stuck tight."

"Goddam it!" I shouted. "Try again! I don't want to spend eight hours waiting for the tide. Give it all you've got!" Nothing gave but our sweat from running and straining.

"Sand's suction now," Nancy said. "Nothing we can do about it. Let's go back, make a camp and go back to sleep."

"Damnit!" I exploded. This kind of hold-up really frustrated me, but Nancy didn't seem ruffled.

"How about a shelter behind those big logs over there," she said, pointing over to the right of our old camp. "That way we won't have to put up the tent."

"I guess if we have to wait, I could use an hour or two more of sleep. I didn't sleep well last night anyway. Kept wondering if the tide would reach our tent. Besides, we have to cook breakfast somewhere. Might as well be here." It was still more dark than light.

We hauled our sleeping bags, cooking gear and food back up the beach over by the logs. We found some old timbers and thin logs that could be wedged to form a framework for a windbreak, using our tarp. It flapped in the wind but served our purpose. We nested our bags down into the sand behind the biggest log and fast were asleep.

CRAAAAAAASH!! BONK-BONK. We both shot upright. "Whaaa –

," and it was immediately obvious. "Wind's come up." A corner of our structure had been blown out of its wedge and over. I looked at my watch. "Six-thirty. Guess we'd better get moving anyway — water could be deep enough in another hour or so."

"Two hours at least," Nancy mumbled. "I'd like another half an hour in the sack."

"You go ahead and sleep. I'll work on this shelter so we can cook out of the wind," I responded, pulling on my pants.

"With you trying to wedge the logs, it'll be like sleeping next to a jackhammer," Nancy returned, sitting up in her bag. "Let's hope for a good camp tonight and we'll sleep in tomorrow. I need to make up about four hours."

By ten, we were off again. We pulled out of Blunden Bay into a stiff westerly and a heaving five-foot swell. It had started to rain just as we finished breakfast; the rain clouds now scudded low over us. Gulls also swept over low, scrounging their breakfast from rocks and shore, voicing their feelings to the wind. "I know this isn't halfway yet, but I kind of feel that it is," I offered as we pulled up the rain-shrouded coast.

"How's that?"

"We've only got about twenty more miles of exposure to open ocean and then we'll be home free in the more protected inside waters. What do you think of that?"

"I'll believe it when I see it. I don't see many easy parts anywhere."

"Nancy, you see only the grim side."

"Remember — I'm the realist."

"Ah yes, but things might change. Believe me; tomorrow may be better."

"Remember — tomorrow we're sleeping in."

After two hours we pulled inside of Egg Island, thankful to be in its lee. "That light looks like it takes a real pounding in the winter." I was looking at the light tower perched up about a hundred feet on top of the island.

"It looks cold and windswept even now," Nancy responded. "It's pretty barren. I'm sure all the fishing boats welcome its beam. With all these rocks this place looks as bad as the west coast of Vancouver Island. I wonder how many ships have sunk around here. This is tough now — think what it'd be like in winter."

"I don't want to think about it, especially in our boat." I looked shoreward. "Jones Cove is just around that next headland. Let's pull in there and eat lunch before attacking Smith Sound."

Jones Cove was murky and wet. A fishing boat was anchored about halfway down the narrow opening. Smoke rose, wind-swirled, from its small deckhouse stack. No one came out on deck as we approached. We passed on by and found an overhanging cedar that afforded us slight shelter. Lunch was quick, simple and damp. On our way out of the cove another troller pulled in and dropped anchor. The skipper and his young grandson made up the crew. While the grandson, perhaps fifteen, remained inside, the skipper leaned over the fantail, clearly wanting to visit. "Hi. That's a nice boat you've got there. Whatta ya doing out here?" He took our bow line, and as we bobbed in the rain, we talked. This hadn't been a good year for him. "The seiners and the Russian and Japanese fishing factories are taking all the fish. They don't leave much for us small guys. In a few years you won't see any of us out here. And the packers have fish in their warehouses from last year's poison scare. They won't pay nothin' for the fish we do bring in. I don't know, this may be my last year. But what else is there to do? Fishin's all I know. Maybe I'm borrowin' trouble, eh? It's given me a pretty good life, though. Where're you goin' tonight? There's no place you can duck into on this side." Looking across the sound – "The bay on the other side is good. Protected from the weather and it has an old fishnet dock right around the inside. Fishing boats use that bay all the time to tuck into. You could tie up there."

"Where's that?"

"Right over there," and he pointed to some land about two miles across the sound.

"Nancy, I hate to cross in this wind, but it looks like we have no choice. It's nearly two – we'd better get going." I turned and looked up to the fisherman. "Thanks, and good luck with your fishing. Maybe we'll see you again sometime."

The wind in Smith Sound was out of the east, blowing strongly out of the mountain snows, funneled through the narrows of Boswell Inlet. Here, it was hitting both a slowing flood current and the ocean swells, producing a high, heavy chop. "We've got to quarter into it or we won't make any headway. We better put our lifejackets on. It's going to take us at least two hours to get across, and it won't be easy."

"At least our backs will be to the rain," Nancy muttered. "Thank God for little favors."

From the start, it was hard going. The breaking chop splashed into the boat. Each stroke was met by the resistance of a combination of several choppy waves, each as high as our bow stem, seeming to come from three directions – dead ahead and off both the port and starboard bows. Our progress was slow. The boat actually staggered as we moved into each wave. To make any headway, we pulled at least thirty-five strokes – hard strokes – every minute.

We hadn't been underway twenty minutes when Nancy announced, "I've got a bite! It's running with the line! It's a salmon. I just know it is!" She let it run for several seconds more then set the hook and horsed and reeled. In the meantime, I worked to keep our bow into the wind, rowing and watching to help Nancy play her fish. "I hate to hold us up, but this is big. It's dinner for tonight and several nights. This is exciting! He's fighting me – whatever it is. I've never had anything work this hard! Get the net ready!" All the time Nancy labored, horsing heavily and reeling in the slack. Finally, it broke water, a glistening silver salmon. Big, at least by our standards.

"Careful, we don't want to lose him" Nancy had become the director on the set. "I'll bring him alongside. You get the net under him. Oh, I wonder if he's too big for the net. Be careful. He is beautiful."

I got the net under him. He folded in, resisting every second in strenuous and violent twists and flips. He probably weighed no more than fourteen pounds, but to us he was a prize for eating, and to Nancy, a trophy for endless days of fruitless trolling. Now, we could get back to the task at hand.

After two and a half hours without letup, we were still a quarter of a mile off the land that was now rain-shrouded. Under the low black clouds, our visibility was greatly reduced, down to no more than a mile. The rain pelted our backs and water ran off our sleeves and down our fingers in streams. "A quarter of a mile to go, Nancy. Can you hang in there?"

"No choice. My hands don't hurt. Just numb. Let's just get over there. Don't know how long I can hold out." By now we had passed through slack current and could feel the resistance of the ebb and the building of the waves. We were wet with sweat and my seat was soaked.

"Watch out for those rocks – we'd better stay away from that island – I'm afraid to go inside." I glanced over my right shoulder at some rocks between us and the shore.

"Yeah – too many rocks. Look at that water pull back off that one over there." Nancy pointed to a frothing rock ledge ten feet across, about twenty-five feet away. When exposed by each swirling, receding wave, its barnacle-crusted, jagged, surface looked like a set bear-trap that could make shards of a small wooden boat like ours.

"Ten minutes more, Nancy. Then we can rest. That cove must be right up ahead."

"I don't see it." Nancy had turned while rowing, trying to make out a cove entrance. "Let's pull into that niche," she said. "I've got to rest." The niche was small; big enough for our boat to anchor in if we chose, but all of its outline was steep and rocky, entirely uninhabitable if we thought of it as a campsite.

"No place for a tent here. Let's rest awhile then work our way up the shoreline. Can't be too much farther."

"My hand is better when the feeling's gone." Nancy was massaging her right hand with her left.

We were out of the force of the wind, but small gusts curled around the sheltering headland like flames to lick at us and let us know that it was waiting for us. Eddies from the current carried the same message. "Let's go and get this over with," I said. "I'm tired and hungry."

When we nosed the bow out, it was like sticking a hand out of a window of a fast-moving car. It whipped us downwind before we could set against it. Turning back upwind was tortuous – agonizingly slow. Inch by inch, not foot by foot, we strained hard, heading into both wind and current. The waves were now three to four feet high. "That must be the opening right up there," I said, pointing just ahead. We were just offshore, maybe twenty feet, outside a sawtooth edge of jutting foam-whitened rock. We had to shout to be heard above the wind. The waves crashed against the rocks and the rain pelted our backs.

"That's no opening. It's just an indentation," Nancy shouted. I glanced at my watch. It had taken us half an hour to cover two hundred yards.

"Oh, no! It must be around that next headland." I pointed further upwind, less than a quarter of a mile. "Can you do it?" We were rowing hard just to keep from losing ground. Each oncoming wave hammered us back.

"I'll try — anything to get out of this," Nancy concurred. Another half hour moved us less than a quarter of a mile.

"This can't be right. I don't see any sign of a bay entrance. Besides, look-up there. We're on an island, not on the north shore — DAMN!!"

"Oh hell! You're right. I can't believe it!" Nancy replied. We turned about and fairly shot down channel. It was now well into dusk, fast darkening. As we moved back down the island, we saw nothing but rock cliffs and outcroppings, no suitable place to anchor or make camp. After about fifteen minutes of fast travel, mostly riding down the fronts of the foamy troughs, it became clear that we had reached a group of small islands that lay about half way across Smith Sound. We still had another three miles to go to reach the other side! "Let's go," Nancy said. '"We've no choice."

"I can't make out any bay entrance," I said, searching over my shoulder. "It's getting too dark. The shoreline all looks the same. According to our chart, it must be over there, in that direction. Wish our chart was better. We have to go by compass, or we'll get all screwed up." We had brought a hand-held compass that we used in the mountains. By wedging it into the grating at my feet, I could make out general direction. We were now quartering across an eighteen knot downwind, lifting up, over and sliding down into the troughs. Each wave, now four to four and half feet, hit our stern to push us broadside into the troughs. With each such thrust, we had to counter-pull hard on our left oars to keep from broadsiding. Broadsiding in these waves meant certain swamping and probable death at this hour of day. There would be no one to rescue us and shore was too far away for swimming. Wind's building," Nancy stated.

"So's the rain. We've got to get out of this. All I want is to get to shore." An hour had passed since we had left the islands, and we were still a mile off-shore.

'"I've got to rest a minute." Nancy dropped her oars. "I'm tired and I hurt. What did we do to deserve this day?" While Nancy talked, I worked to keep the stern into the wind and strained to make out anything on the shoreline. Something caught my eye, then vanished. I strained harder, for we were being jolted up, down and sideways by the waves. I saw nothing. I relaxed my eyes. It was now almost too dark to see anything other than the faint streak of the darker shoreline. Wait. There it is again. Out of the periphery I vaguely made out something on the surface of the water, off our starboard bow. First I'd see it, then it would disappear.

"Nancy! Look hard, over there." I pointed toward what I'd seen. "Do you see something on the surface?"

"No. My glasses are too wet, and I can't see anything without them. My hood keeps flapping over my face in this wind."

"Let's row over that way." We rowed for about ten minutes, now dangerously near the troughs. I paused to look again. "There it is, Nancy. It's a small buoy with a radar reflector on top. I'll bet you dollars to doughnuts it's out there for fishermen. Tells them where the bay entrance is. It's got to be that. Let's take the chance and row directly for shore.'

We took on new strength and pulled hard. The wind was blowing now at least twenty, pushing forcibly. In fifteen minutes we closed on the shore. Nancy turned for a bearing. "There it is," she said, with more excitement than I'd heard for hours. She pointed just off our starboard bow. "There are the two small entrances, with the island in the middle – just like he said." We could make this out, but just barely in the darkness. It was nearly eleven o'clock.

"Let's get inside and out of this wind," I urged. "We'll find a campsite inside." Now, directly downwind, we fairly shot through the narrow western entrance, fast into relative calm.

"Let's row around the edge of the bay until we see a place for our tent. Look, right on the back side of that entrance island. There must be eight fishing boats clustered there."

"They must be tied to the old net-dock the skipper of the Lady Luck mentioned." We couldn't make out individual boats, but we could see a cluster of cabin lights. All we wanted now was a place to sleep. We didn't even care if the boat went aground. We had rowed for over twelve hours, with lunch ten hours ago and only a couple of short breaks. We were both exhausted and soaking wet. Before it became too dark to see anything, we spent half an hour rowing from one shore site to another in search of a campsite. They were either too rocky or too marshy. There was nothing.

"How about the net dock? Maybe there's something over there."

"Quietly," Nancy whispered. "Some of the fishermen might be asleep. "

As we approached the dock, I whispered over my shoulder. "Let's go on the backside of the dock. There might be space there where their boats can't go." We rowed as silently as possible around the dock.

"Look out for that cable," Nancy whispered. "Duck under it." Quietly, we edged the boat alongside and both more or less rolled out to tie up.

"I'm too tired to eat. Our beautiful salmon will have to wait," Nancy whispered. "Let's just put the tarp down, envelope-like and crawl in."

"Suits me," I answered. We unrolled the tarp, trying to keep the underside dry in the rain, pulled our bags in, tucked the tarp so it was both under and over us, then unrolled our bags and somehow managed to crawl in. "Fold under your end and I'll do the same," I whispered. The top covered our heads, putting the sound of the rain right next to our ears, but outside. I reached over and touched Nancy. "Like rain on the roof. You can sleep in in the morning if you like."

"Thanks a lot," she whispered. "The fishing boats will probably start up about four."

As I turned over, I thought, some fishermen will be surprised at what they see on the dock in the morning. With that, I dropped off, oblivious to the plank surface of the dock that met my hips and shoulders hard on.

PART VIII: (Pete) SMITH SOUND TO NAMU; "HOW WOULD YOU LIKE A CABIN TONIGHT WITH A HOT SHOWER AND WARM BED?"

Nancy was right. The sound was the starting of four or five engines and the distinctive jumping, thuds and clanking of mooring lines being untied and deck gear being secured. Under our cover I glanced at my watch. "Four-fifteen," I whispered. "Still dark. Let's sleep for another hour or so."

"You promised," she whispered back, not stirring. "See you in a couple of hours."

By seven the rain had let up to a light drizzle. We smelled coffee and bacon from one of the fishing boats, but felt no tap on our tarp to invite us in. We stuck our noses out like two groundhogs to sniff the day. Our noses got wet. No change there. "Let's drape the tarp over the net ridge there at our feet. It's only three feet high, but it'll make kind of a tent for us. At least we'll stay dry for breakfast," I suggested.

"Good idea. You do that and I'll get the food from the boat." While we ate our breakfast, a couple of fishermen came over to talk with us. They were staying in because it was Sunday and besides, they said, the run wasn't very good. We had lost track of the days. They hadn't heard us come in.

The first to approach said, "We come in yesterday afternoon because it was blowing up. Built until about midnight. You came in in that? And in that boat?"

"Hell, Bill, they was fishing in dories off this coast long before you and me started fishing," his friend countered. "They used to tow 'em offshore and leave 'em. For a week at a time. Some right outside here," he said, pointing offshore. "Had a little canvas-covered cutty forward for sleeping. In boats no bigger'n this. Used all hand lines. Dory's one of the safest boats ever made for rough weather. I like ours better though — 's warmer. Let's go have breakfast." He smiled as he turned back to his boat.

Following him, the first fisherman added, "Gotta hand it to you for doin' something different. Can't even get my wife out on this boat. Good luck."

After they left, I turned to Nancy. "Let's pack up and head out. I'm still anxious to get out of these open ocean waters."

"Maybe tonight we'll find a nice campsite. Wouldn't it be great to find a place with a warm stove?"

"You dreamer," I answered. "Next thing you'll want is a long hot shower and somebody handing you a glass of chilled wine. Come on, let's go."

As we nosed out of the bay the wind was still up and out of the southeast, but not quite as bad as last night. "Wind's with us now, and once we're around the point we'll be in the lee of the shore for most of the day until we round into Rivers Inlet."

"How far's the point?" Nancy asked.

"About a mile. We can stay inside these islands for some protection."

"At least we don't have to make any crossings today," she added. "Yesterday was no fun. I can stand the rain. It's the wind that gets to me."

We took most of the morning edging our way up around Kelp Head, inside of Dugout Rocks, rowing in the rain. We were glad to be out of the wind. The water was still the ocean; the swells were ten to twelve feet and the nearby surf echoed with pounding breakers. We passed just outside of scattered jagged rocks outlined by swirling foam. Psychologically though, we felt some relief in the protection of the land mass from the southwestern expanse of the Pacific. Each stroke on this northeasterly heading brought us more "protection," but in truth, we were still in open ocean. It's just that we were ready to believe anything that offered relief from wind, rain and potential Pacific storms.

"Tomorrow and tomorrow and tomorrow creeps in this petty pace from day to day." As we rowed in our own silences, I thought, Shakespeare certainly understood the pace of rowing, though not the reality of offshore rowing. Dusty death hardly, but death was not something we considered as likely. Always possible, we knew, but we felt we were usually close enough to shore to help ourselves in any emergency. More than risk, we felt a sense of personal accomplishment as we moved north, of besting the elements, of surviving in the open. Such feelings can be shared only with those who are part of the adventure; thought about mostly when alone with ones own thoughts. Such times occur when rowing in the rain, inside your own hood, not talking with your partner, but just going on — dip, pull, glide; dip, pull, glide, twenty-five times a minute, sometimes for as many as three hours without resting, but seldom more than twenty minutes without sharing some brief thought, observation or consideration. Other times we'd talk for hours, all the time rowing: books, authors, our children, old movies, future plans. We seldom have difficulty finding something to talk about. At times, it's more comfortable to drift into silence.

Today was one of those days. We just moved on, not bothered by

PART VIII - SMITH SOUND TO NAMU

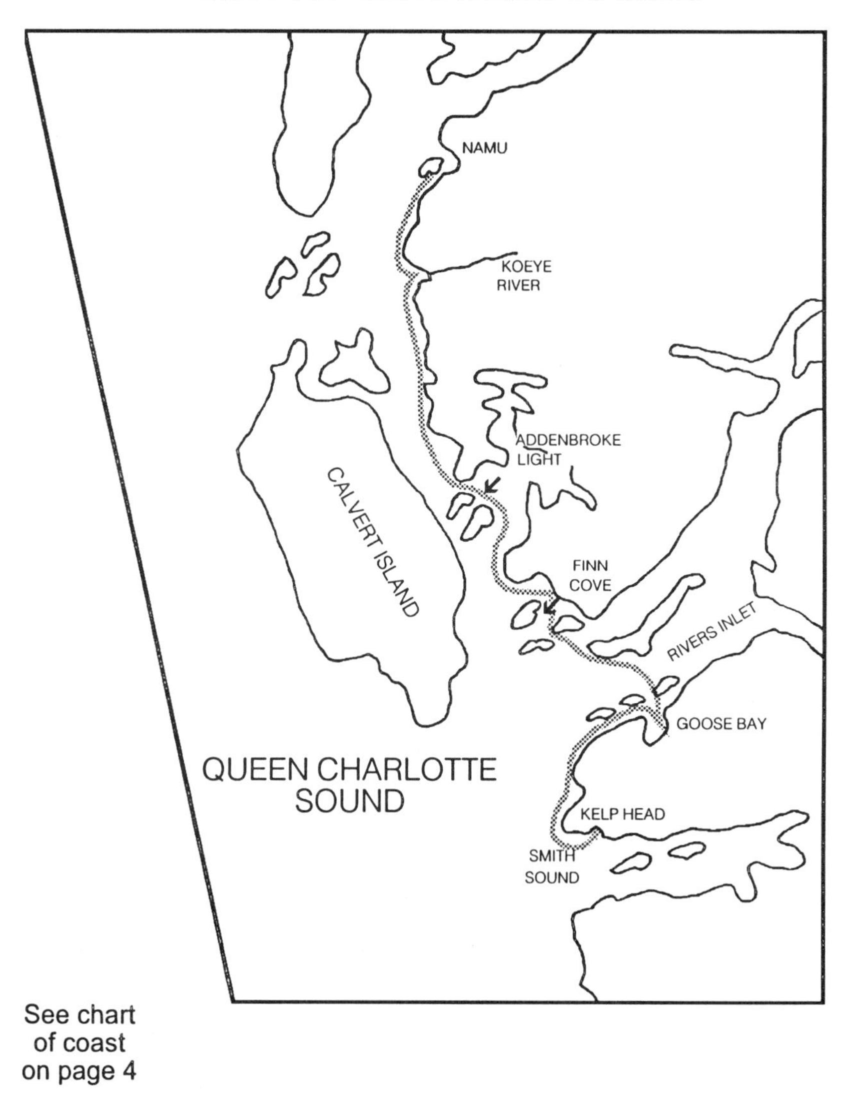

See chart
of coast
on page 4

the rain, simply accepting it as the backdrop on the stage. Today, the elements weren't strutting and fretting their hour upon our stage, and we knew they would indeed be heard again, full of their sound and fury, though perhaps signifying nothing. One has lots of time for wool gathering when rowing.

"This is a wide cove, but look at that beautiful white sandy beach," Nancy said, twisting to look. Before us stretched a long shallow cove with an arcing, unbroken beach, perhaps a mile and a half in length, uncluttered by logs or driftwood and empty of any sign of human visitation.

"Let's go in closer and see if we can find a spot for the night."

"It looks almost tropical," Nancy exclaimed. "White sand and the wind has even bent the trees to look like palms. Even in this rain, it's beautiful." As we approached the shore, I saw one more characteristic of a tropical beach — a breaking surf.

"We can't off-load here, Nancy. The surf would swamp us for sure. Let's go back over there just around the headland and see if that offers more protection." Because of the length of the beach, it took us about an hour to examine five possible campsites. In each case either the surf was too high or the beach too narrow.

"Let's keep rowing up the inlet," I said. "Something better will show up." I was disappointed. It was like looking into the window of a closed pastry shop; all beautiful to see, but untouchable.

As we rowed up the shore in search of a better spot, we both reacted to the sound of a distant outboard. "There's a boat alongside that cliff. Can you see it?" I pointed to a headland about half a mile ahead.

"There's another one out toward the middle of the inlet. It looks like — let me see the binoculars a minute." Nancy reached back toward me keeping her eyes on the nearest boat. I put the glasses in her back-stretched hand. "Yeah. Goose Bay. Goose Bay on the sides of both boats. I wonder what that is?" Nancy now tracked both boats through the binoculars.

"I'll bet there's a fish camp nearby. Those are sport fishermen with guides. Got to be, with those fourteen-foot aluminum boats. We must be close to some bit of civilization," I said. I wasn't sure what it meant to us, but it did add subject for speculation and discussion.

An hour later, we were still rowing up the inlet, looking for a campsite. Inlet is somewhat of a misnomer, for at this point the north shore was four miles away, across open water and the ocean was directly at our backs. We crawled along the south- shore approaching some cloud-covered broken islands. "Here comes another of those boats," Nancy remarked. "He's going to pass close by."

"Looks as though he's coming alongside," I answered, as they approached. The rain was now steady. "Hello!" I hailed, as their bow settled into the water when they throttled down several yards off.

"Hi," the passenger said. "What're you doing out here?"

We briefly explained our journey, ending with, "Right now, we're looking for a place to pitch our tent. Where're you from?"

"To Alaska!" the passenger exclaimed. "That's fantastic! Don't envy you this rain, but that's fantastic. We're out of Goose Bay — not very far from here. It's the old Goose Bay Cannery, now a fish camp for sport fishermen. I'm visiting my buddy, the manager, there."

"Any place there where we might pitch a tent tonight? We're not having much luck along here." I was pointing across the sweep of the shoreline.

The passenger turned to the guide, "The next party isn't due in until tomorrow afternoon. Do you think Gary could find a place for them tonight?"

"I know he can," he answered. "We've got several vacant cabins." Turning to us, "How'd you like a cabin tonight with a warm stove, a hot shower and a soft bed?"

"Where are your wings?" Nancy asked. "Your halos are hidden under your hoods."

"Row between those two islands way up ahead, then turn down the bay. We're down at the very end. A big warehouse on pilings on the left and several small buildings along the shore."

"How far?"

"About three miles."

"It'll take us about an hour and a half, but we'll be there. My, yes, we'll be there!"

"See you later then," and with that they were off, quickly to disappear among the islands. In comparison we crept, but back in our hoods we both smiled through the rain. Our strokes were strong and we sat straight.

"A warm stove," Nancy recited, mostly to herself.

"And a long hot shower," I picked up.

"I wonder what they'll have for dinner? I really don't care, as long as somebody else fixes it," Nancy replied. She nudged the salmon lying in the bottom of the boat. "Salmon, friend, you'll just have to be patient. We'll get to you sooner or later. Stay fresh."

"Maybe we can dry our sleeping bags. God! What a nice break," I went on. "Maybe somebody up there is watching over us. Couldn't come at a nicer time."

It took us about an hour to pass through the islands and into a broader expanse of quiet water. "This must be the bay," Nancy said. "The camp must be down to the left about a mile."

For the last half-hour under lowering heavy gray-black clouds, the rain intensified. With no wind, large heavy drops fell straight onto the flat water, each drop splashing at least six inches off the surface. I had never seen vertical rain fall so densely or hard. We rowed in mid-channel. Though less than half a mile away, the steep heavily-forested shores were barely visible, a dark blur through the near-solid envelopment of rain. Each drop splashed and sent out its own circle of wavelets. The surface of the entire bay was a froth of whipped water, its combined magnitude a low boiling roar. "Strangest water I've ever seen. More like a witches' cauldron than a fishing paradise. If the rain doesn't let up soon, I'll have to bail the boat before we reach the camp."

"I've never seen anything like this," Nancy answered. "If I weren't so wet, I'd say it's beautiful."

"Mesmerizing," I added. We had both let go our oars, quite in awe of what we were experiencing.

"Well," Nancy said, with a tone of finality as she picked up her oars, "back to the warm stove and the shower."

Like many of the old canneries built along this coast before the turn of the century, this one perched on creosoted pilings attached to a narrow, rocky ledge, backed by a sheer cliff or heavily-forested, steep hillside. An outstretched floating dock was kept in line by a single-file of black pilings that marched straight out into the bay. From about a quarter of a mile away we made out a group of aluminum boats pulled up on the floats, and a couple of larger boats tied alongside. There was no activity down on the docks when we tied up. Only the rain, relentless in its intensity. "I'll bail later," I offered. "Let's go see what we can find."

We walked along the floats and up the steep gangway to the top of the dock. Nearby we heard a generator operating, the only sound discernible except for the rain loud on the tin cannery roof. Leading away from the old, silvered corrugated cannery itself was a boardwalk about eight feet wide, shiny and slick from the rain. On the hillside, water ran off the dense salal underbrush and overhanging trees. On the bay side a weathered three-foot high two-by-four railing kept traffic from falling into the water at high tide and into the mud or rocks twenty feet below at low tide. Here and there we saw where new planks had been substituted for rotting originals. Further down the walk we made out several cabins built out on pilings, connected to the bay side of the walk. Several work buildings were squeezed along the hillside. Perched higher on the hill up to our left were a couple of small houses, attached to the walkway by steep narrow steps. "I wonder where we should go?" Nancy asked.

"I don't know. Let's just go along until we see some kind of activity. I'm sure everyone's inside. Only fools out in this."

We had just passed the first set of steps when we heard, "Hi! C'mon up here. We've been waiting for you." We looked up into the rain. It was the passenger we had talked with earlier. When we had climbed up onto the small porch, he and another man, who turned out to be the camp manager, held open the house and screen doors and offered us each a large dry towel. "Come on in and dry off. Take your rain gear off inside. God! You must be soaked!"

The warmth of their stove washed over us immediately as we stepped inside. "What'll you drink? I have scotch, bourbon and some chilled wine in the 'frige'."

Nancy hardly let him finish, "I know Pete would like some scotch with a touch of water. I'll take your wine please." While we toweled, we talked, letting the warmth and the dry take over and the libation work from the inside out. Never had these small pleasures felt better.

Gary, the manager, attended to us as if we were his long absent parents. And well we could have been, for he appeared to be in his mid-thirties, a physically strong, positive person. "I've opened up cabin number eight for you," he said. "Just painted. The stove's been on for an hour, so it should be nice and warm. Lots of hot water and clean linen. If your sleeping bags are wet, bring them over to the mess-hall; we'll dry them on the racks we have over the big stove. Dinner's at six."

The cabin was small but contained a bathroom with shower, a bedroom barely larger than its double bed and a kitchen containing a sink, an oil cookstove and a small table. Though old, the cabin was squeaky clean. As we stepped inside, Nancy turned to me, "I didn't expect heaven to look like this, but I don't know how any place could be nicer."

"You climb in the shower and I'll go get our clothes and the wet bags," I suggested.

"I'll come with you to save you a trip. We have plenty of time. It's only about five."

"OK. While you're showering, I'll spread out the charts that got wet." We each must have spent fifteen minutes under the shower, letting the hot water pour over us. The pleasure in any ordeal is the cessation of pain or discomfort. Recharging the batteries is a marvelous sensation and Goose Bay let us do just that, in abundant style.

The mess hall was fairly new, paneled in rough unstained cedar. Six or seven tables allowed the staff to handle several fishing parties at once. Groups of photos on the walls attested to the successes of many of their guests – big salmon and even bigger smiles on the faces of the catchers. The biggest salmon shown weighed seventy-two pounds. It was huge!

Gary Dewling, the manager, had his Ph.D. in psychology and had worked for several years for the Canadian Government. Because of her counseling background and studies in psychology, Nancy hit it right off with him. She was interested to learn that he had worked very closely with several leading psychologists and psychiatrists in the United States – until he simply tired of the bureaucracy of the government and the hustle of cities. He opted for a simpler life and jumped at the chance to run a fish camp, something for which he also had considerable qualification. I like the people that come to us," he stated. "The small crew we have – everyone pitches in guiding, dishes, serving, maintenance – the whole shebang." He smiled. "Wouldn't trade it for anything. Off season, we work to improve the place. What could be better, eh?" "What about the rain?"

"Oh yeah, the rain." He looked outside. It was nearly dark for the heavy low clouds and the steady tatoo on the roof. "We get 180-200 inches a year here. That's a lot; but you get used to it – have to or you don't last. Some folks don't – too gray, too wet and too isolated. Depends on what you want." We talked on, a group of us sitting around one of the tables drinking coffee, one subject leading to another until late. It was a welcome change for us.

Around one in the morning I awakened to a surge of rain on the roof. "I'd better go check the boat. It must be near full and I'd sure hate to find it on the bottom in the morning."

I think I'll let you go alone – but do you have an aspirin? My hands are really bad tonight – too much luxury – they can't adjust. Besides, there's only one bailer." With that, Nancy crawled back under . . . . .

Getting into my boots and yellows was OK – they were warm on a chair by the kitchen stove. Along the walkway, hooded light bulbs swung, isolated in the wind. Small circles of light danced along the boardwalk, highlighting the rain that streaked by and splashed on the wet black timbers. Shadows of overhanging branches moved stealthily in the rain, giving some bit of life to the outer blackness. Ahead in the darkness and the shadows loomed the faint outline of the lifeless old cannery. I made my way down the walk, alone and surrounded by the ghosts of the Chinese, Japanese and Finnish laborers who had worked here so many years ago.

The tide was out; the gangway down to the floats steep. When I reached the boat, it was clear I was in time – but just barely. The water inside was within six inches of the rails. I bailed fast. In twenty minutes the water was down to the gratings – good enough until we'd come down in the morning, even if it didn't stop raining. I was ready for another shower, which I would take in the morning I thought, smiling at the prospect.

A breakfast for four finally filled the two of us. We lingered over a third cup of coffee, then gathered and packed our warm dry belongings. After hugs, good-byes and well-wishes, we made our way down to the boat. Their hospitality had been magnificent.

The rain had slackened to light. While Nancy stowed, I bailed. As we pulled away, several of the crew were up on the boardwalk, waving. "We keep running into such great people," Nancy said, as we headed down the bay. "It's so different from living in the city. The only new person I've met during the past year is one of the checkout women at Safeway. There seems to be a sharing and mutual dependence that goes with more isolated living that I find appealing. What's the big difference?"

"For one thing," I reflected, "there's not nearly the emphasis on things, or position, or advancement and darn little outside pressures such as commuting traffic, or PTA, or Little League, or service clubs or all that stuff that goes with urban living. So much hassle. Out here's not for everyone though – not easy to make a living, let along helping kids through college or being able to build anything for retirement. A lot of these old fishermen still fish because they have to. It's pretty much hand-to-mouth. We all have to make choices, I guess. What's important?"

"I know," Nancy answered. "Like you say – it's a complex world, with few easy solutions and fewer that're absolutely right. Sitting offshore on our boat for a couple of months is kinda like sitting in a front row seat to life. We get to look at our world and our life, free of everyday hassle."

"But with a few unique types of hassles substituted – like wind, rain, current," I quickly added.

"You're right, but they're different," Nancy countered. "Although I do appreciate having the rain stop." While we moved through the islands on the north side of Rivers Inlet, a bush pilot made several low passes over us in his Beaver float plane. Our first thought was that something had happened to one of our children. With eight, that is always a possibility. Since none of our family knew exactly where we were, it was logical that in an emergency, they might send out a bush pilot to look for us. After three sweeps, he flew off. "Must not be looking for us," I offered.

"Probably had a passenger who wanted to photograph my gray hair and your bald head in an open boat – strange sights along the North Pacific Coast. Peaceful, isn't it, now that he's gone? Miles and miles of islands and wilderness. And no people," Nancy went on. "I like this."

"Finn Cove is on the northwest corner of Penrose Island. That'd be about ten miles today. Considering our late start, why don't we look there for a site for tonight?"

"Sounds good to me – then tomorrow, we can start up the Inside Passage." Nancy thought a minute, then added, "It'll be nice to have Calvert Island between us and the ocean. With luck, we'll be in Namu day after tomorrow."

"Maybe I can find a new pair of rainpants," I added. "It'll be nice to touch in at a settlement with a store."

Late in the day we pulled into Finn Cove, leaving the influence and swell of Queen Charlotte Sound for the first time in over a week. Just inside the cove we saw a house and some outbuildings built on floats. A troller was tied up at the dock. We stopped there to ask if there was a suitable camping site in the cove. As we approached, a man pulled out to meet us in his small outboard skiff. He made it clear that people were not welcome on his property and suggested we set up camp on a dock down the bay. We thanked him and started off. With a grimace of conflicting emotion he said, "You might as well come in for tea. Tie up anywhere and come on." This was said loudly without a smile, and it appeared against his natural inclinations. Fascinated now, we followed him into his cozy boat home and introduced ourselves.

"I'm Ken," he countered. "I'm not very hospitable," he added vehemently. "I don't like people. I came here to get away from the bloody city. Hate cities!" As he served us tea and packaged cookies, we sat at his small kitchen table. His only companion, an ancient canary, teetered on its perch. The bird became upset, Ken told us, if moved from the table. It would fall off its perch to the bottom of the cage; so Ken let it remain near him.

Hummingbird feeders hung at every window and the tiny creatures visited Ken in droves, their throats gleaming brilliant red flashes and their wings vibrating like miniature helicopters. He had invested in over thirty-five pounds of sugar for them since spring.

Ken had been an early gold prospector in the B.C. interior near Lake Williams. He also had served in the Army and then had made fishing his career. He moved to his present bankside location thirty-three years ago alone, and has remained so since. During that span of time, Ken has created a miracle on the hillside behind his water-based home. Originally a rocky wasteland, he has built it into a lush vegetable garden complete with fruit trees. He did it by bringing in one bucket of top soil a week, which he obtained from an abandoned truck farm near his mail pick-up location, about twelve miles up the inlet. He started with carrots and lettuce and gradually expanded his crop with each additional bucket of dirt. He is also building a small house on the hillside where he will live at its completion.

We thanked him for the tea and cookies and Nancy climbed back in our boat as I released the lines. Ken's inner struggle began again. "Look here," he said gruffly, pointing to a net shack at the end of his dock, "you can stay here tonight if you don't bother me."

The shack was complete with an old mattress and some foam pads — and it had a roof to ward off possible rain. We accepted with pleasure. Ken indicated where to tie up, then disappeared into his house.

We settled in and laid out our limited supply of pots and pans to prepare dinner on the dock. It was finally time to cook our Smith Sound salmon. Nancy had turned to pull it from the boat when Ken appeared carrying a huge chum salmon he had caught that day. He hacked off a hunk and left it, saying, "You might as well have some of this for your dinner — but don't bother me."

Within five minutes he was back again with two cans of salmon he had canned last year. "Here — take these, but leave me alone."

After dinner, Nancy risked his annoyance by taking him some hot pan bread for dessert. He avoided eye contact, but grabbed the bread eagerly and took it into his home mumbling something about honey.

We left early the next morning after tacking a note of thanks on the shack door. We never saw Ken again, but he has entered our thoughts and conversation many times since.

Around ten next morning, our running commentary was interrupted by an approaching outboard motorboat. We had started early from Ken's net shack and were just north of Addenbroke Island, making good time with the current and our sail. So far, eleven miles in three and a half hours, all easy going and pretty through these islands off Addenbroke. "Hello," the approaching boater called. "Saw your sail, so thought I'd come over." We quickly lowered the sail to stop our progress, letting the boom rest on the boat sides. "I'm the lightkeeper over at Addenbroke Light. Don't see many lug sails around here. Wanted to see what you were. You sure look nice under sail. I like your dory."

As we briefly explained our undertaking, he interrupted to say, "A younger fellow, two years ago, stopped by and spent a night with me. He was also rowing a dory to Alaska. From down near Seattle."

"That must have been Steve Gropp," I interjected.

"That's right. Steve Gropp. Do you know him?"

"We sure do. He's why we're here today." After about fifteen minutes of visiting, we felt it time to go.

"Koeye River is about ten miles this side of Namu. About eight miles up the sound. If you can make it there tonight, there's an old miners' shack about a mile upstream. Hunters and fishers use it. It used to have a stove. Don't know what condition it's in. Haven't been there in years. You might want to look."

"Thanks — nice talking with you," we both enjoined. With that he pulled off and headed back to his light, while we raised our sail to move on.

In its estuary, the Koeye River flows lightly. We easily made our way upstream. Our course stayed midstream around the gradual bends to avoid the shallow gravelbars that projected into the river at each bend. In this area the river was about a hundred feet across. The north side, on our left, was heavily forested with evergreens; the south side more an open valley, with high grass and berry bushes in the areas between irregular clumps of deciduous trees.

Half a mile upstream we saw the remnants of four ancient one-room shacks, built along the river. These were not far from some old timbers and a pile of rock tailings lined out higher on the backing hillside, stemming from the entrance of a long-abandoned, hand-operated mine. The cabins, all built out on pilings to the river's edge, were near exhaustion. Three were more open than enclosed. One was better than the rest, but not much. "Looks terrible," Nancy offered, as we glided into a shallow cove.

"Let's go look. If it's no good, there are lots of places here for our tent." We tied the boat and walked up to the cabin through grown-over brush. Broken glass, old cans and dried bits of lumber and shingles lay strewn about. And plastic - containers, wrappers, envelopes, sheeting: junk left by scores of previous shelter seekers.

A newer piece of plywood had more recently been cut, hinged and hooked to form a closed door. We opened it slowly to peek in. More junk: more plastic, more cans, more bottles, more wrappers. "Oh yuck," Nancy managed. "What a pig sty!"

"But it does look dry inside and there is a stove — such as it is." The stove was a rusty fifty-gallon steel barrel, on its side, resting just off the floor on some larger river rocks. Where its rusty chimney passed through the ceiling, enough sky was revealed to permit weather forecasting. The windows, long glassless, were covered by opaque plastic to keep out the elements and larger four-legged intruders. "Let's go look for a tent site," I suggested.

"I agree. This is pretty bad." Just as we arrived back at the boat, we heard an approaching outboard. A lone rider in a small aluminum boat approached. He wore some kind of official uniform.

"Maybe we shouldn't be here," Nancy said.

"We'll soon find out." I turned toward the visitor who had now edged his bow onto the shore on the far side of our boat. "Hi. How're you?"

He returned the greeting with a smile. Though he had shut off his motor, he made no motion to leave his boat. "Saw you come in. I was in that cabin at the entrance. Don't see many rowers — especially our age." He smiled again. "I work summers along here with the Fisheries Department, trying for better fishing management."

"Is it OK if we stay here tonight?"

"Oh yeah. Some people who fish stay here. Cabin isn't much. We get a lot of bear in these parts. They like the berries here. Little early now, but a fella did see one just the other day, down past the mine there, couple hundred yards."

We asked him about Namu.

"Lots of boats in. They're talking strike against the canneries. Mostly the younger guys. Store's pretty empty — so many boats in, they're cleaning it out." We visited a little longer before he returned to the fisheries cabin.

"Well," Nancy announced, "it looks like rain. Let's go work on our cabin."

"I'll cut a couple of fir boughs for brooms."

"I'll start mucking out," she answered. Half an hour later, the cabin was as clean as it probably ever was since the last permanent residents had left. It was still filthy, but much better by comparison. We didn't quite know what to do with all the trash, so we piled it neatly outside. In its greater junk yard there, our neat stack was a spot of light in a world of darkness.

While Nancy started dinner, I gathered wood for the fire I had built in the stove. As much smoke leaked out of the chimney into the room as passed on up and out. "It'll keep the mosquitoes out," I volunteered.

"And cure cheese too," Nancy answered, wiping her eyes.

We turned in early after dinner. Although it wasn't even dark, we both quickly dropped off.

"What was that?" I whispered, sitting up. I knew Nancy was also awake.

"I don't know," she whispered back. "Something's thrashing around outside."

"There it is again. It is thrashing, in the underbrush."

"Definite steps. Too big to be any kind of small animal."

"Sounds like two of them now. They're coming closer to the cabin!"

"We should have put the food back in the boat and anchored it out. They can probably smell it." We were still whispering.

"I just saw something move outside through that crack in the door. And there! Over on the back wall! Look at that outline ! It's a head! At least six feet high!!"

"My God! One's right at the back door. It's only wedged shut with a little stick!" We both sat fully upright on our sleeping bags, waiting for the bears to burst through the door.

The first heavy pound on the door burst it easily open. "Hello – anybody inside?"

"Whewwwww! Come in," we both answered, expelling our breath with relief.

"Saw your boat and thought you might be in the cabin. We just sailed up Queen Charlotte Sound and are a little weather-weary. We thought that was something, but you're rowing. To Alaska, according to the Fisheries officer.

That's something else."

Nancy had rustled about to find and light a candle. Our visitors were two male teachers in their early thirties, summering aboard their twenty-six foot sloop. They were thinking of sailing to the Queen Charlotte Islands. Their boat was anchored down by the Fisheries cabin. Shortly they left us to go back to fix their supper.

"I don't know if I can sleep now or not," Nancy sighed. "That was scary."

"Let's try. I'm still tired from Smith Sound."

Around one-thirty, I awakened, startled by the sound of water lapping closely under the thin floor. I quickly recalled that tonight's tide was to be very high – twenty-one plus feet. I wonder if it rises higher than the floor? No. The floor is too dry. But it is close. What time is high tide? Maybe right now. I'll wait a few minutes. If it begins to sound worse, I'll get up and see. So I lay there in the dark staring up, seeing nothing, fully awake and straining to hear if the water was rising.

Sometime later, I heard some light rustling over in the far corner.

"What was that?" Nancy had shot upright to a sitting position.

"I think it's a mouse," I answered. "Probably lives here."

"Oh God!" Nancy shuddered, cinching her sleeping bag around her throat.

"He's a little field mouse. Can't hurt you, I'm sure. Relax and go back to sleep."

"I can't."

"Why not?"

"I'm afraid he'll get inside my bag. Hear him? He's coming closer!"

"He's more afraid of you than you are of him. Go back to sleep."

"How do you know? Did you ask him? I can't go back to sleep."

"You stand watch then, and I'll go back to sleep." As I rolled over, I cinched my bag around my neck. I don't know how long Nancy lasted, but she was asleep when I awakened at 0430. Under our roof we did stay dry when the rain started sometime around dawn.

Halfway to Namu, the light following wind veered to the northwest and strengthened, producing a tight chop. It took us four hours of hard pulling to cover the last five miles into Namu. The rain was heavy, the clouds low and dark.

Namu is not a town as we know one. It is a cannery with its own community. A company town. A private town. In addition to the familiar dock-side sheet metal warehouse/processing plant, there are several nearby buildings, including an old dormitory, an office, a company store, a generator building, a bathhouse, some individual houses on the hill and a small coffee shop on the dock. Just down from the coffee shop is a large marina for fishing boats. Today, it was full: over a hundred fishing boats, mostly gillnetters and trollers, singled and rafted. On the docks milled hundreds of fisher people, male and female, with a sprinkling of younger children. Their talk was all strike. Bitterness cast a pall over the whole community. We heard the same ing on the dock, in the office, in the company store and in the coffee shop.

"They won't pay nothin' for any fish."

"Twenty-five cents for pinks."

"Twenty-five cents is better than nothin'."

"If we don't fish, the seiners'll come in."

"Them and the Japs and Russian factories is runnin' us out of business."

"The company's got us by the balls and they know it."

Not a happy place, and there clearly was no place for us to stay. Cheeseburgers in the coffee shop tasted good, but the store was nearly cleaned out of groceries. I couldn't find a pair of foul-weather pants that came close to fitting me. "Let's get out of here, Nancy. The assistant manager said we could stay with him tonight. He's got one of those cabins up on the hill, but I'm afraid to leave the boat alone all night. Too tempting to rip off some of our gear, and I don't want to haul everything up to his cabin."

"That's OK by me," Nancy answered. We stood in the rain in our yellows and looked out over the marina. "I'm for getting away from here. Almost anything would be better than this."

We hauled the few groceries we had bought back down to the boat, balancing our way down a steep rickety gangway and then along a group of slippery, waterlogged, narrow wooden floats. We didn't even take time to stow the food, preferring instead to cast off and move further up the bay.

Past some islands, about a half mile further inland, we came upon an abandoned net-float, fifty feet wide and a hundred feet long. It was tied alongside some boomsticks that were cabled to the shore. The nearby shore was dense evergreen wilderness. "A campsite complete with toilet," I said. I pointed to an outhouse constructed on the boomsticks, doubtless complete with tidal flushing.

"This looks beautiful to me," Nancy said. "I like the peace and quiet." We set up our tent on the float, rigged the big tarp over it, off-loaded the gear we needed and fixed our dinner. Though the deck was hard, we took considerable comfort in its isolation.

"Don't have to worry about the tide coming either," I offered. "Small pleasures from small things, huh?"

"Right," Nancy responded. "I was just plain uncomfortable around that group of angry people back there."

"They've got a tough problem. Damned if they do and damned if they don't. I sympathize with them, but I'm glad I'm not in their shoes."

"Not much easier for the guys running the canneries. They're just trying to do their jobs," Nancy added.

"Strikes are ugly any time," I said. "Somebody usually gets hurt, and they're all people just trying to get along. You've said it so often — the world cries for the application of communication skills."

"Let's read in the tent for awhile, before it gets too dark." Nancy had unzipped the mosquito netting on the tent and had crawled in.

We had been reading about twenty minutes when we heard an outboard motor approaching at high speed. Quickly following, we heard male voices laughing and shouting as their boat turned fast in a tight circle just off our float. "Look, there's a tent on that float," one of them shouted above the whine of the motor. "Let's go over and visit 'em." More laughter as the boat noise circled away from the float and suddenly drew louder, as if in an attacking run. By now, we were both up out of our bags and on our knees, looking out of the tent.

"They're drunk," I said. "Looks like three or four of them. They're heading straight for us." They hit the dock head-on, twenty feet away from where our boat was tied alongside. They were going about ten to fourteen miles an hour. Their boat bounced straight back, the motor maintaining its high pitch, the voices of the occupants now a loud jumble of laughter, obscenities and excitement.

"Hit it again!" one managed. Back in they came, this time a little further down the dock, where two logs were tied alongside the float. This time, the bow of their boat was lifted by the lower riding logs, high enough to clear the edge of the float. Their momentum carried them up and over, the boat finally coming to rest on the float, its propeller biting air in a wild frenzy of sound.

"They're either drunk or on drugs," Nancy said. "Either way we may be in trouble."

"Are they kids?" I asked.

"I can't tell. Late teens or early twenties. Here they come. Let's go meet 'em before they start something." We both crawled out.

"Hi, anything we can do for you?" I asked. "We're rowing that dory to Alaska. Trying to get a little rest. What are you guys up to?"

The three of them were spread out, separated by about ten feet apiece. They approached slowly. Now they stopped. I don't know what they had in mind. Perhaps nothing, but both of us knew fear as we saw them survey our tent and gear.

"You guys look like kids I taught in school last year," Nancy said. "I do like boys. Where are you from?" That did it. If they had any mischief in mind, they were instantly disarmed. Few kids are going to act openly malicious to a gray-haired lady teacher. Worse, they were caught, as if she had pulled each up by his ear. We could see them visibly sag.

They didn't depart immediately. Rather, they wanted to visit, which we did for about fifteen minutes. They were off a Canadian seiner, the skipper of which was the father of the driver of this boat. As they pulled away, much quieter than when they had come, I turned to Nancy, "That was close, I think. Nice going. You may have saved us a lot of misery."

"They were on dope. That one would just as soon his dad never knew. I think they all feel a little bad about what they had started – if they can remember."

The next morning as we rowed up the coast out of Namu, we were overtaken by a seiner, the same name the boys had mentioned the night before. On the after deck, three figures waved enthusiastically at us. And continued waving long after they passed us by.

"We'll remember Namu for more than being just the capturing place of a famous Killer Whale," Nancy reflected.

"It's also the end of the first half of our trip. I wonder if the second half will be as interesting," I replied.

"Hard to believe it could be any more exciting or varied," Nancy said.

PART IX: (Nancy) NAMU TO BELLA BELLA: "WHOEVER HEARD OF WALKER POINT?"

Kissameet Bay, our evening's destination, appeared on the chart to be an easy twelve miles up Fisher Channel, after an initial two-mile crossing of Burke Channel. This seventy-five mile long passage empties into Fitzhugh Sound from Bella Coola, in the interior of British Columbia, and brings with it currents which meet ocean swells at the point we were crossing.

The chart was pocked with little crosses indicating partially submerged rocks, potential death-traps to mariners in any size craft. We were particularly sensitive to these hazards after our circumnavigation of Vancouver Island in a sailboat. The west coast of that huge island is the graveyard for more than twenty-five vessels. Their shattered hulls remain on the bottom of the ocean floor impaled on those killer-rocks.

We didn't anticipate any problems from rocks, though, as our wavetop viewpoint allowed us to see the white water breaking over their crests at close range. All we had to do was row around them, wasn't it?

The wind had come up out of the west and it was still raining. We hadn't seen the sun for over five days. Everything was damp, especially our spirits. A chop built rapidly on the surface as we started across Burke Channel. Normally, a two-mile crossing would take us an hour, but today the wind pushed us to the east and up the mouth of the large waterway.

Two hours later we were still struggling to get around the end of Walker Point, which marked the southern tip of King Island and the start of Fisher Channel. Having been forced so far east, we had to work directly against the building wind to gain entry into the channel. "We'll have to pull harder if we're going to beat this bastard,"' yelled Pete over his shoulder. The water was now roiled with the combination of wind-powered waves, tide rips and chop. We were being bounced, tossed and churned all at the same time.

"I'm pulling as hard as I can," I screamed to be heard over the wind. I could feel my hands reacting to the strain as streaks of pain shot up my arms.

Hang on hands, I thought. It will all be over in a month or so.

The wind tore at our backs and frequently caused us to take bites of air with the oar blades instead of water. Pete crashed off his seat and onto my feet during one particularly vigorous air- stroke. "DAMN! This is going to be a battle. We're not making much headway and the wind's pushing us toward those rocks! We better quarter into the waves a little more. This is too tough!" By angling into the wind, we were able to gain slowly on the point, but were continually pushed sideways to the building troughs of water and in danger of turning turtle. This was one spot where we could not rest for a moment. Waiting rocks loomed ominously .

"Put on your lifejacket," I screeched. "We're beginning to take on water!" Pete struggled into his jacket as I battled to keep our position and maintain the precious inches we had gained. We reversed roles and continued the fight. (Because lifejackets are restrictive to rowing and hot, we normally kept them handy, but held off putting them on until prudence or panic prevailed.)

"Whoever heard of Walker Point, anyway?" I yelled. It seemed that our most fierce combat so far had been in unheard of and unlikely locations: Lasqueti Island, Smith Sound and now Walker Point.

"We've got to go harder if we're going to get around this cougar," Pete shouted. "Let's point up a little more. Those rocks are getting too damn close!" Sweat poured down our sides and dripped off Pete's nose. The boat took on water over the bow with every lurch and wallow. I clenched my jaw and dug hard. Our grunts and groans sounded like Jimmy Connors attacking the net.

It took us a full hour to finally wallow around the point. We pitched dangerously close to the rocks, each foot fought for with at least a half-dozen hard strokes. We pulled into a small protected cove, dropped our oars and sat for awhile – totally spent and dripping with sweat. Here was today's challenge; today's unforeseen crisis that again tested all our resources. In these situations there seldom was time to think or analyze our options. We simply had to react.

Kissameet Bay greeted us with quiet reflecting water, dotted with mounds of rocky islets. It was a relief to be out of the wind. We slipped easily through the quiet waters searching for an old fisheries' cabin we had heard about in Namu. Like the manned cabin at the mouth of the Koeye River, these little shelters dotted the B.C. coastline. Most were unused now because of a reduction in Fisheries Department spending. Most had fallen into disrepair as well, but they offered us dry nights and protection from bears.

"There it is," said Pete.

"It looks pretty bad, but let's get closer. Anything's okay if it's dry." We slipped Surfbird's bow into the shore, secured the line and scrambled up the muddy slope to the cabin. Salal and ocean spray had almost obliterated the entrance.

"Afraid it won't work, Nancy. The floor and siding have disintegrated

PART IX - NAMU TO BELLA BELLA

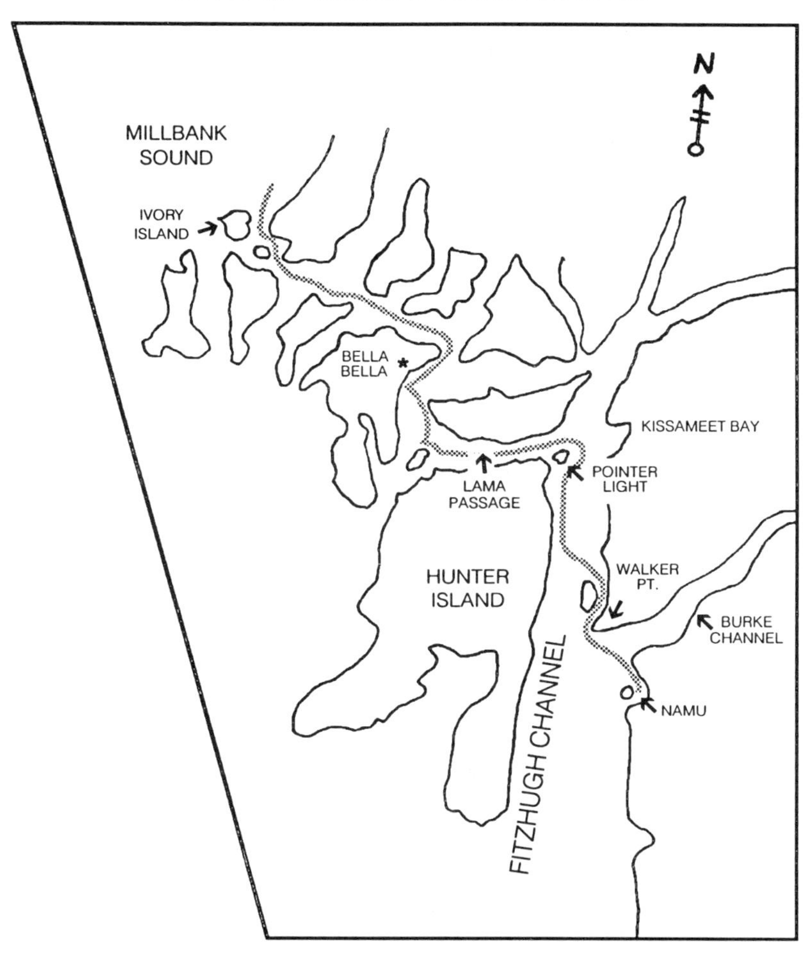

See chart
of coast
on page 4

and there are holes in the roof. Our tent is dryer than this." Discouraged, we slithered down to the boat and pushed off again.

"Let's look back in the northeast corner of the bay. Maybe we'll find a good site there." The shoreline was murky. Wet grass, mud and rocks lined the islands and mainland. Again we searched for a flat dry campsite above the projected high tide line.

"Look, Nancy – what's that on the little rise back in the woods?"

"Where?"

"Look back in those trees. See – there's a flash of white siding or something."

"You're right. Something's there. Looks like a cabin. Let's go investigate."

We squished through the muddy, grass-lined shore and scrambled up a steep incline to a weathered, but clean, unfinished, one-room cabin perched on stubby pilings. The door stood about four feet off the ground so Pete hauled over a board he found nearby and set it up as a slanting walkway to the doorsill. He cautiously turned the knob KAROMP! The door fell off its rusty hinges and crashed onto the sod below.

"Talk about a dramatic entrance, Pete. You sure aren't going to sneak up on anyone." We stepped in to find a snug dry haven for the night. The floor space was taken up by several dozen cartons of large round plastic lids – hundreds of them. "What do you suppose these are for?"

"I don't know. They look like they'd fit on paint buckets, but I don't see any around."

"There are so many though. Do you suppose someone ships something out of here?"

We decided to explore the area to see if we could solve our "mystery." We had noticed a plank walkway extending into the woods, so we followed its winding trail for a mile or so. As we walked along, we filled our pockets with red and blue huckleberries from the laden bushes lining the walkway. A Steller's jay harangued us from above. He hopped overhead from branch to branch and scolded us harshly. The wooden path meandered a long way back into the woods. Seeing nothing of interest, we decided it was a trip to nowhere and turned back to unload the boat and settle in for the night.

"I bet someone grows dope back there. That's why it's so remote and secretive."

"Who knows? Maybe we'll be raided tonight. We could use a little excitement."

"Walker Point was enough excitement for me today, thanks. My old bones need food and sleep – in that order."

There is comfort in rain falling on a wooden roof. We slept well in our haven that night.

We rounded the corner into Lama Pass around 10:00 A.M. the next morning. The two-mile crossing of Fitzhugh Channel had been uneventful in the early morning calm.

We were grateful for that, for in this narrow passageway the wind comes up fast. There was activity at the Pointer Island Lighthouse. People were hammering and painting. We pulled in close to the shoreline to see what was happening. Dave Edginton, the junior lightkeeper, came down to squat on the rocks, introduce himself and talk with us. "Where are you folks going?"

"We're halfway to Ketchikan, our destination."

"Fantastic! We had a couple of kayakers stay here with us a few weeks ago, but they flew back from Bella Bella. The wife didn't want any more rain or wild water conditions."

"I can sympathize," I said, nodding my understanding, "but we hope to stick it out. We're planning to restock in Bella Bella tomorrow and pick up some mail."

"You might have a problem there. Tomorrow is Saturday and the post office will be closed."

"Damn! We've lost track of time out here. It didn't cross our minds that a weekend was coming up."

"Tell you what," Dave said. "I'm going into town around 1:00 today. I'll look for your boat and take one of you in to the post office and store. Okay?"

"Super! We'll look for you after lunch." We waved a goodbye and pulled away up Lama Passage toward our evening's destination near Hunter Channel where the passage turns hard right toward Bella Bella.

At 1:00 P.M. sharp, Dave's high-powered runabout appeared from down-channel and rapidly drew abreast of Surfbird. "Climb aboard, Nancy, and we'll be off to Bella Bella." Once aboard, he introduced me to the senior lightkeeper's wife. She and her husband had been lightkeepers on Pointer Island for twenty-five years. They had raised six children there, educating them at home until seventh or eighth grade with correspondence courses provided by the government. Friends in town then boarded each child through their high school years. This, according to Dave, was common practice among lightkeepers. What a different life than that of our children who were raised in a suburban community near Seattle. I tried to envision no television, no school activities, no organized sports, no dances, no requests for the car, no drugs. Somehow, it didn't sound bad at all. The only trouble kids could get into would be falling off the rock!

After dropping the lady off at the dock, the afternoon passed swiftly. Dave filled me in on all the lighthouse gossip as we scurried from post office in Old Bella Bella to store in New Bella Bella, to bakery in another cove. As we sat over steaming cups of coffee and brownies – what a treat – I asked Dave what had urged him to become a lightkeeper. "To be honest with you, Nancy, I answered an ad because I was out of work. I had been in the military, but when I came out of the service it was hard to find work anywhere in B.C. I thought it would be a challenge to give lightkeeping a try."

"How has it been for you – living in such isolation?"

"Not bad at all. I can adjust to most personalities all right, so the senior lightkeeper and I get along fine. We keep busy maintaining the radio beacon, the light and the horn, as well as all the mechanical and electrical equipment on the property. We also have to keep records of sea conditions and weather to pass on to the Coast Guard for their VHF communications.

"What do you do for entertainment?"

"We have a garden, play cards, bake bread and read a lot," he added with a grin.

"I bet you do. I'll send you Pete's cracked-wheat recipe when we get home."

"Great. I'd like that."

We found Pete on an islet in Ada's Cove taking advantage of a late afternoon sun break. All our gear was spread out to dry on the grass and rocks. We unloaded mail and groceries from Dave's boat, thanked him and waved goodbye as he turned to roar back to his little island.

It was pleasant to be able to share my afternoon's experience with Pete. I rattled on about all the details of my shopping trip, including the lighthouse gossip. Pete listened attentively as he had always harbored a desire to live in a lighthouse for a year or so.

"When we get home, Pete, I'm going to read up on manned lighthouses of the B.C. coastline. I wonder how many are left?" (See Appendix E: Lighthouses of the B.C. Coast.)

The sinking sun lit our islet with a glow of soft orange and pink light. We sat avidly pouring over the letters and packages we had received. "Sounds as if Molly's in love again. She's having a wonderful time this summer it seems."

"Ummmmmm," murmured Pete, engrossed in his letter. "Looks like Bobbi's having a little trouble."

"Like what?"

"I'll trade you letters in a minute – Martha's doing okay in summer school, but she's looking forward to the end."

"I'm sure – oh, good – here are the Gaz canisters we asked Jay to send up. There's a note tucked inside too."

"That's a relief. We'd be literally dead in the water without that little burner. Did our package of food arrive – the one we sent ourselves?"

"Yep. It's all here: oatmeal, Jami's fruit, hot chocolate, Bisquick, nuts. Look Pete – what a sweetheart – Patty sent up a 'care package: tea, dried fruit, snacks – how thoughtful!"

We felt warmed by the touch of family and friends. They all seemed so far away. There was nothing we could do to relieve Bobbi's pain or share in Molly's excitement. The isolation was complete. Only the lightkeeper knew where we were at this moment.

"Want to fly home from Bella Bella? It's your last chance until Prince Rupert."

"Hell no. I want to make it to Alaska – don't you?" Pete nodded agreement. We went to work setting up camp and folding our dry clothes.

Moss-draped trees decorate the shoreline.

PART X: (Nancy) BELLA BELLA TO BUTEDALE: "THERE IS NEITHER LOGIC NOR CONSISTENCY TO THE CURRENTS."

A few days later in a campsite off the Seaforth Channel we awakened to a blanket of fog and the raucous screaming of a crow trying to unseat a raven from a nearby snag. He cawed and cawed, hunching his wings around his head until the raven wearied of the racket and flew to an adjacent cedar to watch the group of crows which had now gathered around their victorious comrade. A close-by clump of firs was full of the noisy creatures gabbling and cackling away contentedly. The raven watched awhile then flapped into the center of the crows' tree. They, predictably, arose screaming and yelling and began dive-bombing the raven. He bore this uproar for several minutes then returned to his original perch. After the crows had settled into peaceful cackling again, he looked over, shrugged his wings and headed over to stir up another fracas. It was as if he were saying to himself, "Well, it's time to bug 'em again."

We were constantly amused and fascinated by wildlife. Steller's jays invariably greeted us with scolding caws and crackles as we set up camp in their territory. It seemed almost nightly that one would be waiting in its tree, about five feet above our heads. It would carry on for fifteen minutes or so, then give up to fly to a branch a bit higher and wait for our handouts of leftover rice or bread. Their perky topknots and audacious challenges have always amused me.

The fog cover was pervasive. It crept into our tent, curled around the boat and obscured our vision. Since we planned to move in a straight shot up Seaforth Channel, we decided to take a fix on the sun, a hazy orb in the mist, and work west toward Milbanke Sound. Our plan was to cross the channel, cutting inside Ivory Island and duck between Watch Island and the Don Peninsula to avoid the unpredictable waters of the sound.

Keeping the sun at our backs and land on the port, we rowed slowly up the coastline. Trees and rocks materialized out of the fog, then dissolved back into obscurity. It was as if they were made of vapors instead of solids.

PART X - BELLA BELLA TO BUTEDALE

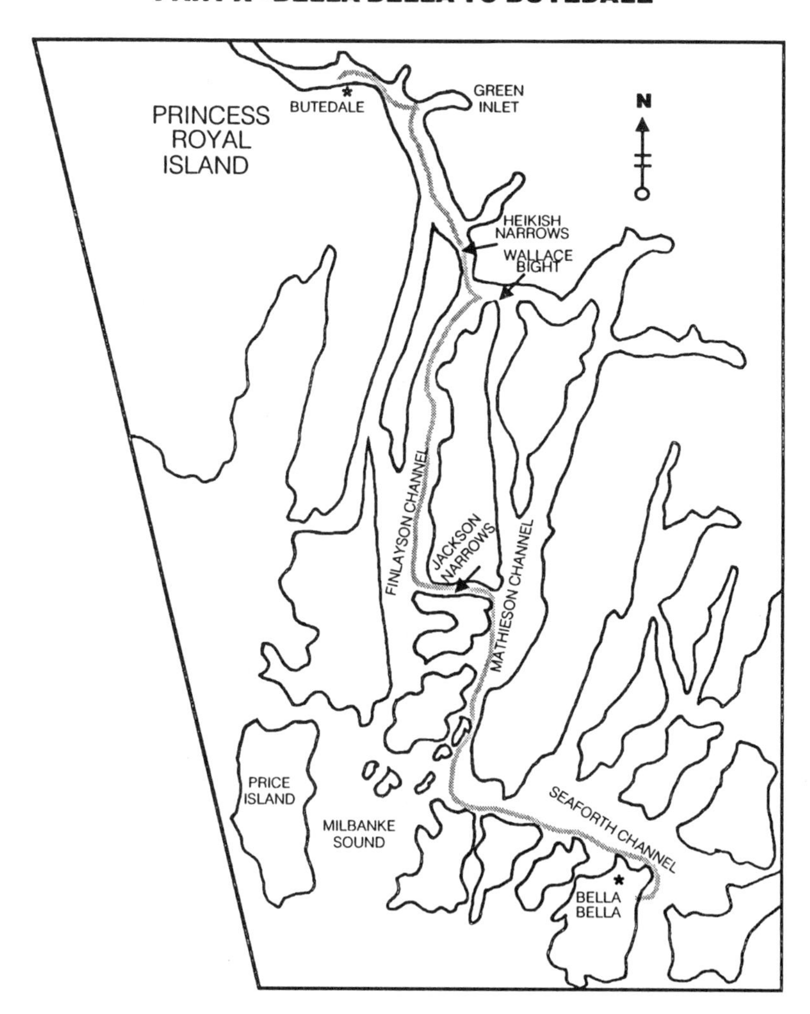

See chart of coast on page 4

Except for the dips of our oars, silence hung over us like a wet gray shroud. When crossing small inlets and baylets we lost sight of land. Only the sun's faint glow at our backs reassured us of our direction. We continued on until land appeared on our port side once again. "The sun seems to be changing direction," I observed.

"Ummmmmmmmmmm. You're right. We must be turning south."

"What's that noise?"

"What noise?" Pete's hearing is not as acute as mine, but I knew I'd heard something, and it was getting louder.

"My God, it's an engine! There must be a boat coming at us. Shall I start yelling?"

"It's near all right – quick – duck into shore. It'll hit rocks before it hits us!"

"There it is! It's a fishing boat heading right for the shore. My God!" We both screamed, "HEY!" At that instant someone of the boat's bridge saw us and the oncoming shoreline and jerked the wheel around. "WHEW! That was close." We pulled in behind a large rock and waited for his wake to flatten. After he left, a low engine sound remained constant, neither increasing nor diminishing.

"Sounds like a boat that's not moving. Let's pull slowly toward it and see if they're in trouble."

Suddenly, out of the mist, loomed a huge white box-like barge. It was anchored, with generator humming. That was the sound we had heard earlier, not an engine. An older gentleman was peering over the deck railing at us in amazement. "Hello there. What're you doing out here in a row boat?"

"We're working our way north to Alaska from Washington State," I responded.

"My God – I don't believe it. Wait'll the crew hears this. Come aboard and join us for breakfast."

"Thank you. We've already eaten, but coffee would be great." Once aboard and smelling bacon, eggs and apple pancakes, Pete snarfed down his second full meal in two hours, complete with hot maple syrup. I sipped a cup of coffee and marveled at his capacity.

We were aboard the Canadian Hydrographic and Fisheries boat, Pender. Alex, the crew chief, explained their function. "We're a crew of twelve who go out and make soundings for depths and obstructions. We gather information during the day, break for dinner then do plotting, graphing and charting in the evenings."

"How long are you stationed out here?" asked Pete.

"We're aboard from May through October with four days off a month. The food is great and we're all pretty compatible, so it's very pleasant duty. Right now we're charting these waters between Dufferin and Horsfall Islands." He pulled out a chart and pinpointed our exact location. We had wandered down into a bay off Horsfall Island and had headed due south.

"Maybe you can tell us how to figure these currents better than we have been doing," I said. "We study the charts and think we have figured the logical way for the current to flow in a given area; then we arrive on the scene only to find the water rushing the other way."

"Well," said Alex, "I hate to say this, as it sounds so stupid, but in all our years out here we have determined that there is neither logic nor consistency to the currents. They seem to be affected by the winds, the Japanese Current and some unknowns. We just read the situation where we are and go from there."

"Well, at least we're not as inept as we'd thought," I said with a grin.

After sharing their food and good conversation, they pressed us to take a sorely needed chart before we returned to little Surfbird. We waved goodbye with warm thanks for a pleasant interlude.

The fog still lay heavily on the water as we cautiously rounded Idol Point. "We better duck into this cove and wait out the fog. We can't possible cross Seaforth Channel in this." The channel was over three miles wide where we planned to cross – a one-and-a-half to two hour row for us. Barges and luxury liners frequented it on voyages to Alaska, so we knew we needed good visibility.

Several fishing boats and one packer, the Juno, came into focus as we entered the cove. A man was on Juno's deck waving us over to his bright blue work boat. As we pulled alongside, he said, "Hi. I'm Roy Robinson. The Pender radioed for us to look out for you. Please come aboard. The coffee pot's on."

Roy was the skipper of a crew of three: engineer, deckhand and cook. They anchored in coves off main seaways and took in fish caught by Canadian gillnetters, seiners and trollers. This day Juno was anchored off Seaforth Channel waiting for the fog to lift before moving on to a new location. Since it was still too dense to navigate further, we tied up alongside and climbed aboard, using their tire fenders as a ladder. Roy greeted us with warm hospitality and a firm handshake. "Come on down to the galley. I want to hear all about your trip."

We sat around the galley table and downed quarts of coffee, heavenly cheesecake and chocolate chip cookies, while relating our experiences to Roy and his crew. Pete, replete with two breakfasts, managed a full helping of both delicacies with no complaints from his digestive system.

If anyone could share our trip vicariously, it was Roy. His interest and excitement were boundless. He was enthused and inspired by our adventure. "You must send me a postcard at the end of your trip," he insisted. "Here – I'll give you a self-addressed one."

"No," I assured him. "I promise to send you one from Ketchikan. I won't forget. If we make it, I'll want to tell the world."

After good food and conversation, we pushed off with thanks and headed slowly up the coast, constantly checking for clear visibility to make the crossing.

A sheltered, pristine pebble beach greeted us as we rounded a reef.

Temptation won out. We pulled in, secured the boat and stretched full length on the warm rocks to nap in the filtered sunlight while digesting our meals and biding time.

The fog blanket lifted around two o'clock. We were greeted by choppy waters and a brisk ocean wind out of the west. Our passage was to be almost due north, so we decided to go for it, angling slightly northwest to slice into the waves rather than take them broadside. The pull was hard. The waves built at mid-channel. The wind stiffened. We were both straining without let-up. Once midway, there was no return. Looking down toward the Idol Point Light we could see a huge white blob moving in our direction. "What the hell is that?" I gasped.

"Looks like a luxury liner to me."

"Oh my God – how fast do they go?"

"Sixteen to eighteen knots, I think."

"We better get outta here, fast!"

"You're right. They'll never see us on their radar." We quit talking and pulled. Once again we frantically battled an unexpected obstacle. The huge bow seemed to point straight at us no matter how hard we fought.

"I think they're deliberately aiming at us," I grunted.

"Keep hauling – they're coming fast." We gauged our progress constantly by fixing an outcropping of rocks or a headland against an island backdrop. Bit by bit we were gaining the north shore. Ivory Island gradually increased in size as we struggled toward it.

"I think we're across her bow now, Pete. She's got to turn soon to head into Milbanke Sound."

"It's going to be close! – The Cunard Princess. What a beauty, huh?"

"I think I would appreciate her beauty from a bit further out, thank you." I had long ago quit wearing my glasses because of salt spray and constant slippage down my nose. My eyesight was a hyperoptic blur. Everything was a little fuzzy around the edges, except this enormous vessel which came into dramatic focus, much too close for peace of mind.

"She's going to clear us okay, but you can see the passengers. I wonder what they think about us."

"Probably that we're a bit daft to be out here at all."

"Well, this time I agree with them." The giant ship slipped by, leaving us riding the huge waves of her wake. They'll be in Alaska tomorrow, I thought.

Our anchorage that night was in Passage Cove on a lump of grassy rock. Fresh bear scat was near our tent site. We scanned the area carefully before bringing out our food for dinner. We were unprepared to handle a bear attack – no weapons, except a veri-pistol and flares. We pulled them out of the emergency sack and kept them at hand. While Pete scouted for more traces of four-legged marauders, I battled the six-legged variety. Mosquitoes lined up at their diving stations and flew in formation to zing in for the kill. One after another screamed in to sink its proboscis into the exposed skin of my neck, hands or face. In desperation, I threw a loose piece of netting over my head and tucked it into my collar. That denied them two of their targets and gave me some relief, but it was like breathing inside a gas mask-slightly claustrophobic.

We slept lightly that night, reacting to every snapping twig and rustling in the underbrush. It was with relief that we pushed off in the morning.

A soft following breeze allowed us a rare and pleasant sail up Mathieson Channel until strong head winds sweeping out of Oscar Pass forced us to drop sail and fight across. Once around Miall Point, we again raised the sail and laid back to enjoy the drift toward Rescue Bay at the lower end of Jackson Passage. The sun was warm and for once no rain clouds skulked on the horizon. A fisherman out of Prince George swung alongside and called out. "Where are you headed?"

"Ketchikan," we yelled in unison.

He shook his head in disbelief and with a wave headed back out to drop his line in mid-channel.

Rescue Bay provided us with clams, mussels and a refreshing dip in relatively warm water. It felt wonderful to wash bodies and clothes and then crawl into the sun-warmed tent for a late afternoon nap.

In the evening cool we cooked our chowder and hot pan-bread. No bear visions disturbed our rest on our tiny islet in the middle of the cove. We preferred islands to mainland camping for that reason, and whenever possible selected them for our stopovers. Someone, (probably an old wife,) once told us that bears lived only on the mainland. Even though we learned differently from Bob and Eileen Wood on Cracroft Island, we tended to select an island over a peninsula or mainland campground. Psychologically, at least, we felt more secure.

The voyage up Jackson Passage the next morning, was magically lovely. This is a narrow inlet leading into the much wider Finlayson Channel. Unspoiled wilderness surrounded us. Solid forest everywhere we looked. No floating debris or hacked-down trees gave hint of man's presence. It was as if we were stroking into an undiscovered and pristine water-world. Again we related the scenery to Indians' designs for bowls, blankets and rugs. The continuous rock cliffs looked hand-painted in bold strokes of rust, brown, umber, black and white. Images of ravens, bear, eagle and wolf seemed embedded in their surface, easily discernible.

We emerged from this fairyland into the wide shipping lanes of Finlayson Channel to be greeted by a soft following wind. We set sail and floated serenely up to Wallace Bight, over nineteen miles from our last campsite.

Before ducking through the narrow entrance to the enclosed baylet, I dropped the jig to catch dinner. Within seconds two fat rockfish, a small lingcod and a copper, jumped onto my hook and hung there apathetically. With dinner aboard we squeezed through the tiny pass with only three feet of water beneath us and rowed to the back of the cove. "Why is this called a bight, instead of a bay?" I queried.

"Damned if I know," said Pete. "Let's look it up when we get home." (See Appendix D)

Our six-legged winged zingers attacked with fury as we stepped ashore. It was time to take stronger action. I was tired of them winning the war. I reached deep into the clothing bag and pulled out our rainhats, those khaki-hued formless objects usually worn with Macintoshes, some mosquito netting, needle and thread. I artlessly stitched the netting inside the hats and formed two safari-like bonnets designed to keep the buggers in their place – away from our heads and faces. It changed the atmospheric pressure near our noses, but accomplished my goal. That night I cooked the fish without the constant annoyance of a high-pitched whine in my ears and itching bites on my neck.

Weird animal cries pierced the quiet of the night and punctured our sleep. The sound seemed to come from across the bay. I pictured a cougar or a bobcat yowling for its lost mate. The cry was eerie and somehow sad. It continued intermittently throughout the night and into the morning.

Bolstering ourselves with huckleberry pancakes, we set off early to secure a fresh load of water from a roaring stream feeding into the bight, then pushed through the narrow entrance one more time. Our early rising was partly from lifelong habit and partly because many boaters and fishermen told us that's the time to be on the water is early morning. "Yep – get out there before dawn and travel 'til noon. That's when the wind starts up. Head for cover in the afternoon."

Our past sailing experiences in the San Juan and Gulf Islands had, for the most part, verified this belief. We had observed the wind picking up in the late morning and blowing until late afternoon. Usually it quieted toward evening.

Feeling confident that this would be the case today, we stuck our bow out into the channel. WHAAAMMM! The wind tore up the passageway from the southwest and slammed into the boat with a vengeance. "Damn those fishermen and their calm-morning garbage. I'm never going to believe anything I hear again!"

"Do you want to head back in?" asked Pete.

"No – we'll just have to listen to that howling critter all day. It shouldn't take long to fight around this point. Then we'll be with the wind."

"OK – let's go!" We hauled back hard on the oars – the pain shooting from fingers to elbow on each strain. After every fifty strokes or 50, I turned to check our position on the rocks jutting out into the channel. We were making progress, but ever so slowly. The wind gathered speed down near Milbanke Sound and shot full length up Finlayson Channel. The waves built up in direct proportion to that speed, slammed into the point of Roderick Island and rebounded off the rocks into our path. The result was a choppy, churning, bouncy mess.

"Aughhhh – I lost my oar!" I screamed from my position on the sole.

I had pulled a bite of air with my last stroke. The force threw me off my seat and the oar out of the oarlock. It was now floating and bouncing toward the rocks. Pete quickly pursued the errant object and we scooped it back to safety without too much delay.

"Now we know why we have six oars aboard — just in case." I nodded my understanding while quickly slipping the oar back in place.

Two hours of hard pulling finally nosed us around the point and let us move with the wind once again.

"That was one tough mile," Pete mumbled more in comment to himself than to me. We pulled swiftly into the Hiekish Narrows where we were able to set sail and glide through effortlessly with wind and tide in our favor — a nice break after that early energy expenditure.

The narrows fed into the Tolmie Channel, which separated huge Princess Royal Island first from Susan Island and then from the mainland. Mountains rose out of the water on our left and inviting inlets headed inland on our right — always luring us to explore their waters. No one could thoroughly inspect all the waters of British Columbia. You would run out of years long before running out of inlets, bays or coves and uninhabited wilderness. Somebody once figured out that between the Strait of Juan de Fuca and the Portland Inlet north of Prince Rupert, there are 17,000 miles of tidewater coastal shoreline within approximately 500 miles of latitude. Every mile of distance includes an average of 33 miles of shoreline.

Green Inlet was our destination for that day, in spite of a cove near its entrance with the unappealing name of Horsefly. It was bad enough battling mosquitoes. I was not anxious to take on the big-mouthed biters. Just before making the turn into the inlet, I dropped the hook and caught a nice kelp greenling for dinner. Now we could search for a campsite with a nourishing meal assured. "What's that up on the bluff, Nancy?"

"Oh boy, I think it's a cabin. Let's go see."

"Yep — looks like rain again. It would be nice to be dry tonight." A tiny cove tucked in behind the entrance bluff gave us a perfect anchoring spot. It was deep enough to keep the boat afloat and close enough to shore to tie our lines securely to a log. The cabin sat overlooking the length of Tolmie Channel. It was made of pre-cut cedar logs, fairly sound, although the front deck was rotting. It was complete with a rusty bed, open cabinets and a small sink that drained to the ground outside. It looked as if it hadn't been used for several years. We set to work like the seven dwarves. (I felt we should be singing, "Heigh-ho, heigh-ho") We swept out the accumulated debris: twigs, dirt, spider webs. Cedar boughs worked nicely as brooms and left a crisp Christmasy odor behind. The open window stared at us sans glass. Hornets flew in and out at will and were clustered around the sill. I decided to take apart our "safari-helmets" and screen the window with the netting. Pete scrounged some nails from a rusty coffee can on the entrance decking and hammered the netting in place with a rock. A few well-placed swats killed the remaining hornets and our little haven was secure for the night.

We slept on the floor as it was more appealing than the moldy mattress. About midnight we awoke to the sound of an engine accompanied by a strobe light shining through the window. "Oh my God," I groaned. "I sure hope it isn't the cabin owners coming home." Pete snaked out of his sleeping bag and peered into the night.

"Looks like a fishing boat or a tug. They're turning into the inlet. I suspect just to anchor." Sure enough, the engine throb moved down the inlet and soon stopped. We both dropped back to sleep with the sound of raindrops drumming on our cedar roof.

Butedale was only about seventeen miles away. With a light following breeze we row-sailed up the channel admiring the scenery on the way. Great granite outcroppings peeked through the dense evergreens forming the sheer walls of the channel. Waterfalls plunged down the cliffs from myriad lakes nestled in the high valleys above. The peaks of the mountains rimming the channel materialized out of the mist to reveal snowy tops, then faded back into the clouds. It was astonishingly lovely and we were completely alone.

We pulled into Butedale around 1:00 P.M., water rivuleting off our yellows and feeling a bit chilled from the breeze. A pleasant young man greeted us at the long wooden dock. "Hello there. Welcome to Butedale. Here, let me take your bow line." We scrambled out of the boat, introduced ourselves and followed him up the steep gangplank to the main dock above. "Come on in the store and have a cup of coffee. The pot's always on." Wonderful words. They should go down as among the most pleasant in the English language.

The store was clean and the shelves neatly stocked. It was operated by an energetic group of Canadians. They were renovating the old cannery site into a resort. Included in the restoration were an old hotel, a superintendent's home and the store itself.

Behind, and to one side of the building, was a roaring waterfall, a viewing stopover for cruise and pleasure boats alike. The wide falls cascaded from Butedale Lake above, providing a dramatic backdrop for their project.

Ample dock space, gas and diesel supplies and good fishing in the area promised to attract both pleasure boaters and fishermen. They intelligently stocked a good selection of fishing gear on the store shelves.

A young woman was in the kitchen kneading bread dough. We assured her we would be eager customers after it came out of the oven. Again the hospitality of British Columbia people surfaced. We were invited to spend the night in the superintendent's home up on the hill behind the store. There were several rooms to choose from for our sleeping area, plus a dining/living room, kitchen, laundry and shower. What luxury for two murky rowers. We washed some accumulated dirty clothing, showered in warm water with real soap, cooked a good meal and ate in splendor in the dining room overlooking the bay. It was easy to imagine a family living here years ago when the cannery was in operation. Their garden, also being rejuvenated, spilled down the hillside in bursts of color: golden marigolds, blue lobelia, red geraniums.

After dinner we explored the area, climbing above the house toward the lake then back through all the outbuildings and docks. Two huge pigs grubbed in the garden next to our cottage. Cats were everywhere. They had been brought in to bring down the large mice and rat population. The whole area bustled with activity and purpose.

We sauntered down to the dock and were invited aboard the Chase by a couple from Secret Cove, B.C., who had built the boat and their home by themselves. The boat's interior gleamed from immaculate care. We sat at their table over steaming mugs of coffee and shared boating tales of pleasure and pain. "You must detour by way of Bishop Bay Hot Springs," they urged. "We stopped there and had a wonderful time. It's our favorite spot to soak and relax." Visions of hot soaking baths at Hot Springs Cove on the west side of Vancouver Island flashed into my head. Pete and I had spent a glorious afternoon there one summer day during a circumnavigation of the immense island. It had been one of the highlights of the trip.

"Whattaya think Pete? A hot bath would feel good. How far is it?" Our new friends pulled out their chart and we all poured over it.

"The bay is only ten miles up Ursula Channel from the corner of McKay Reach. It might be fun to row all around Gribbell Island instead of backtracking. That way we'd see a section of the country that most people miss. It would probably take us three extra days."

"Well, let's go for it. We have the time, don't we?"

"Sure," said Pete, confident that the detour would work into our time-schedule without a major disruption.

We left Butedale the next morning replete with rest, good food, two loaves of freshly baked bread and warm wishes from the staff.

Butedale

PART XI: (Nancy) BUTEDALE TO HAWKESBURY ISLAND: "IF WE DON'T FIND A BAY OR INLET SOON, WE COULD BE IN FOR DEEP TROUBLE."

A northwest breeze pushed against us all morning as we pulled diagonally across Fraser Reach. This part of the channel is rimmed by 4,000 foot cliffs which soar skyward straight out of the water. We wanted to work up the eastern shore to see the waterfalls and granite out-thrustings a bit better. The going was tough, but we were able to gain steadily until the current changed and we found ourselves stroking futilely – going nowhere. It's an odd sensation to be working as hard as you can and realize you are standing still. (I understand there are small swimming pools manufactured now that allow you to swim against a current. I wonder what happens if you stop to rest. Are you flattened against the end of the pool?)

"Let's attach the bowline to that snag over there, Pete."

"OK. I think we have to get past it and then I'll row like hell while you secure the line." We accomplished the awkward task, then sat back and watched the waters rip by, swirling and gurgling. We pulled out a loaf of freshly baked bread, slathered peanut butter on thick chunks of it and munched it down while waiting out the current. We tended to be content when stuffing our faces.

The wind shifted in the early afternoon and helped us fight northward against the slackening current. At the bottom of McKay Reach a shallow bay opened up to our right. It was indicated as Angler Cove on the chart, but no fish leaped onto my line as we entered. "I don't think there's enough water in here to anchor," Pete said, peering over the side of Surfbird.

"How far is the next inlet?" I sighed wearily.

"It's at least two miles north."

"That's a whole hour of rowing," I whined. "It's getting late, my hands hurt and I'm hungry."

"So am I, but I hate to anchor where we know we're going aground at night. If bears got into our food, we'd be in real trouble." Pete's voice had taken on a testy quality – a warning that his patience was being pushed.

PART XI - BUTEDALE TO HAWKESBURY

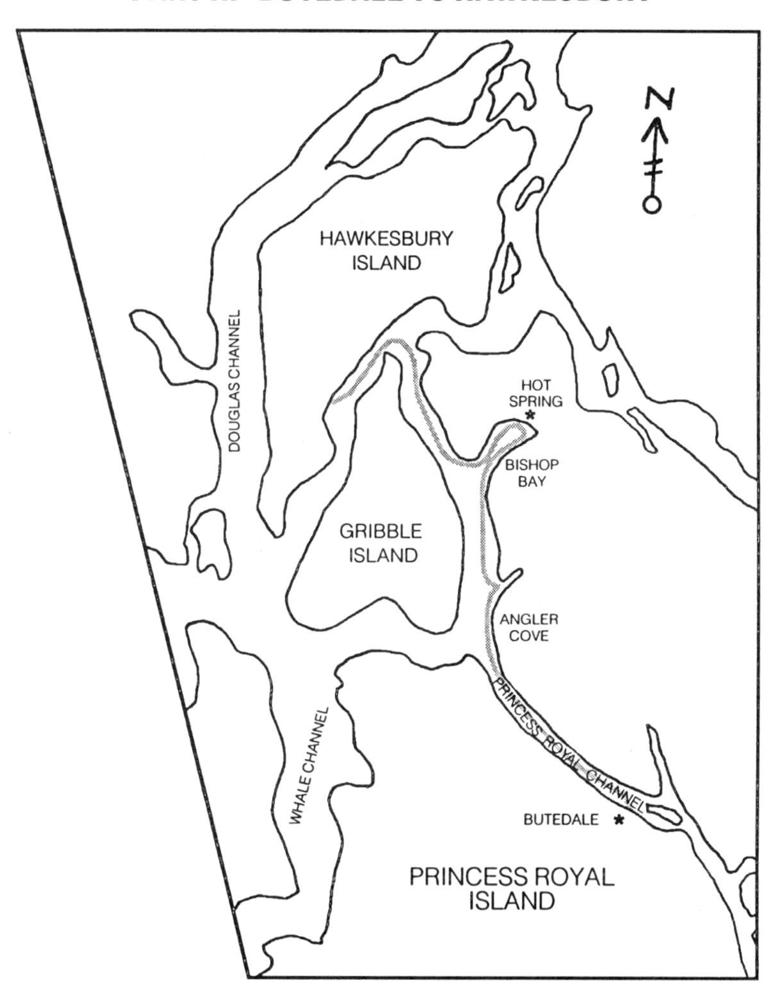

See chart
of coast
on page 4

"Well, let's drop a lead-line. The water's only going out seven feet tonight," I persisted. "We might be OK in here." Pete dropped the line several times in various locations and finally acknowledged that one spot seemed to have enough depth. We quickly beached and unloaded the gear so he could return to that exact spot to anchor.

Our search for a campsite ended in the shadowy woods, high above the tideline. The forest floor was covered with a spongy layer of moss which made the best beds. We selected a flat spot, erected the tent and tarp then set out the cookware down on the beach. Sun-bleached driftwood logs were laid out in a ready-made kitchen/ dining area – a nice protected spot out of the wind for cooking. Big round slabs of cut trees served as table and counter. Clean pea-sized gravel surrounded it and there were no bugs. My idea of heaven. I felt like a little girl playing house.

We slept much better on our bed of moss than we had on the sagging mattresses at Butedale and awoke refreshed to find the boat still afloat and all things right with our world.

The cove was backed by waterfalls and a roaring stream which poured into the bay on the right side of the inlet. Needing to refill our water jugs, we walked over to the bubbling waters and dipped in our containers. "Hey – this water feels warm."

"I doubt that. It's coming right off the snow fields."

"Well, try it." Pete wriggled his fingers under the surface.

"You're right. It's almost bathtub warm. This must have a hot springs under it. I wonder how it affects the plants and animals around here?"

"I don't know, but if I were a deer or an eagle, I'd choose to live around warm water if I had my druthers. It would sure feel nicer on the wing-pits than an ice cold stream."

We managed to break camp and reload before the boat went aground then rowed leisurely toward Bishop Bay, nine miles up channel. We enjoyed the scenery and stopped to fish at the mouth of the bay. A tiny fawn, still spotted with youth, walked delicately out onto a rock ledge near our boat. It surveyed us with its innocent gaze then quietly merged back into the forest.

WHAP! "Salmon on!" I shrieked, grabbing the stub pole excitedly. Pete lunged for the net and we both salivated as we imagined dinner already cooked and going down. I brought it up to the side of the boat, grinning with pride when – SNAP – off he went to the depths with my lure and sinker and my hopes. "DAMN-IT! I sure wanted that one!"

"Get the line rigged again. Maybe he has a sister or brother lurking around," urged Pete.

"Maybe – but they've been damned elusive so far." We continued the slow pull into the back of Bishop Bay, futilely dragging our trolling line behind us. "What is all this guck on the water?" I asked.

"I don't know. Looks like some kind of red-orange algae. Do you suppose it's Red Tide?"

"Well, it's reddish and thick and looks ominous. I don't think we'd better eat any more clams and mussels for awhile."

"I think you're right. Let's tie up to the dock and see what the hot springs are like. So far, it looks pretty murky." Several small cruisers and one sailboat were tied to the dock, indicating a popular stopover in this region. We angled in near the head of the dock and clambered out to explore the area and look for a campsite. The path was slippery and steep. Black sticky mud made climbing and walking a trial of patience and body control. We hung on to branches and twigs to keep from falling into the mire.

"I'm not too impressed yet," I grunted as I slid down an embankment. "Where's the pool?"

"Looks like a roofed shelter up ahead." Sounds of voices and soft splashing caused us to stay on the path and not interrupt others' pleasure. We slithered on – over a short bridge, up a rock-strewn path to another structure laid out on a point of land overlooking the bay. "Here's a covered tent platform. It's got a campfire site too."

"Great! It's perfect."

"I'll go back and get the boat and row it over here so we can off-load on that big rock," offered Pete. "Maybe we can use the pool after we've set-up camp."

"OK. I'll clean up this mess while you're gone. People are such slobs! Can't believe what they leave behind." I busied myself picking up aluminum cans, papers, bits of plastic. A path led to a dumping area not far from the campsite. I hauled my booty to its final resting place and returned to sweep the platform with sweet cedar boughs.

That afternoon, dressed in swimsuits in deference to the public, we eased into the near-boiling waters of the hot springs pool. "This is what a crab must feel like in his final minutes of life."

"Ahhhhhhhhhh," Pete sighed, as he slipped beneath the surface and leaned his head back against the rock-lined wall. "It's not a bad way to go at all; sure beats those cold saltwater dips, huh?"

"Thank you, citizens of Kitimat, for maintaining this facility." I saluted weakly, then lay back to gaze at my legs and arms floating in the warm water. "You know, I think I've lost a lot of weight. I don't have as many thigh ripples as I used to."

"You look slim and sylph-like to me," Pete said gallantly, his eyes barely open.

"You're absolutely gaunt, Pete – you've lost so much weight. It's interesting to me physiologically. I wouldn't think people our ages could actually change our body types. I've lost weight in the bust too. I'm almost flat now. Shoulders are wider too. Don't you think that's interesting?"

"Ummmmmmmmmm," murmured Pete. Obviously I wasn't going to get much reaction out of my rowing partner while he was in sodden bliss.

After dinner we carried the food bag back to the boat to secure it for the night. A man popped his head out of the cruiser tied up behind

Surfbird. "Do you have a way to cover your entire boat tightly?"

"No – we just keep everything in waterproof bags."

"Well, you might have some trouble tonight. There are mice here that run all over the docks at night. They board all the boats and eat anything they can find. We always lock up tight when we're here."

"Oh-oh," I responded. "I guess we'd better anchor out, Pete."

"I tried to anchor off the rock, but it didn't work. Let's tie off the dock a ways." Pete figured out a system which suspended the boat between the dock and an onshore fir tree. Surfbird rode happily through the night undisturbed by marauding rodents.

In the morning we reloaded and cast off, waving to a couple from Ketchikan we had met the night before. "We'll call you when we get to Ketchikan!"

"We'll be looking for you – good luck!" they responded.

The reddish slime filled the bay. It was like rowing through tomato soup. "Ick. I hope this doesn't stain Surfbird's hull. She won't like it."

"We'll be out of it soon. Looks like it's concentrated at this end of the bay."

It was quiet on the water. A soft, misty rain began to fall as we approached the bay's mouth where it emptied into Ursula Channel. "Look, Pete – just off the starboard side. Two porpoises!"

"Looks like they're having a good time – what sleek swimmers – beautiful motion." The lovely mammals cavorted down channel, slicing in and out of the water in graceful arched dives.

We pulled on our right oars simultaneously to make the turn up Boxer Reach which led to the northeast tip of Gribbell Island. Once again we settled into the familiar pattern of mechanical rowing, our arms and bodies locked into motion without benefit of conscious thought. Our minds were free to wander through mazes of disconnected memory, ideas or creative thinking.

Turning the point of land at the top of the island, we entered the wider and virtually untraveled Verney Pass. Only an occasional boat passed this way to or from Kitimat, a logging and smelter town connected by highway to Terrace, B.C.

Mountain peaks on Gribbell Island had been flirting with us all day, peeking out of their veil of mist alluringly, then quickly retreating – just enough to pique our curiosity. Hawkesbury Island, in contrast, revealed its considerable charms. Sheer granite walls laced with thick white strippings resembling frosting, sliced into the waters from hundreds of feet over our heads. Waterfalls plummeted from every indentation in the cliffs. Rock pictures abounded – this time in vertical stripes rather than the more common horizontal patterns: orange men, black ravens, gray whales, white horses, with brown stripes running through all.

Crossing over to the Hawkesbury side, we marveled at the awesome beauty close up, while acutely aware of the dangerous situation evolving from the afternoon breeze. It had freshened in short order into a wind against us, sweeping down the pass with building power. We hugged the sheer walls, hiding in every niche from the full force of the blow. "If we don't find a bay or inlet soon, we could be in for deep trouble," said Pete, his concern reflected in his eyes.

"Yeah. I don't look forward to hanging onto a branch all night while flattened against this wall. Let's try to get around that next corner." The next corner revealed only more vertical granite — no indentations — no hidey-holes. "Check the chart, Pete. Is there anything down channel?"

"There might be something around that point, but that's the only possibility," he responded, indicating a land mass about a mile away. "It's getting late in the day. We might have to cross over to Gribbell, and I don't look forward to that in this much wind."

"Neither do I. Let's try to get around that point. Maybe we'll be lucky." The wind strengthened and pushed against our oar blades on every backstroke. Our forward progress was hampered considerably. We stayed in close to the wall taking advantage of every dip inward that gave us any protection. The mile seemed more like three as we struggled to pull around the point. It was 4:00 P.M. and beginning to sock in. "Not much farther now. We're almost there."

As if a magician had waved his wand as we rounded the point, a lovely bay appeared. A long, curving, sandy beach complete with driftwood wind-barriers revealed itself. The beach was nestled into a backdrop of sheer granite cliffs accented by seven waterfalls flowing down their flanks in lacy white banners. The roar created by the wall of water, combined with lapping wavelets on the beach, gave the area an aura of enchantment. "It's like entering Yosemite Valley for the first time,"' I said, staring.

"Look Nancy, we have a friend."' A large seal had popped up nearby as we entered the bay. He withdrew momentarily to safety below the surface, then reappeared nearer to us than before.

"He wants to make our acquaintance, I guess," I said, reaching out my hand toward the round-eyed creature. "Hello, Mr. Seal. Come on over here." He submerged with a whoosh, then popped up again to push head and shoulders high out of the water as if to say, "Who are you guys?" He remained just offshore and cruised slowly back and forth as we unloaded. He stayed nearby, scrutinizing us with intense inquisitiveness for almost half an hour.

As we headed into the woods to set up camp on a mossy knoll, a mink ran down the logs, saw us and stopped to stare. It remained motionless for over a minute. Then, as I raised the camera, off it ran, humping dexterously across the driftwood.

We decided to stay an extra day to enjoy some relaxation and exploration. We slept well that night knowing we didn't have to arise early to meet the tides.

In the first light before dawn I heard a strange clucking approaching from deep in the forest. It was rhythmical and different from anything I had heard before. "Pete – Pete," I hissed. "What's that noise?"

He listened awhile, then said sleepily, "I'm not sure. Sounds like a regiment of chickens coming our way." I lifted myself partially out of my bag and peered through the netting as the "army" approached. One foot from my nose, and in single file, a row of about a dozen spruce grouse came marching by. They kept in perfect step, hooting softly in synchronized song as they traversed the length of the log, their perky heads bobbing in rhythm with their steps.

The entire area teemed with life. While breakfasting, we were visited by an offspring of the mink we had seen earlier. The tiny creature scurried across our "kitchen" and ducked into a hollowed-out log. It exhibited no fear. Neither did the sharp-tailed sandpipers moving along the tide line. They allowed me to come within three feet to capture them on film. A family of otters cavorted on the rocky shoreline, slithering in and out of the water playfully. Two deer stood by our boat, aground at low tide. They too, stood ground as I approached within six feet. They moved off slowly after satisfying their curiosity, but in no rush of fear or panic. They stopped and turned their liquid eyes back for another look then wandered peacefully down the beach.

Our stay stretched into three days, as Pete was attacked by a fast-acting virus or bacteria which laid him low with diarrhea. He lay in the tent incapacitated for two days, managing only to struggle feebly into the woods from time to time at nature's insistence. It was a scary period for us both. Pete wondered if he would ever regain his strength, and I worried about what I would do if he didn't. I knew I couldn't row the boat alone very far unless it had no load, and with no load I couldn't survive long. I could return – to Butedale for help, or call the Coast Guard on our VHF, but didn't relish the thought of either solution.

Our First Aid kit contained everything but medication for diarrhea. We have vowed to correct that deficiency in the future. Buried deep in my subconscious a faint memory stirred. It surfaced in the form of "tea and rice." Was it my grandmother's cure for the runs? I don't know where it came from, but it was worth a try. I boiled a huge pot of rice on a crackling beach fire and also water for tea, then carried them in to Pete. "Tastes good," he said weakly. "Maybe I'll be able to sleep through tonight." The old fashioned remedy seemed to turn the tide on the disturbance. He felt noticeably better in the morning and was able to move on by the fourth day on the island.

I had not been idle during his illness. I had explored up to the foot of one of the waterfalls and along the entire coastline of the half-moon bay. I also had managed to snag the fishing pole on the bottom of the bay and had lost it overboard, so two of my days had been spent searching for it in vain at minus tide.

As I had wandered the beach alone during that time, the isolation of the area had dominated my thoughts. No boats had passed by. I had neither seen nor heard any planes. The only sounds had been from nature and wildlife: grackles, caws and screams of the birds, whispers and moans of the wind in the trees, roaring of the falls, squeaks of playful otters. I had felt much as I imagined Robinson Crusoe must have felt alone on his beach. I had wondered how I would handle the situation if Pete had become more ill. In frustration, and to change my mood, I had taken everything out of the boat — even the floorboards — and given it a thorough cleaning, rewarding myself with an Almond Joy for a job well done.

The third day had been wet. It had rained all day — hard at times. I had joined my sick companion in the tent and read most of the day, arising occasionally to stretch my legs on a long beach walk.

When the time came to leave Hawkesbury Island, we both knew we had been in touch with a magical world — one which would probably not be experienced again in our lifetimes.

Bishop Bay bath house.

PART XII: (Pete) HAWKESBURY TO CHATHAM SOUND: "THIS IS AN EERIE PLACE."

At Hawkesbury, we were about ninety miles south of Prince Rupert. Already we were talking about cheeseburgers, a warm room and long hot showers. Prince Rupert is a modern town of about twenty thousand, a worthy destination. In between was nothing of social significance. No canneries, no villages, no nothing. Grenville Channel, our main route to Prince Rupert, is a straight, narrow, highsided waterway that stretches northwest for nearly fifty miles before it opens into Ogden Channel and Telegraph Passage. With mountains close on both sides, the lower half of Grenville Channel ranges from a mile to half a mile wide. At its northern end the channel broadens gradually to about two miles. A handful of bays offer possible campsites. Otherwise, the steep, rocky cliffs provide little relief, especially from the winds that funnel through this tight passageway. There would be no crosswinds. The wind would be either with us or against us. We were to have both before we passed out of Grenville.

I was weak. Two days of diarrhea with no intake but Nancy's tea and rice had left me wobbly and uninspired.

"Are you sure you're up to rowing?" Nancy asked as we finished packing the boat. "We could lay over another day."

"I feel OK now. Not strong, but also not weak enough to remain here, nice as it is." We had gotten up at four; it was now about five-thirty. As we headed out of the cove, I continued, "I wonder what brought it on? Strange that something would hit me and not you. At one point, lying there two nights ago, I wondered if I was going to make it."

"I don't know what caused it. I feel great except for my hands. I wonder if you picked up something in the hot spring?"

"Sure could be. We don't know who or what's been in that water. Looked clean. Couldn't have picked a prettier place for a layover though, than here. In terms of spectacular beauty, this part of Hawkesbury sure qualifies as a national park.

"Yeah, it reminds me a lot of Yosemite. This valley backed by towering mountains – positively beautiful."

"Well, we're back to reality fast," I interjected. "Let's put on our

PART XII - HAWKESBURY ISLAND TO CHATHAM SOUND

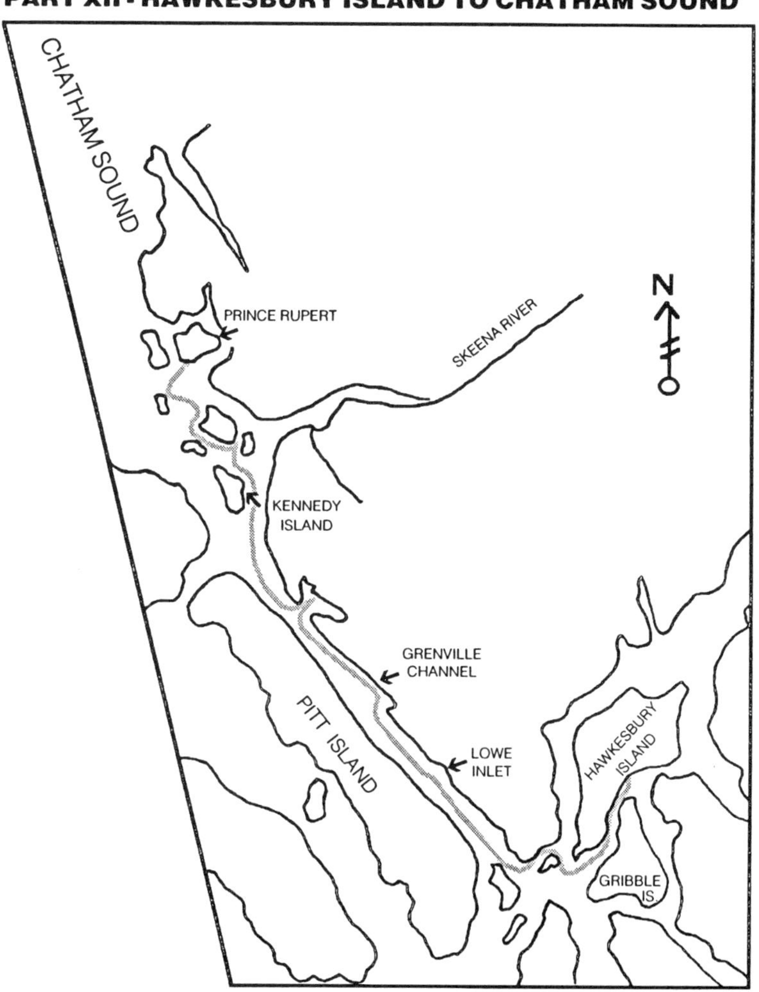

See chart
of coast
on page 4

yellows." The clouds had lowered, and a steady rain had opened up.

"I knew this dry wouldn't last," Nancy added.

"This wind isn't helping, either." It took us over five hours to cover the eight miles down to the tip of Hawkesbury Island. By then the wind was blowing about twenty knots, hard at us out of the south from Wright Sound. We headed to round Sainty Point on the southern tip of Promise Island, so we could turn up Grenville Channel. The wind refused to let us go that way. Rowing hard, now into the sixth hour without rest, we were being pushed up two-mile-wide Douglas Channel against our wills.

"We've got to change heading," I shouted to Nancy over my shoulder. "If we change now and run with it, we can probably make it across to the north tip of Promise Island before we get blown past. I don't like this." We were now in three-foot breaking waves.

"I'm for it," she answered. "These swells are getting worse. Let's get out of the middle of this channel."

Forty-five minutes later, we pulled around the north tip of the island, both wet from the steady exertion. "I need to rest Nancy. I need lunch. I need a rubdown with a velvet glove." And with that, it came natural for me to sing: " . . . . There is nothing I can take, to relieve this pleasant ache. I'm not sick, I'm just in love."

"Don't try to dance, Donald; you'll rock the boat." Nancy had stopped rowing and was reaching for our lunch bag. "If you can get us to the lee of that rock, I'll pull out our crackers and peanut butter. It's been a long morning."

"Just like lunch on the waterfront," I offered as I honked down my rye cracker disk.

Rowing down the back side of Promise was easy, but the rain continued steady and hard. By four, we had rowed over sixteen miles but it had taken us nearly twelve hours, with few breaks. I was beat. Nancy, I'm sure, was no better off.

"The chart shows a cove around the point. Let's look there and quit if there's any place halfway suitable for camp." I was talking while studying the chart on my lap. Under its wet transparent cover, the printing was all distorted.

"How far to the next inlet?"

"That's Lowe Inlet, a good fifteen miles."

"We'll make this place do," Nancy concluded. The rain continued without letup. We found a flat spot above the tideline on the north shore of the cove. The tarp went up quickly. Everything we unpacked was either wet or damp. Dinner consisted of bouillon, rice and tea, all made quickly on the single burner, eaten or drunk while standing hunch-shouldered under our tarp. Despite the warmth of the liquids and rice, we were both chilled. It was about six o'clock, but the rain and heavy cloud-cover brought on a darkness that made it seem much later. "I'm going to crawl in," Nancy said. "Maybe I'll be able to warm up a bit."

"I'll put the boat out and then do the same," I responded. To crawl in and lie down sounded wonderful. To become warm sounded heavenly.

"How do you feel?" Nancy asked when I had returned and had crawled backward into the tent, leaving my boots just outside the opening.

"I don't feel sick today, and I've held on to everything I've eaten. Just tired. The day was harder than I'd set myself for. The pull down Hawkesbury was hard, but getting across Douglas Channel was even worse. I don't think I'll read very long."

"The rain on the tarp does sound nice," Nancy commented, as she rolled over onto her elbow to read.

"Yes, it does," I replied, "but I'd sure appreciate it if it drained itself out tonight. Two more days like this and everything will be soaked, including these bags."

"I don't even want to think about that. It sure feels good now."

"I know." By now I was back in my book, immersed in the Fall of Singapore. But not for long. I needed sleep more than enlightenment.

"This spot looks OK, Nancy; it's about all there is anyway, but look over there – where that creek dumps out."

"Oh WOW!" I pointed to a black bear that was browsing along the creek, about a hundred yards away, waddling along on all fours. "He's big," Nancy whispered.

"As far as I'm concerned, all bears are big," I replied, not taking my eyes off him. "He's working up the creek and I don't think he's noticed us yet. The next inlet is about twelve miles away. We just about have to stay here and hope he goes away. We'll anchor the boat out as far as we can tonight."

"OK," Nancy agreed, "but I'm sure not comfortable here. I prefer islands to this kind of set-up. Seeing one up this close reminds me of The Night of the Grizzlies – remember? In Glacier National Park?"

"Don't think about it. Remember, he's more afraid of you than you of him."

"Then how come you're taking the veri-pistol ashore?"

"I feel better thinking I can scare him off in a crisis,"' I answered.

By my estimate next morning, there were upwards of a hundred and forty-three bears along the south shore of Lowe Inlet that night, and both of us heard every one of them. Many moved back and forth, breaking sticks and breathing heavily right outside our tent. How they managed much traffic with so little disturbance, I'll never know. Next morning, easily forty-two hours later, careful inspection revealed absolutely no sign of any wildlife. "Whew!" I offered, "that was close."

"Apparently they leave you alone if they think you're not afraid," Nancy returned. "Or the rain all night sent them to their own hidey-holes."

We hadn't been alone in Lowe Inlet that night. Along about dusk, a white cruiser of about fifty feet had passed by to anchor farther inland. Our site was about a mile in from the channel.

By seven A.M. after rowing for half an hour, we re-entered Grenville Channel heading north. At the same time the cruiser was coming up to depart the inlet. On his flying bridge, it was impossible for the skipper not to see us. Just before entering the channel, which is at its narrowest here, he cranked in a heavy throttle setting. With an echoing roar, his bow wave frothed viciously in response and built. By the time he reached us, he had attained his cruising speed, and by his heading, was not going to give us more than thirty feet leeway. We were about the same distance from the sheer rock wall of the channel.

"That son-of-a-bitch!" I yelled. "He's deliberately trying to swamp us! That bastard! Get the stern to him. Be ready to back! He's going to drive us into the wall!"

His bow wave hit our stern with jarring Force, lifting and driving us straight for the wall. "Back hard Nancy!" I shouted. We were trying to back row to stop our forward momentum. "Here comes the stern wave! Get ready!"

By the time we had recovered, his bow wave, little diminished, bounced back off the wall and hit our bow, lifting us up and over and pitching us backward toward our port rail into his high wake. "Pull on your right oar! Get the bow back into these waves!"

A minute later, the waves were gone and so was the cruiser. We sat, rocking in the final disturbance of his waves, as his wake gradually dissipated.

"The —— out of Seattle," I read off his stern. "That son-of-a bitch! That God damned son-of-a-bitch! That arrogant bastard! I hope I never run into him. I'll deck him, so help me, if I have to use a two-by-four!"

"I can't believe he did that," Nancy added, equally as angry as I.

"It's like drivers on a freeway—they're animals when they have a few hundred horsepower. Self-centered bastard!" I was still churning inside.

We rowed on silently for several minutes. "When I think about it though, most of the boaters we have met have been good people. It's just one jerk like this that ruins the image." By now I had calmed down and we were rowing steadily over oily gray water, now quiet but for the ripple of the rain. The sound of his diesel had long been swallowed by distance.

In the Navy I had flown for several thousand hours and still hold a commercial pilot's license. We have also boated for many years. It has long struck me that private boating could use some of the organization of private aviation. Mainly, qualification and licensing of operators. Such things as Power Squadron courses are not mandatory. They should be. Courtesies afloat are simply actions for boating safety, no different from Rules of the Road. They need to be required and taught if it is expected that they will be learned.

"That salmon was good last night, even if we did have to eat it in the rain." The sound of my voice broke the spell of our silence over the past ten minutes as we were both thinking of the passing boater, for Nancy countered.

"He was probably a very nice guy who suffered from near-sightedness and had forgotten to put his glasses on." After a pause, she added, "That was good salmon though. We'll have the other half tonight. Maybe I should use huckleberries all the time. Sure cheaper than lures."

In the course of trolling mile after mile, we had lost most of our lures. Yesterday we were down so far that Nancy had decided to use huckleberries on a hook. "What the heck – they're red, and if they stay on, the salmon won't know the difference – or maybe it'll even be curious enough to bite."

Midday, in the middle of Douglas Channel, she found out. A twelve-pound Chinook decided to go for the new experience and we acquired a delicate dinner for two nights. Catching a salmon is always exciting, for it fights and must be played. We have lost many in that play. Yesterday's catch was particularly rewarding for the creativity of the lure.

With no wind and steady rain, we just rowed and talked little. In times like these, it was possible to row and drowse at the same time – not quite asleep, but close to it. After nearly four hundred miles, the rowing motion had become nearly automatic. We slipped into this state from time to time to be pulled back by the splash of a fish, the sound of a bird or of a distant boat engine, or, more often, one of us hit the other's oar. When that happened, we got back in step, like marching. Without words, we each knew what had happened. With my back always to her, Nancy could never see my face, unless I twisted around. She could tell if I was nodding. I could only guess when she was drowsing by the action of her oars.

Today, in the tranquil hollow of my hood, I was thinking about Nancy. Every night, mostly in the rain, while I dinked with the boat and made camp, she fixed dinner. It was always good. Everything so well-organized. No complaints. Just continued on day after day. Anything that came up was just part of the trip. I should be so lucky to have her as my partner.

"Nancy," I said, breaking the silence.

"What?" She obviously was pulled out of a drowse.

"I love you. Thanks for being you."

"What brought that on?"

"I was thinking of hot bouillon and that reminded me of you."

"That makes no sense, but thanks. I love you too. I wish this rain would stop."

Around noon, the rain did stop, to be replaced by mist and fog. Though the channel was narrow, we couldn't see across or very far up or down. We hugged the eastern side. From time to time we heard the muffled sounds of a passing fishing boat. Once, the sudden roar of an approaching airplane frightened us for his nearness. When he passed over, he couldn't have been more than fifty feet above the water.

"Did you see that?" Nancy asked excitedly. "He smiled and waved! I swear he almost hit our mast!"

"These bush pilots sure do earn their keep. The gunk they have to fly through. They sure have to know their territory like the backs of their hands. And be incredibly skillful."

"I think you'd still like to be flying Beavers. Aren't you a little old now for that kind of stuff?"

"I guess I am, but I wonder if that wouldn't have been a better life after I left the Navy. Better than working for a corporation,"

"Better for you, maybe, but five kids of your own and three of mine – but dream on, Roscoe. Too bad you don't have your helmet, goggles and scarf."

Later in the afternoon, as we rounded into Klewnugget Inlet, we were greeted by a dozen or more rare, black oystercatchers working the rocks and kelp off the entrance. With their long, bright orange beaks and orange legs and feet, they stand in marked distinction. Their cry is a piercing, high-pitched whistle, heard often when they're around. We were thrilled to be so close to so many. Again, we were reminded how unafraid wildlife was, especially birds. A couple of mornings ago, Nancy had "talked" with a raven, who had chosen to sit on a nearby branch while she had fixed breakfast. "Hello. Hello." Over and over, Nancy had called out, pausing between each call. At first he had answered each call with a deep-throated, "Awwkk." After several goes, he had clearly sounded out an answering hello. The amazing thing was that he had mimicked Nancy's voice. The sound had been close.

We observed along the way north that crows, ravens, gulls and even eagles have a wide range of communicating sounds: lots of chatter and talk, using a wide range of sounds, in addition to their traditional and characteristic "calls."

That evening, as we were off-loading the boat to make camp, we both noticed a small brown Lincoln's sparrow. He remained near us the whole time, perching close by and watching as we put up our tent and tarp. Throughout the dinner preparation, he moved frequently, but never more than four or five feet away, often approaching closer to examine something of particular interest. When we sat down to eat, he jumped first onto my shoes and then up onto my plate, accepting the bits of pan bread I pushed over to him. Later, when we went down to the water's edge to load the food aboard and put the boat out to anchor, he sat on a rock, close by Nancy, and watched the entire proceeding, cocking his head first to one side and then to the other. His interest was personal and keen and quite unique in our experience .

Since leaving Westview, down in southern British Columbia, we had heard horror stories from fishermen about two areas. One, the mouth of the Skeena River, this side of Prince Rupert; the other, Portland Inlet, the body of water that separates British Columbia from Alaska. Right now, our concern was for the Skeena River.

Our choice was to pass on the inside of ten-mile-long Kennedy Island and take on the Skeena River waters, or pass on the outside of

Kennedy and expose ourselves early to the infamous weather of Dixon Entrance. Our compromise, to save time, was to stay inside of Kennedy and outside of Smith Island, next up the coast.

The Coast Pilot is a book that tells mariners what to expect in most waters and anchorages up and down the coast. Based on years of updating, it usually is thorough and accurate. Since they can't cover small coves and inlets, The Coast Pilot was of limited use to us. Still, we referred to our water-wrinkled copy whenever we could – usually to our advantage.

For the Skeena River estuary, The Coast Pilot virtually throws up its hands. Experienced fishermen and tugboat skippers will tell you no two days are the same, and most of the time is bad. Not predictable, is the conclusion one draws: always potentially dangerous. Four things contribute to this condition. First, the river pours a heavy flow of water down from the mountains into the salt water estuary. Second, tides in the area run sometimes over twenty feet, bringing in and taking out large volumes of water. Third, the entire estuary is shallow, one-to-eight fathoms, with many outreaching sandbars and some areas less than a fathom at low tide. Fourth, and finally, is the wind, which can blow up quickly and fiercely. It can come either from the northwest out of Dixon Entrance, or from the east to southeast, down off the glaciers, out of the mountains. Combinations of any of these wreak havoc on the waters of Telegraph Passage and behind and around Kennedy, DeHorsey and Smith Islands, mostly in the name of unbelievably high and punishing chop on top of the waves and current.

When we approached this area, the day was calm. We stayed near shore, pulling against the current until we were just off the southern tip of DeHorsey Island. The crossing around DeHorsey to Smith Island was a little over four miles-three hours for us, the currents being what they were. "Whatta you think Nancy? Should we try it? If we leave now, we'll reach the other side around seven. Still plenty of light."

"The weather looks OK, but it's so hard to tell with this overcast."

"Sure wish we had a barometer. I'd like to know what's building in this area."

"I know," Nancy answered, still scanning the sky. "Is this a calm, or the calm before a storm?"

"I don't know. I guess we'll soon find out. Let's head for the other side. There are still quite a few fishing boats out here. They must think it's OK." We started across, angling northwest by north to counter the current. The chop was light, for which we were grateful. I had an uneasy feeling, even though the crossing was no different from dozens of others we had made.

"I hope this water stays like it is. This we can handle," I offered.

"I just want to get to the other side. This is an eerie place. If it's possible to row on pins and needles, I feel like that's what we're doing. Something feels wrong – like something is going to happen." Nancy said. It was the first time I had heard her express any negative feelings of this sort.

"It's all in your mind, Nancy. Think of hot shower; and cheeseburgers in Prince Rupert. It's only about twenty miles away and we'll get in another six today. It's four o'clock now. We'll be in Prince Rupert tomorrow night. I'll take you out to dinner. Wine, steak, two desserts if you want. It'll be nice." OK words, but I still couldn't shake the strange feeling I carried.

"Let's just get across the Skeena first," Nancy responded. "We're making fair progress."

We reached the southern tip of DeHorsey Island after an hour and a half of steady pulling. Rather than relief there, we found the currents from the ebbing tide running strong between Smith and DeHorsey. We used another half hour of even harder rowing just to get around that point.

"The chart shows a cove about two miles up shore. It's shallow, but maybe we can find a campsite. Let's go look. I'm ready to call it a day."

The cove we approached was calm and circular, about a half-mile in diameter inside a narrow entrance. All around, dense forest matted to the waterline. In three places, light green coloring on the surface of the water suggested patches of grass at the water's edge. The mosquitoes were thick, covering our hands and faces as we rowed. "Let's go look in that patch over there." I pointed to the nearest patch of light green. "Once we get our tent up, we can close out these damned mosquitoes."

Nancy had put on her netted hat. "I don't like this place at all."

As we approached the green, the appearance of grass dissolved. "That's saltwater grass, Nancy. Growing on the bottom. The green is all marsh. Look. We can see bottom There's no place for a tent – no solid ground."

"Let's go look at one more patch," Nancy suggested. We headed for the other side. I stopped rowing and turned to Nancy.

"Wait a minute. Let me poke an oar."

"Why? What's wrong?"

"Just as I thought. Three and a half feet. This place is all marsh. At low tide this whole cove'll be dry-muddy, rather. Can't stay here. We have to go on until we find something better."

"I'm tired. Where can we go?"

"We can go around to the back of Smith Island, along Inverness Passage. It's about three or four miles, but I don't see any coves on the chart. Besides, from the contours, there's high cliffs on both sides, a real funnel for any wind and no place to anchor. I think we're better off on this side. There are some smaller islands up ahead. Surely we can find some place there to camp."

We rowed automatically, our bodies, not our minds, propelling us across the calm channel. An hour of silence was finally broken when we reached a narrow passageway between Smith Island and a smaller offshore flanking island. "Let's go up this channel and see what we can find," I suggested.

"It's getting dark and I know we've got to keep moving to find something, but we need to eat something. It's been eight hours since lunch."

Nancy was drained of all energy.

"You're right – let's take five," I answered, feeling no stronger. Peanut butter on hardtack. Chateaubriand never tasted better. Water instead of wine was our emollient – a very poor substitute. While still swiping with my tongue at crackers glued around my teeth, I picked up my oars. "We better go while we have a little light."

We rowed on for another hour, finding no possible place for tent or boat.

"What if we don't find anything?" Nancy asked. "We can't sleep in the boat."

"We might keep on rowing. Row all night, right on up the channel," I answered, feeling down and thinking rather numbly. "There's a little island up ahead – there, about a quarter of a mile. Let's go look at it."

The island was low and small, about a hundred feet long and fifty feet wide, crescent shaped, with a dense patch of scrub evergreens along its west edge. "A place for the boat, some screen from the wind and a not very flat tent site. This is our room for the night," I observed. "Motel Three."

Nancy stepped out of the boat to look for the best campsite. "There's nothing very good," she called back. "This marsh grass is growing out of solid rock, but I don't think we should go any further." We put the tent and the tarp up by using boulders for the stays. There was no ground into which pegs could be driven. Makeshift, but it seemed OK. Scrounging boulders was the hardest part, for we both simply wanted to crawl in. A light rain started just as I set the boat at anchor.

"Just in time," I said, as I crawled into the tent. "I'm too tired to eat anything else. Let's sleep first and have a big breakfast in the morning."

"You read my mind. I need rest more than food," Nancy answered.

Rest we didn't get. Around midnight, the rain intensified, now driven by heavy, gusting winds. As if looking for weaknesses, the wind searched the corners of our tarp and tugged, like hungry wolves tearing at the flesh of a crippled moose. Some of the stay-lines just loosened and snapped in the wind. Others remained tied to rocks, but the wind became powerful enough to whip those rocks around. Three times I had to get up to re-tie the tarp. We feared it might tear, possibly even blow away. Keeping it up and whole was essential to our well-being. So the wind challenged and threatened the rest of the night, hard out of the southeast, allowing us little sleep. Outside our tent, we heard the rivulets of the hard rain gushing around and over the rocks. Around five, we were both wide awake and concerned.

Through the broken crackle of our pocket VHF, we heard, "Small craft warning in Dixon Entrance – gusts to thirty – low pressure area-"

"We can't stay here," I said. "This open part of the island will be under water in another couple of hours and the tarp won't last much longer in this wind."

"You think there might be something better up on the lee side of Smith?"

"Anything's better than this. The wind'll be with us up the island. Let's eat first though. The wind may let up after the low passes through."

It was a miserable breakfast, eaten on our knees in the tent: hardtack and peanut butter again, along with some lumpy oatmeal and thin coffee. Moving as quickly as possible in our yellows, we stowed everything in the boat and pulled out. Rowing with the wind, now gusting well over twenty, we slipped down close along Smith Island. Being somewhat in the lee, the sea was running with us, the waves unobjectionable.

About two hours later, we rounded the northwest corner of Smith, only to be hit by a strong head wind, funneled right at us off the back wall of Inverness Passage. We turned in to it to look for shelter but could make no progress whatsoever. The wind was too strong. Though there were whitecaps, there wasn't enough distance from the wall for the waves to have built.

"There's plenty of shelter on the other side if we can just get across this channel." I pointed to some land almost due north, about two miles away. "I think we can quarter into it."

"That's the only relief I see any place," Nancy answered. "We have to try for it." With that, we pulled on our left oars and headed northeast, quartering into the wind, waves and current. From each oncoming wave, spray whipped up and over us, adding to the driven rain. Pulling hard, we plowed on and away from Smith Island into murky, gray Chatham Sound. After about an hour of silent rowing, the distance away from Smith had grown to about a mile, but hard as we pulled, we could make no headway toward our target land, still two miles away. We simply remained in mid-channel. About a mile away on our left was a small, tree-covered island, all that was between us and miles of open water in Dixon Entrance.

"I think we should turn and run for that island while we can," I shouted into the wind. "This is all too much. If we wait much longer and if the wind becomes any stronger, we could be blown right out to sea." I now felt a definite sense of urgency, and was as wet inside as out.

"You're right," Nancy answered. "We can't make it to the far side. The wind may slacken, but it also might build. Let's go over there and wait it out. Tide's still ebbing, which isn't helping any. Now I understand why the fishermen have respect for this area."

The wind moved us quickly toward the island — almost past it. We had to pull extra hard and fast the last quarter mile just to keep from passing beyond the island's north end. In the rain-mist, we couldn't tell if the island was all rock, or if it might have a sandy beach. "Let's try to get around it for something on the lee side," Nancy suggested.

"I think we can do that, if we hug the shore," I answered trying to gauge the situation looking over my shoulder, while still rowing hard. As we came closer, a cove appeared dead ahead.

"There's a cove, right inside the point. It appears to have a sandy beach. Maybe we should head right for it and not take the chance of not getting back on the other side. Whatta you think?" Nancy asked.

"How's the surf?" I was thinking of Lasqueti Island.

"It doesn't look too bad. Let's go in and see."

The narrow pocket beach came up on us quickly. It was set in between two jagged rocky arms about a hundred feet apart that seemed to reach out to embrace us. "Looks OK," Nancy shouted, just as a bigger wave deposited us on the beach with a thunk and a jolt. One more pull of our oars in open air and we were on the beach, settling in soft sand, trying to catch our balance. "It's not dry," Nancy observed, "but at least it's on land."

"You watch the boat and I'll look around," I volunteered, climbing out into a receding wave. Everything was drenched from the heavy wind-driven rain. I found a suitable place for our tent, but nothing looked good. Everything, in fact, was miserable. We were tired, hungry and wet. The thought of spending another wet day and night out was depressing. I climbed up on the rock outcropping to have a look up-channel. In the distance, I could make out some large, orange, construction cranes. These I took to be in Prince Rupert. They weren't. They were four miles this side of town, but my chart was too small a scale to show that. This also was a clear case of falling into that mariner's trap of seeing what you want to see. "Damn," I said to Nancy, as I returned to the boat. "I can see the town. It's right there. I can almost touch it. And smell it. It smells like cheeseburgers and feels like hot water. And here we are, stuck on this island, pinned by the wind. DAMN!"

"And stuck in the sand too, if we don't move the boat," Nancy added. "Tide's going out." The soft sand held like a suction cup that we could overcome, but only with hernia-producing tugs, each lifting and hauling on a side of the boat. In between these efforts, we hunched in back of a rocky outcropping, somewhat out of the wind, each staring at the rain that drove onto the beach. Though still early morning, everything was dark: dark water, black wet sand, green-black trees, dark brown rock outcroppings and low, gray-black clouds scudding by fast under a heavy low overcast. The only brightness around were our glistening wet yellows. We were too down to even try to eat. If spirits could be dark, ours were.

More to break my numbed inertia than anything else, I turned to Nancy, "I'm going to have another look." I glanced at my watch. It was just after ten. We had been there over two hours.

As I climbed and slipped up the wet rocks, things felt a little different. Was it real, or did I just want it to be that way? I looked carefully at the water and turned my face both ways to feel the wind. It definitely had slackened — no doubt about it. I looked some more. The waves clearly were smaller. I turned back toward the beach. Nancy was walking toward me as I dropped down off the rocks onto the sand. "It's better. I think we should give it a try. Wind is letting up. What do you think?"

"I don't want to spend the rest of the day and night here," Nancy answered. "Let's give it a try."

With the receding tide, the surf had diminished. We had no trouble launching the boat, but as soon as we turned the bow about, we faced directly into the wind and waves.

"Let's quarter over and see if we can make some progress. We'll head for the other side. If we can't we know we can come back here." I talked over my shoulder as we pulled out of the cove.

When we were on course, I took a rough fix on a channel marker that was in line with a distant small island. After about fifteen minutes, I took another fix. "We're moving on our track, Nancy. We're making headway. Positively and not at a bad rate. We can make it across!"

"The wind has slackened," Nancy answered. "It feels like the front or low, or whatever, has moved on."

The tone of our voices had quickly changed to upbeat, our strokes more confident. In another half hour, we were halfway across the southern approach to the channel and the rain had stopped.

I smiled. The sun wasn't shining. The clouds hadn't even risen any. My spirits had though, and from looking at Nancy, so had hers.

"I'll buy you lunch. It'll be a little late, but worth the wait. You'll be my date." Nancy was almost singing, so I did.

"There'll be a hot time in the old town, tonight."

Lincoln's Sparrow

PART XIII: (Pete) DISASTER! "HANG ON! JUST HANG ON!"

WHAAAAAMMMMMMMM! A thunderclap of wind out of the southeast tipped the boat over violently, nearly burying our port rail. "My God! What the – ?"

WHAAAAAMMMMMMMM! Another blast, only this time it was a wind that didn't give. It held and built. Waters that only a minute before were calm, now had foot-high waves. The tops became instant froth. Fortunately, our sail was down and furled on the mast, or we would have capsized for sure.

"I don't know what's going on, but let's pull for shore," Nancy shouted. We were about a hundred yards offshore. I had just looked at my watch. It was twenty to one. It had taken us two and a half hours to cross the channel entrance. We had just entered the marked channel leading into Prince Rupert, weaving our way through some new construction and a group of cranes, towers and barges situated just offshore when the wind hit. These were the cranes and towers I had seen earlier from the island down-channel. This was not Prince Rupert as I had imagined. The town still lay four and a half miles up-channel due north of us.

"We can't turn into shore, Nancy. Wind's too strong! We'll swamp!" I yelled over my shoulder, straining hard on my oars to miss a steel stanchion. The first blast of wind was at least thirty-five knots and was building. It picked us up as a toy and threw us straight at the first of several barges anchored out. "Pull hard on the right," I shouted, "or we'll hit!" I had dropped my left oar to pull with both hands on my right oar. The waves were now two feet high. Spray drenched our faces. We raced by the barge, not three feet separating us. We had little control over our direction. "Keep the stern into the wind or we'll capsize!" I shouted. Another barge loomed. To hit anything now would smash both us and the boat. The wind was treating us as a small wooden chip.

"Hard on your left!" Nancy screamed. "Harder!" The barge shot by us just off the tip of our oars. I saw it only as a blur. In turning to miss it, the stern was quickly picked up by the wind and thrown broadside. I dropped my left oar and picked up my right, muscling with both hands to get the stern

PART XIII - DISASTER!

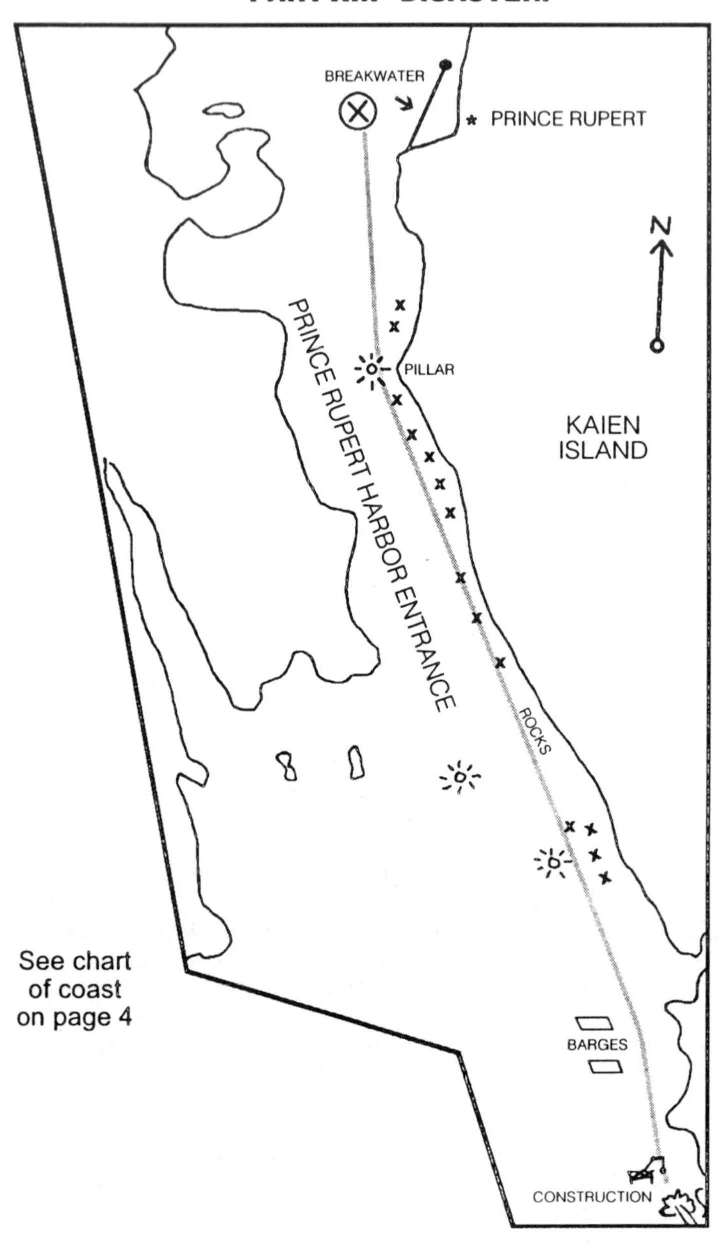

See chart of coast on page 4

back into the wind. The forces were so great. The oars bent. If one broke, we were through. Sometimes I grabbed air. The waves were now at least four feet. Wave tops and rain mixed to pellet us horizontally. Our faces stung, especially our eyes. I could barely see. It was like we faced into a sandblaster, only this ran off us and down inside our yellows by gallons. I was oblivious to being wet.

Nancy took her lead from me, pulling on her matching oar – right or left. To be broadside in a trough now meant certain capsizing. Each wave now broke; its top exploded downwind. The top of the water in every direction was streaked white – on the waves, in the troughs, spewing off the crests. Violence surrounded us. We weren't rowing. We simply fought to keep our stern into the wind, now forty-five to fifty knots. We shot over the tops of all this – so fast, we pounded into each successive downwind wave.

The shore was less than a hundred yards away – large, jagged rocks pounded by frothing waves. For our lives, we had to stay away from them. "GODDAMN!" I yelled at nothing but the wind. "This is enough! You win!" Anger, fear and reaction. No time to think. To stay afloat was all that counted. We had no plan. We simply reacted, clawing in desperation.

"PETE!" Nancy yelled, trying to make herself heard over the howl of the wind. "Up ahead! That point! We have to pull around it!" I turned briefly to look. Ahead, about three hundred yards, the shoreline edged out into the channel ending in a point, all large rocks. Just off that point, about fifty feet, was a channel market light placed on top of a solid stone pillar. It would take all we could manage to edge around the point, if we were lucky. It came up on us fast.

"We can't make it around that light," I yelled over my shoulder. "Have to try to go between."

"We'll never clear it!" Nancy screamed.

"No choice," I yelled back. "Hope it's deep enough and not a reef!" The balance was now delicate. If the stern moved a foot off the wind in either direction, the boat would bolt broadside. If that happened, we would capsize instantly. Both hands first on the right oar, then on the left. Pain in my legs. Pain in my arms. Pain in my shoulders. My elbows, especially, screamed for relief.

"Hard on the right!" Nancy shouted. Then, "Hard on the left!" We fishtailed down the channel, now at a speed well over fifteen knots, not quite out of control, but within inches by any measurement.

I twisted to look over my right shoulder, then quickly over my left. I had over-corrected. We hurtled straight for the stone pillar. I pulled five hard quick strokes on my right oar, expecting a shattering crunch as we hit. The pillar or a jagged reef. Which would it be? The pillar flashed by at arm's length, and in a second we were through the slot, somehow, still afloat, more flying than in the water. "Oh my God," I heard Nancy yell. Then, "Up ahead, about a mile. Looks like a breakwater. Can we get over there?"

"Maybe," was all I could manage. My physical exertion was greater than anything I knew. When I'd lift the oars out of the turbulence of the water, the wind whipped them back and down. Often I caught little or no stroke at all. When that happened, I had to get the oar out again and back for a bite. Double strain. Double pull.

Now entire wave tops streamed into the wind, leaving five to six feet between troughs and crests. Above the scream of the wind, the rain burst against our lifejackets in pulsating, machine gun staccato. Our hoods had long since been blown back off our heads. My ears and face were stung by thousands of needles. The air around us was now half water, rain and gray-green water in equal amounts. It lashed at us horizontally. I could hardly breathe.

"Half a mile Pete!" Nancy yelled. "Can you hold out?" Now I knew no soreness or physical weakness. That was all past. I moved. I pulled. I responded. I swore. Each pull came from somewhere. We were still afloat. I caught flashes of the town over to the left.

"I'll try!" I yelled. Just then, I looked up. Clearly, as though the seas suddenly turned into slow motion, a hundred yards back, one wave rose slowly above all the rest. I watched, transfixed. I stopped rowing. Here came the end. The wind picked up that whole wave and threw it as though a dam had burst. A solid wall of water rushed down on us. "This is it!" I yelled at Nancy. "Hold onto the boat whatever you do. I love you!" It hit us with the force of a giant breaker. Like a piece of flotsam, our boat was pounded broadside then lifted and rolled over. I was aware of the boat twisting and rising above the waves, almost airborne. Then the lee side went down. As the water rushed in, we were thrown out and down. First it was air and bubbles and froth and water; then it was just water. I kicked and pulled with my arms to resurface, bobbing up quickly with the help of my lifejacket. Ahead about five yards away was our boat, bottom up, mostly submerged. Nancy was the same distance away.

"Swim for the boat!" I yelled before starting a kickless swim. I could see Nancy doing the same. I had no sense of time. We both wore boots, rain gear and lifejackets. Within minutes we reached the boat and draped our upper bodies onto it, coughing, catching our breath.

"How're you doin'?" I managed, grabbing Nancy's hand.

"OK. How about you?"

"I'm all right. Let's rest a minute."

"There's a fishing boat." Nancy pointed toward the breakwater. "It's turning this way. Maybe he saw us."

I stared, wondering, doubting. Then there was no doubt. "He did! He's heading this way – right for us!"

"Oh my God! How lucky," Nancy responded. In about five minutes, he was within fifty feet of us crossing downwind. A face poked out of a pilot house window, then an arm that waved. We both waved back excitedly.

"He sees us!" We both yelled. We each stretched an arm over the other's shoulder.

Slowly he edged up into the wind. Though he sat heavy in the water, he still rose five to six feet with each wave. He was experienced. He pulled upwind to keep us in his lee. Carefully, he crabbed down to us. Along the side of his hull hung three rubber tires used as fenders. "We have to be quick, Nancy. When he's close enough, grab a tire and pull yourself up. I'll hold on 'til you're up. We don't want to get pounded by that hull." Now he was alongside, each of us rising and falling five to six feet, not quite together in motion. He often surged up while we plunged down. "Grab for it Nancy!" I held onto a line that hung over the side of his boat and pointed to the nearest tire. Nancy reached. She couldn't quite touch the tire. "Try again on the next rise!" Again inches separated her. She waited out the next rise, gauging the tire. On the next one she stretched and kicked and caught hold. Somehow, moved under and boosted. It was enough for her to hook her foot into the tire. That's as far as she got.

"Can't pull myself," she managed, looking down at me. "Too weak." She just hung there. There was nothing I could do. We had been in the water for about fifteen minutes. Though out of the Gulf of Alaska, the water didn't seem cold. I knew that hypothermia was taking its toll. Weakness would be the first sign. How long could Nancy hold on, curled around a tire?

"Hang on!" I yelled. "Just hang on!" Nancy made several attempts to lift her other leg, without success.

Just then, a body loomed over the edge of the deck. A shock of black, windblown hair streamed away from the full round face of a stocky man. Holding onto his rail with one hand, he reached over and caught Nancy's wrist. He pulled, but with no success. His deck heaved violently. He couldn't let go with his steadying hand lest he go overboard himself. He tried again to haul Nancy up. I was still in the water hanging onto the line, dunked with every fall of the boat.

"I can't pull myself up," she forced down over her shoulder.

"Try, Nancy, try!" I yelled back. From on deck, our rescuer shouted over the wind. "I can hold on, but I can't pull her up! I need help. There's just my wife. She's got the wheel." We three were fixed in this space for another couple of minutes, slammed from side to side by the pounding hull. We were unable to do anything. All I could think of was Nancy. She twisted from time to time to look down at me, pain on her face. I knew she couldn't hold on for long. Nor could I. I had managed to wrap the line around my wrist, but with each rise of the boat, the pull brought wrenching pain to my wrist and shoulder. With each rise and fall, I slammed into the side of his metal hull, as did Nancy. Our boat had long drifted away. I remember thinking, what a miserable way to end our trip. While holding onto the boat, I had seen things floating away: oars, gratings, bags. The things that had not been tied in.

Nancy made another attempt to pull herself up, but it was feeble. She looked now as if in resignation. Neither of us could hold on much longer.

In a sudden flurry above, two more bodies appeared; two young men out of nowhere. Lying on the deck, they both reached over and down with one hand, locking onto Nancy's wrists. They hauled. As she lifted, they also grabbed a chunk of her rain pants and pulled up and over. In a second, she skidded across the wet deck on her stomach, thrown up as they would have heaved a flounder.

I then swam over to catch onto the same tire. As I reached up, they both reached down and grabbed onto my wrists. They hoisted me enough for me to get a foothold in the tire. In like manner, I was hauled up and onto the deck, out of breath and coughing water.

For a minute I just lay there. I lifted my head to look around. Vaguely, I saw a similar boat move away, just after two figures leaped from our boat to theirs. When I looked around, I saw no sign of Nancy. I pulled to my knees, but felt dizzy. Someone took hold of my arm and lifted me. We staggered for our balance and stumbled toward the wheelhouse. With halting steps and little to hold onto, we finally made it, stepping over the combing and inside. There sat Nancy, shivering on a stool, staring at nothing, a pool of water forming under her. As I came in, she looked up. We both managed weak smiles. I edged over and put my hand on her shoulder. Now I too, shook.

The man who had helped us outside, took over the wheel from a woman. We headed back toward the breakwater. Sam McMillan and his wife, Sarah, were the crew of our rescue boat. They live in a village northwest of Prince Rupert, up near the Alaskan border. Each summer Sam fishes, as did his father and probably most of his ancestors. This year Sarah opted to go with him. On this particular day, even in the face of the storm, they were trying to get out of Prince Rupert and down into their summer base moorage, Just south of the city. They were in company of two other boats of the same make.

As they had swung out of the breakwater and into the teeth of the gale, they had talked with the other two boats to see if they should turn back to wait out the storm. A crewman on one of the other boats had looked down channel and seen us. "There's a rowboat out there with two people in it. They're sure as hell going to capsize!" He had yelled into his radio.

Just as Sam had seen us, we went over. All three boats then changed course to our position. After we were picked up, all three boats returned to the breakwater.

As we sat in the warmth of Sam's pilot house, I looked around. Sarah had some plants growing and some curtains pulled back from one of the windows. A woman's touch was evident. After Sam took over the wheel, Sarah scurried about to get us each dry towels and a cup of hot coffee. I looked up past Sam to a St. Christopher's medal hanging in front of the wheel. Angels, I thought, sure come in various forms. For us, they came as a middle-aged Indian couple, fighting every day for their own survival, who wittingly risked their own lives that they might save ours. None of us said much as we made our way back behind the breakwater. Sam pulled over alongside a tied-up Coast Guard cutter, where several crewmen waited to help us off.

As we moved to leave, we both hugged Sam and Sarah. "Thanks," was about all either of us could mutter, for the watery eyes and choked feeling we each had. "We'll write," Nancy promised, holding up the piece of paper on which Sarah had written their names and address.

"Captain wants to see you on the bridge," one of the Coast Guard crewmen shouted to make himself heard as he helped me over the bulwark of the cutter. We both climbed the ladder. "You guys were lucky those fishing boats were out there. Our engine is dead. Look at that anemometer. Over sixty and gusting to seventy. Caught a lot of us short, but that's weather in the Dixon Entrance." While talking, the skipper was listening to his radio. "Fishing boat's in trouble out near the Charlottes and another off Dundas."

Next to the anemometer was a ship's clock. It was two o'clock. Figuring fifteen minutes in the water and about twenty minutes for rescue and return, our ride had lasted between fifteen and twenty minutes – give or take a few. Four and a half mile. At the last we had to be moving over twenty knots – in a seventeen-foot dory! Standing in the cutter's wheelhouse, I felt weak again. In shock is probably a better evaluation. A sense of failure overwhelmed me. We had failed to make it to Alaska.

Prince Rupert Harbour.

PART XIV: (Nancy) PRINCE RUPERT TO ALASKA: "LET'S GO ON. WE CAN DO IT!"

It was all over. Two months of hard rowing, every day, was for nothing. We stood on the Prince Rupert docks like two half-drowned mongrels. Our boots were filled with water, our clothing soaked and so were our spirits. I started to shiver and shake involuntarily. I felt inert and unresponsive. I just stood and stared. Discouragement was complete. After a while some activity out by the breakwater tugged for my attention. I looked dully out at the entrance to the harbor, trying to focus my hyperoptic eyes on an approaching vessel. "Look Pete. Isn't that Surfbird?" I was looking at a fishing boat just rounding the breakwater.

"My God, it is! They've got her under tow." Our jaunty little boat, filled to the gunwales with water, wallowed behind another gillnetter. Fred, a friend of Sam's and Sarah's, swung alongside the dock, a huge smile creasing his face.

"We picked up what we could for you – some of it got away – but here's your boat." Pete took the bowline from him and quickly secured it to the dock.

"How can we thank you?" Pete asked.

"Someone helped me once when I was in trouble. It's nice to be able to repay. Good luck to you folks." Fred pulled away, a thumbs-up sign accompanying his wide grin.

Pete was ecstatic. He hopped into the boat and threw her entire contents up onto the dock, making a verbal inventory as he worked. I stood by, shivering convulsively, in shock, unable to participate. With the bags, line and remaining oars up on the dock, all of which had been tied in or secured under the cuddy, he started bailing. The need for activity and accomplishment was stronger than his distress or exhaustion.

"Pete, I've got to get to a motel and get dry. I can't stop shivering," I said weakly. Pete stopped his frantic bailing, finally realizing there might be another priority.

PART XIV - PRINCE RUPERT TO ALASKA

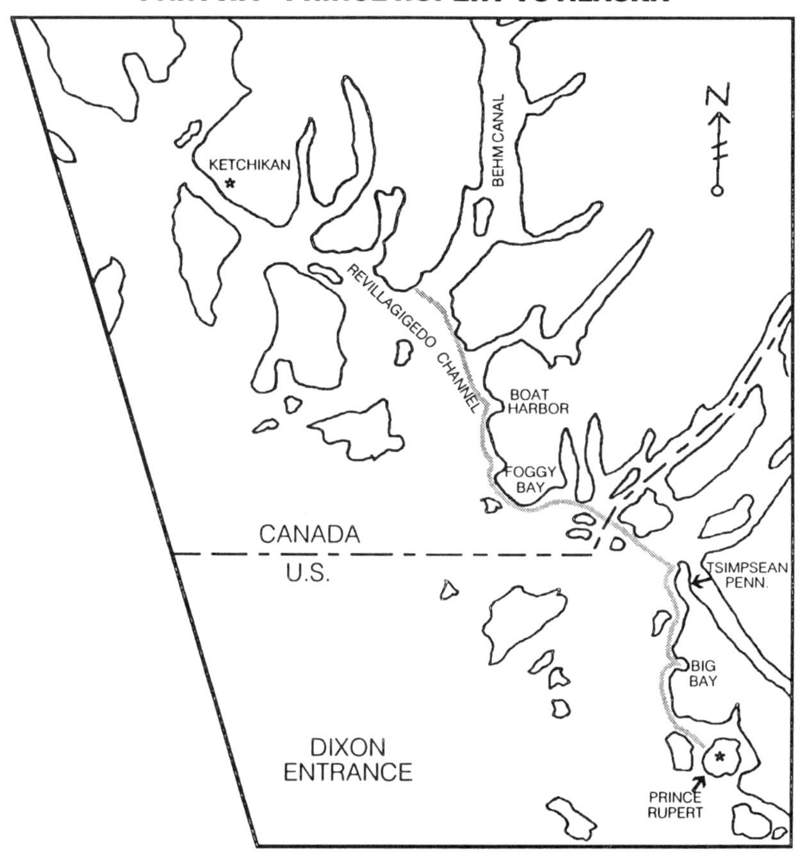

See chart
of coast
on page 4

"OK. Let's take all these bags with us and sort out what we have and what we've lost." We threw the oars, one remaining seat and all the line back into the boat, gathered the bags together and followed a coast guardsman up to his car. He drove us into town and dropped us at the nearest motel.

Squish, squash, squwrinsh. We sloshed into the lobby, dropping soggy bags on the floor and leaving a trail of sea water behind us. "You folks been out biking in this storm?" queried the desk clerk.

"No, but you'd never believe us. Do you have a room with a nice, hot shower?" It came home to us again, that life ashore is vastly separate from life on the water. Winds go unnoticed unless trees or wires blow down and electric service is interrupted. It doesn't matter if waves build over six feet, or foam blows horizontally off their tops. Rain is ignored unless one is caught in a downpour without a waterproof jacket or umbrella. Life revolves around a different axis on land. Only fish folk or mariners truly comprehend the fury of the sea. It would be an exercise in futility to attempt to explain our current situation to anyone unfamiliar with the water.

"Let's get cleaned up and go find that cheeseburger."

"It better be a good one. We've earned it!"

Within minutes our motel room resembled the proverbial "Chinese Laundry." All our remaining possessions cluttered the room and adjoining bath. Sopping wet sleeping bags were hauled out of their "waterproof bags" and draped over the shower rod. The tent adorned the sofa. Wet pants, shirts, underwear and socks filled the closet and spilled out to hang over chairs and dresser drawers. Pete disassembled the VHF, dried each part and laid them out on the carpet. (We later learned that it was damaged beyond repair.) The binoculars, emergency flares, survival suits and lifejackets filled the remaining floor space.

"Looks as if we've carried those bulky survival suits along just to take up space in the boat," I volunteered.

"Yeah. It was a good idea, but I don't see how in hell we could get into them anyway in a rowboat."

"I don't think we could. Even if we could, we couldn't row any more. It would be like wearing a deep-diving suit — the old fashioned kind."

"Looks like we lost three oars, all our camping equipment, the fishing gear, some food bags — what else?" queried Pete.

"The floor boards and two seats were gone. Where's the camera? Wasn't it tied in?"

"No. I remember putting it on the sole, thinking I'd secure it later. It's the only time I didn't tie it in. Wouldn't you know?"

"Oh damn! All our negatives were in that bag too. We've lost all our pictures of the whole trip!" Tears welled up behind my eyes. The loss of the camera and the film recording our adventure hurt. Another thought entered my barely functioning brain. "Do we still have our journals?"

"Yep. All the stuff under the cuddy staying in. How — I don't know — but it did. Lucky, huh?" Pete, the eternal optimist, was trying to find something to be cheerful about.

"I don't know what I'd do if we'd lost the journals — that's a relief. Our money and credit cards are here too. What would we have done without them?"

"It would have been tough, but a challenge to our ingenuity — do you want first shower?"

"No, you go ahead — I'll sort through more stuff while you're in there."

Pete came out of the bathroom with a look of bliss on his face. "That was the best shower I have ever had in my entire life. I'm going to write the shower-head manufacturer and compliment them on their product."

"I suspect it's in contrast to the dip you took earlier today," I said, as I snatched up some dry clothing I had found in the bottom of my bag and rushed into the bathroom for my turn.

Pete was right. There is nothing to compare with a blast of hot water directed over a chilled surface of skin. The showers, combined with a couple of thick, steaming cheeseburgers helped us regain our equilibrium.

We sat in a motel coffee shop the next morning over hot mugs of coffee and drearily began to plan how to transport the boat, its contents and ourselves home. Our hearts weren't in it. We pushed our food around and looked bleakly out the window. "Somehow, rowing to Prince Rupert is like kissing your mother-in-law," said Pete. "We're only eight or nine days away from Ketchikan — only three days from the Alaskan border. It all seems so anticlimactic."

"Well, let's walk down to the boat and finish cleaning her up. We can talk about it on the way." It felt good to stretch our legs again after being restricted to upper body workouts for two months. We felt stiff and in need of a good constitutional. Both of us were bruised from the battering we had taken.

"I just hate to quit," Pete reiterated. "It seems so pointless to struggle all this way just to catch a ferry home."

"We'll have to take a ferry from somewhere," I answered. "What's the difference?"

"It's not Alaska, and Alaska was our goal. Besides, whoever heard of Prince Rupert?"

"Well, Canadians, for starters, and the people who live here. Who are we doing this for — us, or other people?"

"Us, of course, but we set out to get over the border into Alaska and I hate giving up."

"I know. I feel the same." I reflected for a moment, then added, "Let's go on then. We can put it back together. We can buy some cooking pots, a new set of oars and a fishing drop line. We can do it."

"We won't be able to sail anymore. The sail ripped and the rudder's gone."

"That's OK, we've rowed mostly getting this far. It'll be no different.

I think I'm afraid to sail now anyway. If the wind comes up over ten knots, I'll want to head to shelter."

"Me too. We have to get across the Portland Inlet though. That's the scary one. You really want to do it?"

"Yeah. Let's do it!"

....

Three days later, with the assistance of our Visa card, we had minimally re-outfitted the boat and purchased a new pair of heavy-duty rainpants for Pete. He cheerfully jettisoned the old, ducting-taped britches in a city trash can.

The sun was shining on the now docile waters of Prince Rupert Harbour. It was hardly recognizable as the setting for a gale's fury only four days earlier. I could still close my eyes and relive those terrifying moments. The wind ripped through my mind and the fear resurfaced. Both of us had had dreams during the past few nights where we again rode that wild passage down the channel. The experience was hard to shake.

But for now the sun was out and the breeze just a whisper on the water's surface. We cut swiftly across the bay and entered Venn Passage, a narrow, twisting waterway, winding past Metlakatla, a native village founded in 1885 by Reverend William Duncan, an early missionary. Another Metlakatla was a few miles north on Annette Island in Alaska. It had been founded by the same man two years later.

The waters were very shallow along the western shore of the Tsimpsean Peninsula, so there was no boat traffic near us once we turned the corner to head north. It was pretty here. The coastline was pocketed with small bays and coves, with islets and shoals guarding their entrances. The tides moved twenty-three feet of water in and out during these August days, so we knew we had to plan our camping spot well.

We entered Big Bay in late afternoon and found a spot in clean gravel behind some driftwood. It looked to be above the tide line and proved to be just barely that. Around midnight the water lapped against our log barricade before it started to recede. It was always a bit unnerving to hear waves approach the tent flaps. These were moments of uncertainty and insecurity, usually accompanied by startled checking of wrist watch and tide book.

Big Bay was a large shallow basin. Around 4:00 A.M. someone pulled the plug. The waters drained out before we could shove Surfbird into a comfortable depth. Pete, who hated to be bested, stamped his booted feet around the periphery and swore in frustration. Damnit," he exploded. "Now we won't get off until afternoon. I wanted to be in position to cross the Portland Inlet before the weather deteriorates again!"

It was noon before the water rose high enough to float the boat. We pushed off — our destination the tip of the Tsimpsean Peninsula. We spent the afternoon threading our way through the nets of some Canadian purse seiners whose operations are different from their American counterparts. In the U.S. the seiners send out a small, high-powered work boat to hold one end of their net taut across an inlet or mouth of a bay. In Canada, when working close in, two men with the end of the net hop into a row boat and stroke rapidly to shore where they leap out onto the rocks and secure the net with sturdy lines. They perch on the rocks, momentarily abandoned, until the large vessel circles around and starts the net recovery process. It is a dangerous job, only for the young and nimble.

By late afternoon we pulled into a narrow bay to set up camp. Our selected site was well up in the forest. We didn't want to play guessing games with those enormous tides tonight. We intended to arise early to make it across the awesome Portland Inlet, a five-mile stretch from our anchorage to the nearest group of islets, the Boston Islands. We were still frightened from our capsizing and terribly aware of the heavy wind that could come in off the Gulf of Alaska. We were also aware of winds in excess of ninety knots recorded out of the Portland Inlet. We had no VHF with us now and with it died our only chance of contacting help in another emergency.

Pete, with his built-in alarm clock, woke me at 4:00 A.M. We stumbled around in the dark, rolling up our bags and folding the tent. Staggering down to the beach with our burdens, I went to work preparing breakfast while Pete turned to loading the boat. He tugged on the bow line expecting the usual immediate response. He received nothing but stubborn resistance. Surfbird refused to budge from her anchored position. Pete peered through the darkness trying to determine the problem. "What's happening, Nancy? Can you see anything out there?"

I abandoned my oatmeal pot and ran to the edge of the water. "Looks like some branches are twisted around the line. I can barely make out their outline. Maybe it's one of those floating cedar tops we've seen along the way."

"DAMN!" exploded Pete. "I'll have to go in after her. I can't see any other way. Come hold the lines and keep the pressure on. It'll help me balance on the way out."

I held on grimly and watched Pete's chalk-white legs and bottom gradually submerge into the icy water. The water was filled with phosphorescence in the predawn darkness. Little diamonds of brightness dripped off the length of line and from my fingers. Each of Pete's tenuous steps produced radiant swirls of liquid light. It was mystically lovely in spite of the ludicrous situation.

"God Almighty," grumbled Pete. "It's a whole goddamn tree wound around the line."

"Can you get it off?"

"I think so," he said, reaching down deep. "Just one more branch here." After another series of grunts and mutterings, I felt the tension in the line release. In came Surfbird, following her leash-line like a well trained beagle.

"Damn! That's cold!," Pete said, picking his way barefoot among the barnacled rocks on the beach.

"Here's a towel. You dress and I'll serve up," I said.

"Let's eat fast and get out of here," Pete answered as he grabbed for the towel. "It's calm out there right now and I sure don't want to tackle that baby in any wind."

It took us two hours to make it across. The seas were calm and the wind only an occasional whisper. The current pushed us down the inlet a ways, but we tucked in behind the starkly beautiful Boston Islands with a sense of relief. These islets were pocketed with brilliant white-sand beaches surrounded by multi-colored rocks. Trees clung to those rocks defying gravity and the water was clear and clean. We pulled in to one for a relief stop and to stretch our legs. Tiny worm-like fish scattered out from under our boots as we walked in the surf. They burrowed in the sand right at water's edge, probably as a survival technique.

Back aboard, we pulled past the Proctor Islands and up the Tongass Passage toward the northern end of Sitklan Island. Around noon we crossed into the United States. "Alaska! We made it! Hooray for us!" I chortled.

"Strange — it doesn't look any different from Canada. Do you see a boundary stripe in the water?"

"No — but now we'll be back in harbors instead of harbours and we might not see any more Canadian geese. Well, we better find a spot on this island for the night. Wind's picking up."

The rain started shortly after we set up camp. We crawled into the tent to read and doze away the afternoon, rather enjoying the sound of the rain on the tarp. We felt proud of having reached Alaska.

Around 4:00 P.M. we were startled awake by a woman's voice calling from the edge of the water. "Hello — is anyone there? Hello — " We scrambled into our jeans and boots and slid down the embankment to the beach. A woman of our generation was seated in a yellow inflated kayak just off the beach. We quickly invited her ashore and helped her disentangle herself from her tiny craft. "I'm Audrey Sutherland," she pronounced. "I'm from Hawaii and I'm working my way south from Ketchikan to the San Juan Islands."

"Alone?" I gasped. This trip was difficult enough for two. Attempting it alone was formidable in my eyes.

"Oh my yes. Wouldn't have it any other way. I have already traveled between Ketchikan and Petersburg and Ketchikan to Sitka and Glacier Bay. Now I decided to go south instead of north. Do you know Steve and Mary Gropp by any chance? I thought this might be their boat."

"We sure do. They were our original inspiration for this undertaking."

"Lovely couple — so modest. Tell me, have you found any shelters or deserted cabins along the route?" She hauled out her intricately detailed topographic charts and we helped her pinpoint the few cabins in which we had squatted.

"Won't you join us for dinner and spend the night?" I queried. "There's plenty of room here for your tent."

"No, thank you. I want to be in position to cross Portland Inlet at dawn, so I'll camp on one of the islets nearer that channel. Give my best to Steve and Mary — and good luck."

We watched her paddle around the corner, stroking strongly and unafraid. "Any time you feel like getting a big head and think you're doing something out of the ordinary, along comes an Audrey Sutherland to put you in your place," said Pete.

"It does give you a different perspective, doesn't it?" I agreed. "A remarkable woman. Let's remember to ask the Gropps about her."

The stream near our campsite had other visitors. Three white-tailed deer browsed and a mink scampered through the water. The deer looked up startled at the invasion of their territory, then kangarooed off through the brush, disappearing in seconds.

We passed by Tongass Island that morning. The name evoked images of Indians sitting in their smoky teepees, making baskets, bracelets and belt buckles. The island is apparently a treasure house of relics, but we didn't explore it. We were so intent on getting to Ketchikan in one piece that we drove ourselves always with that goal in mind, an obsession that I regret in retrospect. Fear of the wind accompanied us now that we had experienced its awesome power. Now we knew the fall storms of Alaska clearly were setting early.

Nakat Bay gave us a tussle. It receives winds directly off the Gulf of Alaska and is a body of water we had to cross in order to duck behind the islands off Cape Fox. Even Revillagigedo Channel, which leads into Ketchikan, was not free from those terrifying gales blowing out of the Gulf. We weren't home free yet.

The wind picked up against us on the bay and forced us into another marathon rowing session. We pulled hard for Fox Island against mounting waves and our own trepidation. About halfway across, a young couple in an aluminum whale boat came zooming out of nowhere and pulled up beside us. "Hi! We're looking for some friends who are rowing a dory to Prince Rupert. Have you seen them?"

"No — only a lady in a yellow kayak."

"OK — thanks. Where're you folks going?"

"We're on our way to Ketchikan. We've come up from Washington State."

"You're kidding! That's remarkable! We'll be off now, but good luck to you." They waved goodby and roared off across the bay and disappeared down Tongass Passage.

"I wonder where they were from?" I queried.

"Yeah – we forgot to ask. Do you suppose there's another fish camp around the corner?"

"We should be so lucky – wouldn't that be lovely? Well, let's get across this bugger before we capsize again. Think of peanut butter and candy bars. It's almost lunch time."

Fox Island gave us a brief respite from the unceasing wind. The sun was out, the beach sand was warm and our food tasted great. We had eaten a virtually unchanging menu for two and a half months but neither tired of it. We attacked each meal and snack with the voracity of a boa constrictor gulping his mouse.

We moved into wildly beautiful country off the tip of Cape Fox. A rugged shoreline pocked with huge rocks dominated the landscape. Huge jagged crags marched out to sea and scattered in irregular formation, each froth-based, making rowing difficult and hazardous. Since I was in the bow, it was my job to check our direction and course. Pete adjusted his strokes to my signals: "More on your left – there's another rock ahead – pull harder on the right. OK, now straight ahead. Now on the left a bit – good. Whoops, hard on the right, I didn't see those boulders!" My head swiveled around like a searchlight trying to scope out the dangers ahead. "Stop a minute – I've got something on the line."

We pulled in our oars and assessed our position as I hauled in a nice snapper for dinner. "The wind's beginning to kick up out here," said Pete. "I don't like the way the waves are building."

"Can we make it around the light at Tree Point?"

"Probably, but there's no place to go in until way north of Humpy Point. I think we better head in here. The chart indicates a Boat Harbor, but I don't see it – do you?"

"No, but I think we have to work back behind those giant rocks." Threading our way back toward shore was complicated by hundreds of massive rocks and crashing water. Everywhere we turned, waves broke off barely submerged reefs and rock formations. With the wind coming at us broadside now, we had to work cautiously to avoid smashing onto a protruding obstruction.

"Hard on the left Pete," I yelled. "OK – straight ahead – I think we'll clear the next one hard left again great!" We zig-zagged in behind a huge rock, which was more an islet, and with the cessation of wind, were able to look around for the entrance to the harbor. It opened up invitingly as a winding passage between more monoliths. We followed the trail into a world of flat calm waters.

As we stepped ashore, Pete said, "You know, I bet we're breaking the law."

"How so?"

"We haven't contacted customs yet and we've touched shore twice now."

"Well, if you can think of a way to do it, I'll comply, but I doubt there will be any agents skulking in the woods around here." (We both remembered too well an incident in our naive pasts when we had neglected to touch in at Sydney, B.C., with Canadian Custom officials. We had ended up in court at Ganges, on Saltspring Island, and were fined $100.0 for our negligence. It had been an embarrassment, showcasing our stupidity.)

"Look Pete, here's another perfect campsite." A lovely, clean pebble beach with driftwood rooms greeted us. The forest above the tideline again provided us with a moss-lined platform — this one wonderfully flat and ringed with trees for easy tie-downs for the tent and tarp. I felt a bit like Alice in Wonderland as I discovered each new convenience. "Look — a perfect table over here. We even have backrests on the logs — no bugs either," I chortled.

We sipped at the wine we had purchased in Prince Rupert and watched the sun decline toward the western horizon. "With any luck, we'll be in Ketchikan in three days," said Pete.

"That would be nice. I must admit I get really nervous when the wind blows more than a whisper, don't you?"

"Yes. I wasn't aware of it before. Now we know what it can do."

Near the Foggy Point Light the next morning, we were hailed by several American fishing boat occupants. They all waved and some stopped to ask where we were going. One, a garrulous fellow named Rudy, pulled his boat, the St. Raphael, alongside and chatted for quite awhile. He was from Marysville, Washington, and fished alone. He was lonely. He loved people and talk and seemed content to stay out there visiting with us. We finally pushed on and were just working our way through some slippery kelp beds when the same young couple in the high-powered aluminum whaleboat came roaring around the point. "Hello again," they hailed us. "We thought you should know that the forecast is for deteriorating weather with winds up to twenty knots. Why don't you drop into our wannigan in Foggy Bay? It's the little red one way back at the bottom of the bay. Turn right and just keep rowing until you see it. Can't miss it. We'll be back around noon." Off they shot in a spray of salt water.

"What the hell is a wannigan?" I asked.

"Damned if I know. Must be something they live in. Let's go see. I don't want to be out in twenty-knot winds in this water. We're still not very protected from those Dixon Entrance winds."

Foggy Bay was an anchorage for three packer boats waiting for the seiners and gillnetters to disgorge their daily catch. A huge ice barge was secured further down the bay, a large sign on its hull indicating that fishermen could tie up for a shower. We pulled on down through a narrow passageway into the bottom of the bay. There on a floating dock was a little red cabin, complete with outhouse and deck. "This must be a wannigan."

"Must be. Let's tie up here and eat our lunch while we wait for them. It looks like rain again."

"Yep. In fact I just felt a drop. Sure wish they had a little wood stove, but it doesn't look like it."

"No, it doesn't," said Pete, peering through the windows. "It's all locked up tight, so we better put on our yellows until they come back." We sat, hunkered in the rain, awaiting their return.

Tracy and Michael Whelan worked for the Alaska Fish and Game Department. They filled us in on their responsibilities as we sat over warm mugs of tea in their one-room floating cabin. They went out every day in the whaleboat and checked with the packer boats about the day's catch. They carefully totted up the number of each type of fish caught. This information was shared with the Canadians, who were operating the same way in an effort to coordinate and manage the catches on each salmon run. Bitter rivalries exist in this sensitive border area, and the Whelans were part of a team working to alleviate those problems.

They also collected fish scales from which biologists determined the fish's age and feeding intake. Like the age rings of a tree, this information was indicated in the concentric lines of the scales.

The rain poured down in earnest that afternoon and continued through the night. The Whelans graciously invited us to stay with them, and we eagerly accepted their offer to throw our sleeping bags on their floor. Rain pounding on a cabin roof is somehow comforting as opposed to rain on a tent rainfly. For one thing you know you won't have to fold everything up wet and go through your day chilled and soggy. We reveled in their hospitality and found ourselves talking well into the night.

Michael was working toward his master's degree in Philosophy and Tracy was a Microbiologist. An intellectual pair, they had traveled extensively. They entertained us with vignettes about Japan, India and Europe. Their dream was to live in Germany for at least six months and study the language intensely.

Michael had an insatiable curiosity about the ways of wildlife. His eyes lit up as he told us about witnessing the mating ritual of loons. "I just happened on the scene when walking fish-runs one summer. It looked as if the birds were dancing a Virginia Reel. There were several pairs lined up facing one another, just offshore. One couple would dance down the line just like we would do in the folk dance. Their necks were extended and they skittered across the top of the water. It was absolutely fascinating and I felt very lucky to have been an observer."

We celebrated Pete's sixtieth birthday fighting through a wild tide rip in the Foggy Bay entrance – one of those crazy, no-logic patches of uncontrolled waters through which you bounce, jiggle and whirl with moments of utter panic.

We compounded our problems by going aground during a relief stop. Surfbird hung up on three pointed rocks as the tide deserted her in a quick-drain action. "Hurry, Pete — the boat's hung up! I can't push her off by myself." Pete rushed back down to the water, pulling on his newly purchased rain pants as he ran. We both threw our shoulders into the task, but again Surfbird dug in and refused to budge.

"You keep pushing, Nancy. I'm going to get some leverage going." He ran up the beach about fifty yards and came staggering back with a long driftwood pole. He wedged it under the stern and applied all his weight to the other end. "Push — again — harder — ugh!!" She moved, but almost imperceptibly. CRAAAACK! "DAMN!" The pole snapped, throwing Pete violently backward. He recovered his balance and dashed back up to snatch a bigger pole. "This one won't snap," he said, as he levered it under the bow. "Now, heave!" Again we put our shoulders to the task, digging in hard to apply the strength of our thigh muscles.

"She's moving,"' I grunted.

"One or two more will get her," Pete urged. The rocks finally relinquished their grip on the boat. She surged up and over her captors and slid into the surrounding water. We scrambled back into our floating home with relief and pushed off — exhausted and spent, but pleased to be water borne again.

The wind died and was replaced by rain. The skies opened and it poured, but the waters were calm. "I guess I've gotten to the point where I prefer rain over wind, if I have to choose," I said damply.

"Me too," said Pete, "but it would be nice to try a day with neither."

"I think that's an idle dream."

We pulled across the gaping Boca de Quadra Inlet and worked our way north to an inlet near the wide Behm Canal, one of our last major crossings before Ketchikan. We found a quiet bay where we set up camp and toasted Pete with the last of our wine. I made a special pan-bread decorated with huckleberries spelling out his name. At sixty, Pete looked great — trim, hard and lean. The beard he had grown was a rich mixture of red, black and gray and gave him a strong salty look. I was proud of him, loved him and was very glad he was my partner in life.

An eagle sat on a snag chatting in his strange, squeaky raptor-voice and the water lapped quietly on the gravel beach. We were almost there. If all went well, we could make it to Ketchikan tomorrow.

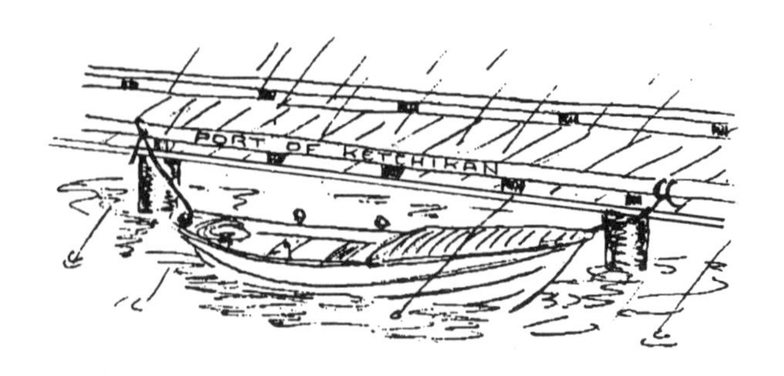

PART XV: (Nancy) THE FINAL LEG: "THERE'S KETCHIKAN — IN SIGHT, BUT OUT OF REACH."

"There it is, Pete — up on the rocks!"

"It sure is — wish we could tell Michael and Tracy." We were just off Lucky Cove working toward Cone Point and the crossing of wide Thorne Arm. There, on the rocks, battered and broken, was the skeletal remains of a little white wannigan. The Whelans had had it under tow two days before our arrival, but had been forced to sever the line when the waters became too wild to control their boat and the barge. They had hoped to fix it and live in it in Ketchikan when their jobs were completed for the Fish and Wildlife Service. Now it would never be lived in. Its shattered remains adorned the rocky shore with the flotsam of their dreams.

"It will eventually break up and wash out to sea, I guess."

"We'll write and let them know where it is. They might be able to get the stove out of it anyway."

Winds off Cone Point were uncomfortably strong. With our awakened sense of anxiety, we ducked inside Cone Island and passed through a narrow corridor to exit into Thorne Arm. A sheer wall of rock and quiet water enticed us to stop for lunch and fish for our dinner. Coho salmon jumped around the perimeter of the boat daring us to catch them. "Take my hook, damn you!" I yelled, annoyed at their taunting antics. "Wouldn't salmon taste great tonight?"

"Sure would — looks like you have something on."

"Just a rockfish — kinda small. Maybe we can catch a friend to accompany it to our dinner plates.

Halfway across Thorne Arm — it always seemed to be at the point of no return — the wind picked up to an uncomfortable fifteen knots. "Let's head right into Moth Bay," said Pete, "instead of angling up the coast. I don't like this blow. Too much chop."

Moth Bay seemed to be in a direct line with the wind's force. We

PART XV - THE FINAL LEG

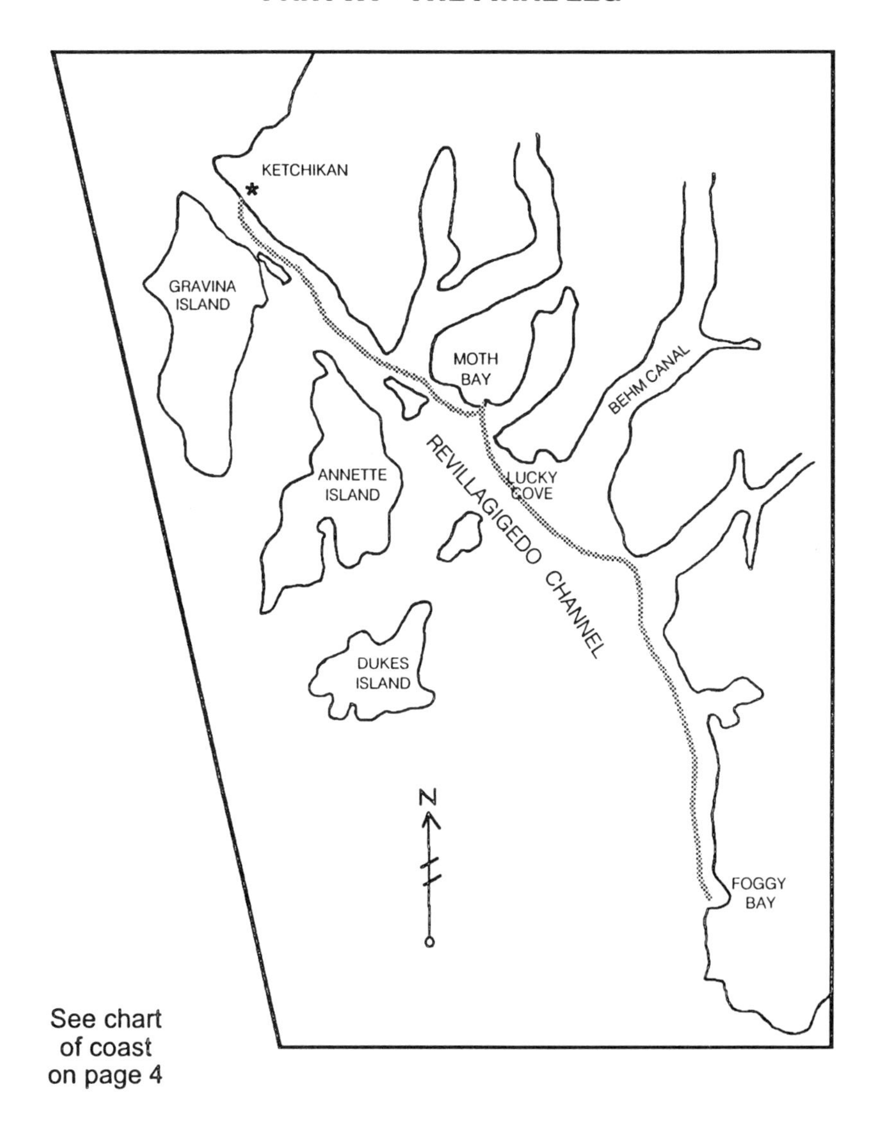

See chart of coast on page 4

checked out an indentation near the mouth, but found no suitable campsite. A red snapper did decide to join our small rockfish at that point, so at least dinner was secured. We moved deeper into the bay, sticking close to the rock walls to duck behind any protuberance we could use as shelter. "That wind's gusting over twenty knots and there's no place to go."

"Here's a niche in the wall," volunteered Pete. "Let's pull in for a candy bar and sit awhile. Maybe it'll blow over in a bit." We clung to an overhanging rock, wedged into a casket-sized indentation in the cliff. Here the wind couldn't touch us, but the rain sure could — and did. It was coming down in earnest. We sat hunched, clinging to our rock. Two more miserable creatures would have been hard to come upon.

From out of nowhere a man garbed in oilskins appeared in his dinghy, his outboard motor chugging away faithfully. "Hello — my wife and I are anchored behind that islet there. We saw you come in. How about coming aboard for a cup of coffee?" There they were again, those wonderful words. We had been uplifted by them so many times on this voyage.

We blew down to the foot of the bay and tied up alongside their handsome forty-foot Willard. Jack and Shirley Converse, from Seattle, welcomed us aboard and plied us with hot coffee and an afternoon of conversation. It was with reluctance that we re-donned our rain gear and pushed off to a cove they had spotted earlier. They said it was all set up for camping — flat tent site and all.

Sure enough, on the west end of the bay was a protected indentation with good anchorage, a cooking platform and a stump table. It would have been ideal had it not been pouring.

We settled in to digest our two fish. Pete leaned across from his sleeping bag to offer a goodnight kiss — a brave feat considering the rancid state I was in. "We'll be in Ketchikan tomorrow — cheeseburgers and showers."

"Don't say that. I've heard those words somewhere before and it didn't work out quite the way we'd envisioned it."

"Oh, ye of little faith — get a good night's sleep and you'll feel better." Our sleep was periodically interrupted by what we believed to be the wind roaring in the cedars overhead. Upon arising, we discovered the stream next to our tent had swollen to double its size during the night. It was now a veritable cascade of water rushing seaward. And the rain continued. "Let's go make a run for Ketchikan," said Pete gamely.

"OK. I'll fix breakfast while you break camp. Maybe it won't be too bad out there."

"It's worth a try."

As we approached the entrance to the bay, wind-tossed waves hit us head on. "Forget this — we better head back in," said Pete. I knew he hated to admit defeat, so I agreed quickly, recognizing that his better judgement had taken over. Back we went, unloaded the boat, set up the tarp and tent and climbed back in our bags to stay warm.

"What a hassle," I groaned. "I so wanted to get to Ketchikan today."

"Me too," murmured Pete glumly, "but maybe it will still work out."

About an hour later, we heard the Converse's engine start with a roar. Pete scrambled out of the tent and hailed Jack. "What's the forecast?" he screamed across the water.

"Flat as a pancake out there," yelled Jack. He ducked back into his warm cabin and they pulled away.

"Let's go, Nancy." We reversed all that had been done before — tarp, tent, bags, gear — and within the hour pulled again for the mouth of the bay.

"Can't see much improvement out here, can you?" asked Pete, as we bobbed and bounced in the rough water.

"No, not really, but I don't feel much wind. This seems to be more of a rip to me."

"I think you're right — let's pull through it and duck into Coho Cove around the corner if we need protection. It should have quieter water than Moth Bay." Just before rounding the point, we saw Jack and Shirley's boat chugging back into Moth Bay. They did not respond to our waves nor come over to tell us what they had discovered.

"Do you want to turn back too, Nancy? They apparently think it's too rough for their boat."

"No, I don't. We're this far now. If we can get inside Bold Island, it should be much calmer." As if by magic, the breeze dropped to a whisper as we entered Coho Cove. The water was still and glassy. Cedars' green reflections were disturbed only by the motion of our oars. A float plane zoomed in at treetop level and dipped his wings to us.

"That must be Michael and Tracy's provision plane. I bet they asked the pilot to check up on us." We waved to reassure him of our safety. "It is comforting to know that someone is aware of our position." We crept around the edges of the bay checking for potential campsites in case we could not go further. But Bold Island did protect us. The channel was quiet and peaceful. We stroked along serenely, confident that we would be in Ketchikan by early afternoon. We crossed the last wide inlet and stroked by the Mountain Point Light. We were now just four miles from our goal. We waved to people fishing off the light and smugly allowed the cheeseburger and shower fantasy to resurface.

WHOMPPPPP! Our boat heeled dangerously toward shore as a blast of wind came sweeping up Nichols Passage directly from the Gulf of Alaska. For some unknown reason, we had not noticed on our chart that last vulnerable section of open water. We had assumed we were safe from wind blasts. But no, here we were again facing mounting waves and intense gusts of wind. "Here comes another one," I yelled, recognizing the telltale lines rushing across the surface of the water.

"We better duck behind this rock for awhile," said Pete, directing us into a shallow, bathtub-sized hidey-hole — just big enough for us to sit in safety while the wind howled on the other side, reaching stormy fingers at us in a futile attempt to force us out. We sat in our tub watching the water drain out beneath us and tried to judge how much time we had left in our prison/haven.

"Look at those people in their warm homes, Pete. They don't even know we're out here. We're so close to our goal – yet it's out of reach. Doesn't it seem strange? Almost like two separate civilizations living side by side but unaware of the other's existence. I think I'm ready to be part of their world for awhile."

"Yes – so am I. Somehow this peanut butter on rye crackers has lost its appeal today."

"That's because you were thinking of those damn cheeseburgers again. There seem to be some gods who want to deny us our simple pleasures. I'm going up on the rock again and see what the wind's doing." I scrambled out of the boat and up the slippery sides of the moss-covered rock. (Everything is moss covered in Ketchikan.) Peering out through the mist-filled air, I sensed a slight decrease in the wind's velocity. The rain was still hammering down, but that had become a damp fact of life. I slid back to Pete and said, "Let's go for it. We only have to make it past the entrance buoy, then it should be much calmer."

'"OK – besides we're almost aground." The tide had left us only about five inches in which to maneuver. We cautiously pushed the bow out and sniffed the wind. "Not bad," Pete agreed. "Let's go for the marker buoy." We bent to the task with vigor. Once around the point, tucked safely behind Pennock Island, we cruised slowly past docks, seaplanes, cruise ships, fishing boats and marinas, feeling smug and just a little proud, oblivious to the pouring rain. We slipped behind the final breakwater and tied up at an empty slip. Our voyage was over. We had made it to Ketchikan. We had realized our crazy dream.

To a passerby we were just two more people standing on the dock with water coursing off our hoods and streaming down our backs. Not an unusual sight in Ketchikan.

Ketchikan

PART XVI: EPILOGUE (Nancy)
COMMITMENT TO CONTRAST

Everywhere we went, Surfbird was admired for the beauty of her lines. We admired her for her sturdy seaworthiness and her responsiveness to our commands. She withstood tide rips, eight to ten foot seas, groundings on barnacled rocks and winds over fifty knots. She sailed at four knots in soft blows of ten to twelve knots, but didn't get too many opportunities to do so. Mostly we rowed - sixty-seven days, 536 hours - from Lopez Island, Washington, to Ketchikan, Alaska. At the end of our trip, we barged her back to Seattle and trailered her home to our island. We left a scraped and battered hulk for Geremy Snapp to restore. She still had her pride, but not her beauty. She resembled a weary dowager.

Of the sixty-seven rowing days, sixty had some amount of rain: sometimes in the form of intermittent showers, but often three to four days of non-stop rain. Some of such intensity that we had to bail the boat three times in one day. At Rivers Inlet, B.C., where the salmon fishing and the downpours are legendary, Pete arose twice in the night, donned full rain gear, and sloshed to the boat to bail her. We both had visions of her wallowing in water to her gunwales. It rains so hard there that raindrops hit the water's surface and rebound three inches. Because of the almost constant dampness, we found ourselves daily climbing into wet socks, soggy jeans and molding boots. We reasoned that the odor in our tent would repel most carnivorous animals, so we didn't waste much energy fearing attacks from the wildlife.

"Wasn't that bear-scat I saw right outside the tent?"

"Not to worry, Nancy - - a bear wouldn't touch us right now. We don't smell like food."

"No, but I hear they're attracted to garbage dumps!"

We later talked to some southeastern Alaska residents who told us the panhandle receives over 180 inches of rain annually, and that this year was the wettest they could ever remember. We did not doubt the veracity of their story.

The flip side of that coin, was our infrequent days of sunshine. They seldom appeared back-to-back, so we treasured each one, and used them to full advantage. Each sunny day found our campsite littered with camping gear and drying clothing, freshly washed in salt water. We usually ducked in ourselves for a salty bath followed by a rinse from our portable bag-shower. We reveled in being able to cook over crackling beach fires instead of the one-pot-at-a-time meals created on our tiny camp stove while huddled under dripping cedars. The sun also allowed us to see to the tops of the surrounding hills and waterfalls, so seldom clear of misty clouds.

Cleanliness became a driving need during the entire trip. As I glance down at my neatly filed and manicured nails, I can't help but remember the broken and dirt-filled nails during the trip. It was impossible to maintain clean hands, or any other body part, while rowing a dory to Alaska. Every chore demanded hand and arm power. Unloading the boat elicited grunts of, "Ugh!" as each waterlogged bag was pulled out and dragged to our campsite. Setting up camp and cooking in soot-covered pots soon turned every piece of clothing or bared skin surface into grime. Squatting between driftwood logs or piles of rock to take care of necessary body functions didn't aid cleanliness either. Nor did our method of dish washing. Somehow swabbing at grease-coated plates and cutlery in cold sea water did little for the dishes and nothing for our hands, except add to the salt crust and wrinkles. The joys of sitting on a clean toilet seat, washing dishes in hot sudsy water and standing under a pelting hot shower are indescribable.

Although we didn't suffer from extremes in temperature, there were days when we would arrive at a potential campsite feeling damp and chilled. Usually it had rained off and on during the day, and the wind had blown from the southwest hard enough to work through our layers of cotton, wool and rubberized rain-gear and cause a slight shiver or two when we ceased rowing. It was on those days that a beach fire was out of the question. We would set up camp quickly and climb into our sleeping bags to catch a brief nap and warm the limbs before dinner.

There were so few days of sun, I can remember each distinctly. One was the day we spent rowing from just north of Quarry Bay, on the Canadian mainland, to Westview. We had a ten-knot following wind, which filled our lug-sail and pushed us along at three-and-a-half knots, when combined with rowing. The sun highlighted the water with silver sparkles and illuminated greens and blues from forest and sky. As the day wore on, we wore less and less, until pulling around Grief Point, we were clad only in underwear and sunburns. Pete, being fair-skinned peeled from that day on to the end of the voyage. His nose must have worked through six layers of skin, and his arms through hundreds of sun-blisters. I reddened and darkened several shades, but shared the nose-peeling syndrome as well.

Now that I am once again counting calories, it is difficult to envision the gross amount of groceries and freshly-caught seafood that we consumed along the way. For the first time in my adult life, I was able to stuff down three big meals a day plus candy bars and snacks. It didn't matter how many calories we consumed, we still lost weight. It was a lovely feeling to have a gap of several inches between me and my jeans, and Pete looked like a survivor of an enforced fast. In the rare occasions that we reached a settlement, we would hit the local cafe and wolf down hot cheeseburgers and french fries. It seems the Canadians include fries with every order. We would scrape the last fry lovingly around the plate to pick up any remaining drips of grease, then buy apple pie-ala-mode to top it off. (As I write these words, I am nibbling on carrot and celery sticks.)

The sea conditions too, presented themselves in bewildering and baffling contrasts. One minute we would be rowing through calm and flat waters, the next, without warning, roaring rivers of rips would appear and give us a wild, jolting ride. We never were able to apply any logic to their appearance or disappearance. We would edge out from our anchorage early in the morning, as we had been told that winds came up in the afternoon. Some days that would be true, but more often we were forced into battle at 6:00 or 7:00 A.M. We could handle fourteen to sixteen-knot winds, and waves up to three feet, but anything beyond that sent us scurrying for cover. Often we would be forced to tuck in against a rock wall or tiny inlet to escape strong headwinds, and then, in a matter of minutes the same roiled waters would be flat and quiet.

We learned early there was no predictability to anything. We simply started each day testing the weather and water. If we had waited for good weather reports, we never would have left Lopez Island. Each day presented some obstacle to overcome. Decisions had to be made quickly and on the spot. Our emotions ranged from joy to stark fear, with many gradations in between.

We have tried to stay connected to some of the people we encountered along the way.

Sam and Sarah McMillan still live in New Aiyansh, north of Prince Rupert. Sam keeps busy working in construction. They are well and happy.

Reinhardt and Doris Kuppers have expanded their floating restaurant and sleeping facilities, and now run Camp Cordero with the assistance of their daughter, Kellie. She graduated from Malaspina College in Nanaimo, and is now managing their restaurant.

The energetic crowd working to upgrade Butedale did not succeed in their endeavors. The old buildings have fallen into disrepair and even the docks are sagging into the water. Boaters tell us that even the roaring waterfall has diminished in size.

Roy Robinson, skipper of the Juno did indeed receive his postcard, and Dave Edginton, the junior lightkeeper at Pointer Light got his recipe for cracked-wheat bread, along with three boxes of cracked wheat.

Tracy and Michael Whelan, of Foggy Bay, did make it to Germany. They studied the language at two live-in institutions. We admired their ability to set goals and work their problems well.

Audrey Sutherland, the lady in the inflatable kayak, taught a paddling course at the University of Hawaii. She is indeed a remarkable woman. She was in her early sixties when we encountered her—firm, trim and strong. Confidence exuded from her like sap from a sugar-maple. She had authored a book titled, Paddling My Own Canoe; an autobiographical account of the numerous tests she has set for herself. She is probably the only woman who has swum the inaccessible side of Maui; around sheer cliffs, where there is no access by land. She accomplished this feat while towing a pack strapped to her forehead. Her rowing ventures have now taken her all over the world – always alone – a new challenge. She creates whatever she needs to survive. On her trip where we met her, she had innovated an outrigger to stabilize her boat and assist her in reentering the boat should she capsize. She was the picture of efficiency, organization and courage. We often think about her and wonder about her experiences on her trip down the British Columbia Coast.

We did connect with the couple we had met in Bishop Bay at the Hot Springs. Kay and Larry Meehan hosted a delicious "welcome-to-shore" dinner at their home when we arrived in Ketchikan.

To sum up the adventure: We accomplished our goals only through unadulterated stubbornness and the desire to finish that which we had started. We came away with renewed appreciation of small pleasures: the warmth of a wood fire, hot running water, clean toilet facilities, a hot pie fresh out of the oven, a good cup of brewed coffee, clean sheets and soap. (While washing my face in a briny stream near Shelter Bay, it occurred to me that the soap I was using was a bar I had taken from the Hyatt Regency Hotel in Kalapani, Maui - - a study in contrasts.)

The company of family and friends is now treasured, as is the deep personal contentment that comes from having accomplished and shared something that was extremely difficult and exhilarating.

AFTERWORD

Pete died on August 19, 1992, of leukemia. Our children and I mourn, and miss a man of enormous integrity, purposefulness, self-discipline, and wry sense-of-humor. We loved him dearly.

APPENDIX A: EQUIPMENT AND SUPPLIES

Camping:

Aluminum foil
Axe
Camp stove
Cast iron fry pan
Cook-set (pans, dishes, cutlery)
Fuel canisters for stove
Line
Liquid detergent
Plastic scrubber
Poly bottles
Shovel
Shower bag
Sleeping bags
Tarp and poles
Tent and poles
Water containers
Water purifier
Waterproof matches
Zip-top baggies

Clothing:

Boots (heavy-duty, rubber)
Gloves (light leather)
Hats (sun and wool)
Jeans
Rain gear
Running shoes
Sandals
Shorts
Sox
Sweat shirts
Sweaters
Swim suits
T-shirts (long and short-sleeved)
Underwear (long and regular)

Emergency Equipment:

Aluminum tape
Bailer
Emergency kits
Flares
Life Jackets
Mirror
Smoke signals
Strobe light
Survival Suits
Veri pistol
VHF hand-held radio
Whistles

First Aid Supplies:

Antibiotic Cream
Aspirin
Bandages
Dental kit: cotton, oil of cloves, toothwax
Ecotrin (arthritis medication)
Elastic wrap
Eye drops
Pain medication (prescription)
Sunscreen
Wide spectrum antibiotic
Wrist braces

Fishing Supplies:

Club
Crab jig
File
Fish net
Hooks
Jigs
Knife
Line
Lures
Plastic worms
Sinkers

Food:

Bisquick
Bouillon
Butter
Carrots
Cheese
Chocolate Bars
Coffee
Dried Fruit
Dried milk
Granola bars
Honey
Hot chocolate mix
Jam
Juice powder
Lemonade mix
Nuts
Oatmeal
Onions
Pancake mix
Peanut butter
Potatoes
Raisins
Rice
Rye crackers
Salt/pepper
Sugar
Tang

Ground Tackle:

Anchors (2)
Block
Nylon line (75′)
Nylon thimble
Polypropylene line (375′)
Styrofoam float

Navigational Aids:

Charts
Coast Pilot
Compass
Current books
Tide books

Personal:

Binoculars
Books
Brush/comb
Camera, film, zoom lens, batteries
Cards
Deodorant
Glasses (eye)
Hand lotion
Jacknives
Journals (writing)
Nail files
Pencils (indelible)
Pens
Sanitary napkins, tampons
Scissors
Shampoo
Shaving gear
Sketch book
Soap (regular and salt-water)
Toilet paper
Toothpaste, toothbrushes, floss
Towels, washcloths

APPENDIX B: BEAUFORT SCALE

Determination of wind speeds by sea conditions:

Knots	Description	Sea Conditions	Wind Force (Beaufort)	Wave Height (in feet)
0-1	Calm	Sea smooth and mirror-like	0	0
1-3	Light air	Scale-like ripples without foam crests	1	¼
4-6	Light breeze	Small, short wavelets; crests have a glassy appearance and do not break	2	½
7-10	Gentle breeze	Large wavelets; some crests begin to break; foam of glassy appearance. Occasional white foam crests.	3	2
11-16	Moderate breeze	Small waves, becoming longer; fairly frequent white foam crests.	4	4
17-21	Fresh breeze	Moderate waves, taking a more pronounced long form; many white foam crests; there may be some spray.	5	6
22-27	Strong breeze	Large waves begin to form; white foam crests are more extensive everywhere; there may be some spray.	6	10
28-33	Near gale	Sea heaps up and white foam from breaking waves begins to be blown in streaks along the direction of the wind; spindrift starts.	7	14
34-40	Gale	Moderately high waves of greater length; edges of crests break into spindrift; foam is blown in well-marked streaks along the direction of the wind.	8	18
41-47	Strong gale	High waves; dense streaks of foam along the direction of the wind; crests of waves begin to topple, tumble and roll over; spray may reduce visibility.	9	23
48-55	Storm	Very high waves with long overhanging crests. Resulting foam in great patches is blown in dense white streaks along the direction of the wind. On the whole, the surface of the sea is white in appearance. The tumbling of the sea becomes heavy and shock-like. Visibility is reduced.	10	29

Knots	Description	Sea Conditions	Wind Force (Beaufort)	Wave Height (in feet)
63	Violent storm	Exceptionally high waves that may obscure small and medium-sized ships. The sea is completely covered with long, white patches of foam lying along the direction of the wind. Everywhere the edges of the wave crests are blown into froth. Visibility reduced.	11	37
64-71	Hurricane	Air is filled with foam and spray. Sea completely white with driving spray; visibility very much reduced.	12	45

APPENDIX C: EILEEN'S BURIAL COVE BREAD (of which I've found none better)

Night before: Immerse one cup cracked wheat in one cup of cold water

Set aside:

1/2 Cup warm water
2 packages powdered yeast - mixed together
1/2 tsp. sugar

Combine:

2 cups warm milk
2 T malt vinegar
5 T salt
2 T brown sugar
2 T vegetable oil
1 cup cold water

Add in: cracked wheat, yeast solution, 1 cup of any other grain desired (bran, oats, etc.,) enough unbleached flour to make a firm dough (5-6 cups). Knead until "right". Let rise until double. Punch down and knead again. Make into four loaves. Let rise again to top of pans. Bake 35 minutes at 350°. Brush tops with butter, just out of the oven and out of the pans.

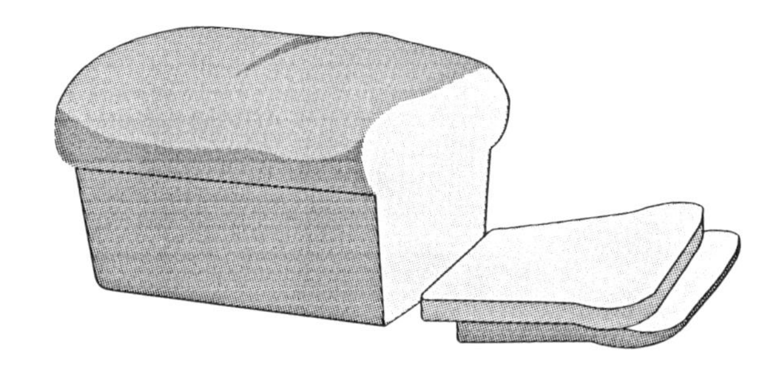

APPENDIX D: DEFINITIONS OF BODIES OF WATER

(As reported in Webster's New World Dictionary, Second College Edition, 1982 Edition)

Arm: Body of water attached or connected to something larger: (arm of the sea.)

Bay: Part of a lake or sea indenting the shoreline; wide inlet not so large as a gulf.

Bight: A curve in a coastline; a bay formed by such a curve.

Canal: An artificial waterway; a river artificially improved by locks, levees,etc.

Channel: The deeper part of a harbor; a body of water joining two larger bodies of water.

Cove: A small bay or inlet.

Gulf: A large area of ocean, larger than a bay, reaching into land.

Inlet: A narrow strip of water extending into a body of land from a river, lake, ocean, etc.; small bay or creek; a narrow strip of water between islands.

Isthmus: A neck, narrow passage.

Narrows: A narrow passage, as between two bodies of water, strait.

Ocean: Great body of salt water that covers approximately 71% of the surface of the earth.

Passage: A way or means of passing; a channel.

Reach: A continuous, uninterrupted extent or stretch of water.

Sea: The continuous body of salt water covering the greater part of the earth's surface; ocean. 2) A large body of salt water wholly or partly enclosed by land.

Sound: A wide channel or strait linking two large bodies of water or separating an island from the mainland. 2) A long inlet or arm of the sea.

Strait: A narrow waterway connecting two large bodies of water.

APPENDIX E: LIGHTHOUSES ON THE B.C. COAST

In 1984 there were forty-two manned lighthouses remaining on the B.C. coast to provide protection for mariners. The waters are treacherous, the winds unpredictable, often ferocious and the currents and rips hazardous. In addition to the manned stations, the Canadian Coast Guard under the mandate of Transport Canada, maintains nearly 1900 aids to navigation on the British Columbia coastline, which is equal to the lengths of Washington and Oregon combined.

The first Canadian lighthouse was built in 1773 at Louisbourg, on Cape Breton Island, near Halifax on the east coast of Canada. It was a tower made of stone and lit by a circle of oil-fed wicks carried in a glazed wooden chamber on top of a sixty-six foot wooden column. This original lighthouse was damaged during the second siege of Louisbourg, five years later, and was not replaced until 1842.

Between 1842 and 1867, 227 light stations were built in Canada, mostly of wood, with a few exceptions. One of those is the oldest west coast light tower. It is located at Race Rocks, ten miles off Victoria. It was built in 1860 of stone blocks, each up to six feet thick. The blocks were quarried and cut in Scotland and transported as ship ballast around Cape Horn. This original tower is still operated and maintained.

Colonel W.P. Anderson, a Canadian architect, pioneered the technique of using reinforced concrete to strengthen the towers. He designed flying buttresses to withstand the high winds common to the west coast.

The light stations play a vital role in keeping the coastline safe for mariners. They provide a geographic reference for determining position. When visibility is low, they send out a radio beacon and a fog horn signal which gives a homing signal or warning.

Lightkeepers must maintain this equipment and keep it in top-notch condition at all times. They also work closely with water or airborne members of the Coast Guard to effect rescue operations. Their communications system is used to relay distress signals or emergency messages. Some stations, such as Entrance Light off Nanaimo Harbour, aid the fishery industry by taking regular samples of sea water and forwarding them to a biological station for analysis.

Lightkeepers usually take pride in their isolated homes. The lawns, flowers and vegetable gardens are generally kept in a tidy fashion.

The hours are irregular, access may be difficult and isolation must be faced. Although most families grow some of their own food and trap or catch seafood, they are resupplied every month and visited at least every two weeks. The supplies arrive by an aid-to-navigation vessel or by helicopter. Even pigs, cows, goats and a piano have been transported to lighthouses.

While electronic navigational gear has changed lightkeeping somewhat, the human touch has proven essential for unpredictable emergencies and essential service to mariners.

West coast history is enriched by lighthouse activity. Triangle Light on the northern tip of Vancouver Island, was built in 1910 and at that time was the most elevated lighthouse in the world. Although only forty-six feet high, it stood on a 700-foot high bluff, twice as high as any other station on the Pacific Coast. It had one million candle power and was visible from thirty-four miles out to sea. The station had to be abandoned though, because fog and low clouds obscured the light for more than half the year. Thus the Cape Scott Light was built in 1924.

Pachena Point Light off Barkley Sound on the lower west coast of Vancouver Island, was constructed in 1907 after the most disastrous shipwreck in B.C. history. The passenger liner, Valencia, crashed on the rocks at midnight and sank. 117 people were lost. Only thirty-seven survived.

Estevan Point, about midway down the west coast of Vancouver Island, built in 1909, is the tallest lighthouse on the Pacific Coast. It is 17 feet from its base to the focal beam of the light. Its design allows it to sway in the gales which sweep in off the Pacific. It is the only place in Canada which was fired upon by the Japanese in World War II. Hearing shots from the submarine guns, the lightkeeper wisely turned off the beacon. Shells whistled by and landed in the forest behind the light.

Nootka Light, also on the west coast of Vancouver Island, marks the site of Captain Cook's first landing on the B.C. coast.

Pointer Island, home of our friend, Dave Edginton, is an island so tiny, it shrinks to a third of its low-tide size every time the tide comes in.

BIBLIOGRAPHY

Blanchet, M. Wylie, The Curve of Time, Gray's Publishing, Ltd., Sidney, B.C. Canada. 1968.

Chapman, Charles F., Piloting, Seamanship and Small Boat Handling, The Hearst Corp., New York, NY. 1972.

United States Coast Pilot 8, Pacific Coast Alaska: Dixon Entrance to Cape Spencer, 20th Edition. National Oceanic and Atmospheric Administration.

Commercial Fishing Guide, Govt. of Canada, Dept. of Fisheries and Oceans, Vancouver, B. C., Canada, 1984.

Conover, David, Once Upon An Island, Crown Publishers, Inc., Canada. 1967

Edwards, Isabel K., Ruffles on my Longjohns, Hancock House Publishers, Ltd., No. Vancouver, B. C., Canada. 1980.

Gibbs, James A., Jr., Sentinels of the North Pacific, Binfords & Mort, Portland, Oregon. 1955.

Lorenz, Konrad, King Solomon's Ring. New Light on Animal Ways, Harper & Row, New York, NY 1982.

Olsen, Jack, The Night of the Grizzlies, G. P. Putnam's Sons. New York, NY. 1971.

Pacific Oyster, Govt. of Canada, Fisheries & Oceans, Vancouver, B. C., Canada. 1984.

Sutherland, Audrey, Paddling My Own Canoe, Univ. of Hawaii Press, Honolulu, HI. 1978.

Webster's New World Dictionary, Second College Edition, Simon & Schuster, New York,

West Coast Lighthouses, Public Affairs, Transport Canada, Vancouver, B.C., Canada. 1984